# MULTICULTURAL EDUCATION SERIES

### James A. Banks, Series Editor

For a complete list of series titles, please visit www.tcpress.com

D1712951

# The Hip-Hop Mindset

## Success Strategies for Educators and Other Professionals

Toby S. Jenkins

Foreword by Walter Kimbrough

TEACHERS COLLEGE PRESS

TEACHERS COLLEGE | COLUMBIA UNIVERSITY
NEW YORK AND LONDON

Published by Teachers College Press,® 1234 Amsterdam Avenue, New York, NY 10027

Front cover design by Peter Donahue. Photo by fatihhoca / iStock by Getty Images.

*Library of Congress Cataloging-in-Publication Data is available at loc.gov*

ISBN 978-0-8077-6870-9 (paper)
ISBN 978-0-8077-6871-6 (hardcover)
ISBN 978-0-8077-8190-6 (ebook)

Printed on acid-free paper
Manufactured in the United States of America

# Contents

# Foreword

In September of 2004, I was invited as one of three finalists to become the next president of Philander Smith College, a small historically Black college in Little Rock, Arkansas. I had been nominated for a couple of positions before, but had been told by the search firms that although I was a good candidate, I didn't have as much experience as others. It didn't deter me. Although I was 37, I knew of a number of presidents selected while in their thirties. But knowing that the average age of presidents at the time was about 58, I knew I would always be a long-shot candidate.

I arrived in Little Rock the day before the interview, and decided I would go incognito to the library archives to see what I could learn about the institution that I couldn't find in a simple Google search. The librarian, Ms. Carter, assumed I was a student. Who could blame her? I had on jeans and my Yankees fitted, and carried a backpack. (She was mortified the following day when she met me as a finalist to become the president!) But in the few hours I spent in the archives, I learned that the college had at least three presidents who were younger than I when they started, including a 29-year-old, M. Lafayette Harris, who also was the longest-serving president in the history of the college.

The interview went well, and within a few weeks I was back in Little Rock to be formally introduced as the next president of the college. This was my first time being a president, so I had to figure out what I was supposed to do at one of these introductions. I quickly learned that I would be expected to make remarks. But what would I say? I was some 20 years younger than the average college president, and I looked even younger. I wrestled with how to handle this public first impression. I decided to lean in to the obvious. I said I didn't look like most presidents. I wasn't from the greatest generation or a Baby Boomer. I was from Generation X, the group often maligned by researchers as the latchkey kids, those with pet rocks and hermit crabs. But my challenge with leaving the comparison at Generation X was that it didn't fully describe Black youth culture for those of us who grew up in the 1970s and 1980s. So I added a better descriptor. I said I was also part of the hip-hop generation. Using the work of Bakari Kitwana and his book, *The Hip Hop Generation: Young Blacks and the Crisis in African-American Culture*, I shared with the crowd that I would be true to who I was and my generation, not trying to fit into the mold of a college president from a different genera-tion. I figured I would be the first college president from the hip-hop genera-tion, and I would embrace it fully.

But what did that really mean? The week after the introduction, the *Arkansas Times* weekly newspaper ran a story with the headline "Philander welcomes 'hip hop' president." Our communications director was worried. She didn't think it was good for a college president to be associated with a musical genre that often had problematic lyrics and images. A few of the locals thought it was undignified that a college president would be com-fortable being associated with hip-hop, and were openly critical. But that's when I realized that the *Arkansas Times* was on to something. So I didn't just say I was from the hip-hop generation; I became the hip-hop president.

I started "Bless the Mic: A Hip-Hop President's Lecture Series," and de-termined that, like hip-hop, I would be willing to address any and all issues. I wouldn't hide from controversy, as the first season included Ann Coulter and Karrine Steffans. I invited hip-hop artists like MC Lyte, David Banner, and Salt-N-Pepa (separately) to speak to the community. That series became an extension of my new brand, and just like hip-hop, it became mainstream. The lectures drew diverse audiences, and averaged 400 to 500 each time, with a few bringing over 1,000 people to the venue. Just as hip-hop words and phrases can be heard by cable news anchors and politicians alike, we had people of all ages and races talking about "Bless the Mic." Surely if hip-hop could be used to sell just about everything, it could be a vehicle to engage not only a new generation of students, but a community with a college.

By the time I moved to New Orleans, the "hip-hop president" was a known quantity. I was told in my interview at Dillard University that with New Orleans being the most countercultural city in the world, a hip-hop president would not be a shock to people. So I continued to lean in, look-ing for new and unconventional ways to reach a new generation of students and a broader community. Hip-hop embraced social media fully, and I did as well, expanding my use of the major platforms as a way to tell stories, which is what good hip-hop does (especially during the golden era of the late 1980s and early 1990s). I used it as a tool to connect not only with members of the Dillard community, but also as a tool for connecting with people in a range of fields all around the world. While Yo Gotti's song "Down in the DM" described how people were arranging clandestine meetings in direct messages, I arranged interviews with reporters and invited people to campus to speak using social media direct messages.

Back in 2004, there were people skeptical of the idea of a hip-hop presi-dent. But they never could have imagined that embracing hip-hop would open unique opportunities. When I received an email saying that MC Lyte wanted to meet with me in 2014, I said yes, and let them know that I would clear my schedule to visit. But no, she was coming to meet with me. She offered an opportunity for the hip-hop president to partner with Hip Hop

Sisters Foundation for a scholarship program targeted toward Black men. Each year one or two men would receive the scholarship, and it brought several high-performing students who were extremely involved as student leaders to Dillard.

MC Lyte further discussed the state of music, and that maybe there was a way we could foster conversations about hip-hop through a course. That fall we launched Hip Hop, Sex, Gender, and Ethical Behavior. Every year, I teach this course to have those conversations, and bring in a who's who in hip-hop, along with journalists, scholars, preachers, attorneys, and even strippers, to discuss the ethics of the hip-hop industry. It has kept me close to the culture, close to my students.

My presidential journey mirrors the ideas that Dr. Toby S. Jenkins describes in *The Hip-Hop Mindset: Success Strategies for Educators and Other Professionals*. Going into a presidency at 37 openly espousing a hip-hop mindfulness was itself a declaration that I would be free in how I led and how I saw education. The creativity of hip-hop inspired me to find new ways to reach students, especially via social media. The braggadocio of hip-hop helped me find confidence as the youngest president for years, often dismissed by elders (especially the unimpressive ones), but over time earning respect like a young rapper in a cypher. Being at an HBCU reinforced to me the importance of placemaking, and how to share that with a generation that saw hip-hop create space and place. And the idea of speaking truth allowed me to write challenging editorials, even calling out a newspaper editor in Little Rock for pimping (and I used that word) Martin Luther King, Jr.'s words to justify a conservative ideology. It is a way that hip-hop closely aligns with the Black prophetic preaching tradition, one that I was steeped in, growing up a preacher's kid in Atlanta.

Dr. Jenkins's work provides a framework for other educators to creatively engage their students and encourages them to lean into their own authentic hip-hop selves as they do their work. For me, this text validates what I knew back in 2004. Being the hip-hop president was a good thing as an educator. It still is.

—Walter Kimbrough
President, Dillard University
#HIPHOPPREZ

# Series Foreword

Recent incidents indicate that race still casts a long and poignant shadow in the United States, over society writ large and schools in particular. The killing of Tyre Nichols, by police in Memphis, Tennessee, on January 7, 2023, shows that the police violence in Black communities that led to the deaths of George Floyd and Breonna Taylor is still an entrenched and intractable problem (Blow, 2023; Rojas et al., 2023). The attacks that conservatives are making on the schools with the invented and deceptive claim that they are teaching Critical Race Theory is another indication of the intensity of problems related to race and culture in the United States (Cineas, 2020; Fortin, 2021; Ladson-Billings, 2021; Schwartz, 2021; Wallace-Wells, 2021). Another indication of racial and cultural polarization is the rejection in Florida of the pilot version of the AP course on African American history that was created by the College Board (Bouie, 2023; Gay, 2023; Hartocollis & Fawcett, 2023; Hartocollis et al., 2023; Makin, 2023; Mervosh, 2022).

This is a propitious time for the publication of this book because it affirms the importance of culture in the lives of African American and other marginalized youth and describes how educators can embrace and use the "hip-hop mindset" in education. Although pedagogy is not the focus of this book, hip-hop pedagogies can be used to increase the academic achievement and social development of students from stigmatized cultures and communities (Ladson-Billings, 2015; Ladson-Billings et al., 2023; Waldock, 2019). Hip-hop's origin is sometimes described as occurring at a particular birthday party in a predominantly African American and low-income South Bronx section of New York City in 1973 (Trebay, 2023). However, Morgan and Bennett (2011) locate the origin of hip-hop in the African diasporic community. Many of the Black and Latino artists who participated in the construction of hip-hop in the Bronx were recent immigrants from the Caribbean and consequently were "shaped by a range of African diasporic cultures" (p. 181).

Hip-hop provides a venue for disempowered youth to experience efficacy, protest racism and discrimination, and articulate their cultural identities and affiliations. It also provides a forum for youths to express their goals, skills, ambitions, worth, and caring in their communities (Alim et al., 2023).

Jenkins's goal in this book is to describe and help educators comprehend the "hip-hop mindset in education." She believes that before educators can effectively incorporate hip-hop into their pedagogical practice, they must understand its values and essence. She writes, "This book is primarily focused on understanding what a hip-hop mindset looks like in the field of education. But the discussion is broad, and the insights are relevant across many industries and fields. A hip-hop mindset benefits any professional" (p. 2). A hip-hop mindset can help teachers construct culturally responsive and culturally sustaining pedagogies and learning environments that will empower students from myriad racial, ethnic, cultural, and social-class groups (Ladson-Billings, 2015; Ladson-Billings et al., 2023). Jenkins details three mindsets and nine values, beliefs, attitudes, and behaviors that emerged from her research for this book and that constitute the hop-hop mindset. They are: (1) *Drive* (hunger, competitiveness, honor); (2) *Approach* (creativity/originality, authenticity/integrity, ingenuity/cultural efficacy); and (3) *Posture* (confidence/claiming space). Jenkins writes, "Exploring hip-hop as a professional mindset in education is not about how you can use hip-hop as a classroom tool, but rather how you can embody it in your practice" (p. 6). A group of interviews with professionals illustrates how they enact the hip-hop mindset in practice.

This is also a propitious time for the publication of this book because 50 years of hip-hop is being celebrated in 2023. The Grammys have had an ambivalent relationship with hip-hop music. Only two hip-hop albums have won the Grammy for Album of the Year—the last recognition was in 2004, almost 20 years ago. Perhaps to make amends, the Grammys devoted a 15-minute segment of its program on Sunday, February 5, 2023, to commemorate 50 years of hip-hop music. The presentations were curated by Questlove of the Roots and consisted of over 20 songs from different decades, regions, and movements (Coscarelli, 2023). An exhibition commemorating the 50th anniversary of hip-hop opened in February 2023 at the Museum at FIT (Fashion Institute of Technology) in New York City, *Fresh, Fly, and Fabulous: Fifty Years of Hip Hop Style* (Trebay, 2023). A similarly-titled book accompanied the exhibition (Way & Romero, 2023).

The major purpose of the Multicultural Education Series is to provide preservice educators, practicing educators, graduate students, scholars, and policymakers with an interrelated and comprehensive set of books that summarizes and analyzes important research, theory, and practice related to the education of ethnic, racial, cultural, and linguistic groups in the United States and the education of mainstream students about diversity. The dimensions of multicultural education, developed by Banks and described in the *Handbook of Research on Multicultural Education* (Banks, 2004), *The Routledge International Companion to Multicultural Education* (Banks, 2009), and in the *Encyclopedia of Diversity in Education* (Banks, 2012), provide the conceptual framework for the development of the publications in the Series.

The dimensions are content integration, the knowledge construction process, prejudice reduction, equity pedagogy, and an empowering institutional culture and social structure. The books in the Multicultural Education Series provide research, theoretical, and practical knowledge about the behaviors and learning characteristics of students of color (Conchas & Vigil, 2012; Lee, 2007), language minority students (Gándara & Hopkins, 2010; Valdés, 2001; Valdés et al., 2011), low-income students (Cookson, 2013), multiracial youth (Joseph & Briscoe-Smith, 2021; Mahiri, 2017); and other minoritized population groups, such as students who speak different varieties of English (Charity Hudley & Mallinson, 2011) and LGBTQ youth (Mayo, 2022).

A major tenet of this book is that teachers and other educators need to incorporate students' languages, cultures, and identities—including those that are embodied in hip-hop—to create culturally responsive and culturally sustaining learning environments. A number of the books in the Multicultural Education Series describe effective ways to implement culturally responsive and culturally sustaining teaching and learning, including Geneva Gay (2018), *Culturally Responsive Teaching: Theory, Research, and Practice* (3rd ed.); Tyrone C. Howard, (2020), *Why Race and Culture Matter in Schools: Closing the Achievement Gap in America's Classrooms* (2nd ed.); Sonia Nieto (2009), *The Light in Their Eyes: Creating Multicultural Learning Communities*; Kia Darling-Hammond and Linda Darling-Hammond (2022), *The Civil Rights Road to Deeper Learning: Five Essentials for Equity*; Catherine S. Taylor with Susan B. Nolen (2022), *Culturally and Socially Responsible Assessment: Theory, Research, and Practice*; Paul C. Gorski (2018), *Reaching and Teaching Students in Poverty: Strategies for Erasing the Opportunity Gap* (2nd ed.), and H. Samy Alim and John Baugh (2006), *Talkin Black Talk: Language, Education, and Social Change.*

The hip-hop mindset and framework described in this book can be used to enrich and revitalize teaching, especially for students who live in marginalized communities who have been considered "culturally deprived" for decades by many mainstream educators. This idea was popularized in the 1960s and 1970s (Riessman, 1962). However, as Alim (2012) states, educators should recognize that hip-hop is a "complex, contradictory, and problematic space" (p. 1065). Within hip-hop there are "difficult tensions around the politics of race, gender, generation, class, and violence" (p. 1065). Some of the lyrics in hip-hop music are violent, sexually explicit, and misogynistic. By the mid- to late 1980s, gangster rap had emerged. It glamorized conspicuous consumption, drugs, and alcohol, and depicted women as sex objects (Ladson-Billings, 2015). At the same time, other hip-hop artists were describing how everyday people were struggling daily to survive, which were counternarratives to the images and themes in gangster rap. Waldock (2019) describes how hip-hop can be used in the classroom to engage students in critical dialogues about the social issues articulated in the negative images in gangster rap:

> The reasons hip-hop has been deemed inappropriate in education by some teachers may be the very ones that justify its place in academia. Challenging

societal issues such as race, class, drug use, violence against women, and so forth, give students an opportunity to discuss relevant issues in modern society and, for some, from their daily lives. . . . Through critical dialogue, students and educators can cultivate the knowledge and tools to form opinions and make a difference within their community. (p. 34)

Teachers can help students understand the problematic characteristics of gangster rap as well as provide counternarratives and counterexamples, as Jenkins states in an engaging and informative section of this book, "Hip-hop culture has always created space particularly for Black women to speak. . . . But when looking at the topic of women in hip-hop, the true power lies in exploring what happens when women bless the mic" (p. 27). Jenkins describes the example of Queen Latifah writing a song called "Ladies First" that depicts the greatness of Black women. Other popular female hip-hop artists are Missy Elliott, Megan Thee Stallion, Cardi B, and Nicki Minaj. An important publication about women hip-hop artists is *Women Rapping Revolution: Hip Hop and Community Building* in *Detroit* by Rebekah Farrugia and Kellie D. Day (2020).

Teachers and other educators will find this book an informative and helpful resource when they use the hip-hop mindset and framework to transform their schools to make them culturally responsive and culturally sustaining. It is an important addition to the multicultural education literature and to the Multicultural Education Series, which it enriches.

—James A. Banks

## REFERENCES

Alim, H. S. (2012). Hip hop and education. In J. A. Banks (Ed.), *Encyclopedia of diversity in education* (Vol. 2, pp. 1062–1066). Sage Publications.

Alim, H. S., & Baugh, J. (2006). *Talkin Black talk: Language, education, and social change*. Teachers College Press.

Alim, H. S., Chang, J., & Wong, C. (Eds). (2023). *Freedom moves: Hip hop knowledges, pedagogies, and futures* (Vol. 3). University of California Press.

Banks, J. A. (2004). Multicultural education: Historical development, dimensions, and practice. In J. A. Banks & C. A. M. Banks (Eds.), *Handbook of research on multicultural education* (pp. 3–29). Jossey-Bass.

Banks, J. A. (Ed.). (2009). *The Routledge international companion to multicultural education*. Routledge.

Banks, J. A. (2012). Multicultural education: Dimensions of. In J. A. Banks (Ed.), *Encyclopedia of diversity in education* (Vol. 3, pp. 1538–1547). Sage Publications.

Blow, C. M. (2023, January 27). Tyre Nichols's death is America's shame. *The New York Times*. https://www.nytimes.com/2023/01/27/opinion/tyre-nichols-video.html

Bouie, J. (2023, January 29). Ron DeSantis likes his culture wars for a reason. *The New York Times*. https://www.nytimes.com/2023/01/24/opinion/desantis-florida -culture-w.html

Charity Hudley, A. H., & Mallinson, C. (2011). *Understanding English language variation in U. S. schools*. Teachers College Press.

Cineas, F. (2020, Sept. 24). Critical race theory, and Trump's war on it, explained. https://www.vox.com/2020/9/24/21451220/critical-race-theory-diversity-training -trump

Conchas, G. Q., & Vigil, J. D. (2012). *Streetsmart schoolsmart: Urban poverty and the education of adolescent boys*. Teachers College Press.

Cookson, P. W., Jr. (2013). *Class rules: Exposing inequality in American high schools*. Teachers College Press.

Coscarelli, J. (2023, February 5). The Grammys celebrate 50 years of hip-hop in a joyous performance. *The New York Times*. https://www.nytimes.com/2023/02 /05/arts/music/grammys-hip-hop-50th-anniversary-performance.html

Darling-Hammond, K., & Darling-Hammond, L. (2022). *The civil rights road to deeper learning: Five essentials for equity*. Teachers College Press.

Farrugia, R., & Day, K. D. (2020). *Women rapping revolution: Hip hop and community building in Detroit*. University of California Press.

Fortin, J. (2021, Nov. 8). Critical race theory: A brief history. *The New York Times*. https://www.nytimes.com/article/what-is-critical-race-theory.html

Gándara, P., & Hopkins, M. (Eds.). (2010). *Forbidden language: English language learners and restrictive language policies*. Teachers College Press.

Gay, G. (2018). *Culturally responsive teaching: Theory, research, and practice* (3rd ed.). Teachers College Press.

Gay, M. (2023, February 4). Erasing Black history is not the role of the College Board. *The New York Times*. https://www.nytimes.com/2023/02/04/opinion /black-history-desantis-college-board.html

Gorski, P. C. (2018). *Reaching and teaching students in poverty: Strategies for erasing the opportunity gap* (2nd ed.). Teachers College Press.

Hartocollis, A., & Fawcett, E. (2023, February 1). The College Board strips down its A. P. curriculum for African American studies. *The New York Times*. https:// www.nytimes.com/2023/02/01/us/college-board-advanced-placement-african -american-studies.html

Hartocollis, A., Goldstein, D., & Saul, S. (2023, February 13). The College Board's rocky path, through Florida, to the A. P. Black studies course. *The New York Times*. https://www.nytimes.com/2023/02/13/us/ap-black-studies-course-college -board-desantis.html

Howard, T. C. (2020). *Why race and culture matter in schools: Closing the achievement gap in America's classrooms* (2nd ed.). Teachers College Press.

Joseph, R. L., & Briscoe-Smith, A. (2021). *Generation mixed goes to school: Radically listening to multiracial kids*. Teachers College Press.

Ladson-Billings, G. (2015). You gotta fight the power: The place of hip hop in social justice education. In C. Benedict, P. Schmidt, G. Spruce, & P. Woodford (Eds.), *The Oxford handbook of social justice in music education* (pp. 406–422). Oxford University Press.

Ladson-Billings, G. (2021). *Critical race theory in education: A scholar's journey*. Teachers College Press.

Ladson-Billings, G., Paris, D., & Alim, H. S. (2023). "Where the beat drops": Culturally relevant and culturally sustaining hip hop pedagogies. In H. S. Alim, J. Chang, & C. Wong, (Eds.), *Freedom moves: Hip hop knowledges, pedagogies, and futures* (Vol. 3, pp. 245–268). University of California Press.

Lee, C. D. (2007). *Culture, literacy, and learning: Taking bloom in the midst of the whirlwind.* Teachers College Press.

Mahiri, J. (2017). *Deconstructing race: Multicultural education beyond the colorbind.* Teachers College Press.

Makin, K. (2023, January 27). AP African American studies: 'Academic legitimacy' or 'indoctrination'? *The Christian Science Monitor.* https://www.csmonitor.com /Commentary/2023/0127/AP-African-American-Studies-Academic-legitimacy -or-indoctrination

Mayo, C. (2022). *LGBTQ youth and education: Policies and practices* (2nd ed.). Teachers College Press.

Mervosh, S. (2022, August 27). Back to school in DeSantis's Florida, as teachers look over their shoulders. *The New York Times.* https://www.nytimes.com /2022/08/27/us/desantis-schools-dont-say-gay.html

Morgan, M., & Bennett, D. (2011). Hip-hop & the global imprint of a Black cultural form. *Daedalus, 61*(2), 176–196. https://www.academia.edu/35412460 /Hip_Hop_and_the_Global_Imprint_of_a_Black_Cultural_Form

Nieto, S. (2009). *The light in their eyes: Creating multicultural learning communities* (10th anniversary edition). Teachers College Press.

Riessman, F. (1962). *The culturally deprived child.* Harper and Row.

Rojas, R., Bohra, N., & Fawcett, E. (2023, February 12). What we know about Tyre Nichols's lethal encounter with Memphis police. *The New York Times.* https:// www.nytimes.com/article/tyre-nichols-memphis-police-dead.html

Schwartz, S. (2021, June 11; updated March 13, 2023). Map: Where critical race theory is under attack. *Education Week.* https://www.edweek.org/policy-politics /map-where-critical-race-theory-is-under-attack/2021/06

Taylor, C., with Nolen, S. B. (2022). *Culturally and socially responsible assessment: Theory, research, and practice.* Teachers College Press.

Trebay, G. (2023, February 8). Hip-hop, still fly at 50. *The New York Times.* https:// www.nytimes.com/2023/02/08/style/hip-hop-50th-anniversary-fashion.html

Valdés, G. (2001). *Learning and not learning English: Latino students in American schools.* Teachers College Press.

Valdés, G., Capitelli, S., & Alvarez, L. (2011). *Latino children learning English: Steps in the journey.* Teachers College Press.

Waldock, S. (2019). "We've got to fight the powers that be": Using hip-hop culture to educate and advocate in the classroom. *Canadian Music Educator, 61*(1), 34–38.

Wallace-Wells, B. (2021). How a conservative activist invented the conflict over critical race theory. *The New Yorker.* https://www.newyorker.com/news/annals-of-inquiry /how-a-conservative-activist-invented-the-conflict-over-critical-race-theory

Way, E., & Romero, E. (2023). *Fresh fly fabulous: 50 years of hip hop style.* Rizzoli Electa.

# Preface

## Trash-Talking

After spending many years leading university cultural centers and working with students within soul-filled, love-filled, culture-filled programs, I know that there is something deeper to cultural engagement. It is not simply enjoyment, socializing, and celebration. Particularly within hip-hop–based environments, the culture builds something in us. It gives us a gift. The power of cultural education is that it gives you more of yourself (more of your history, more of your values, more of your language, more of your ways of thinking, being, and doing).

This work is important to me because I can see very clearly how the hip-hop sides of myself have saved my professional life. I share these personal insights and experiences throughout the book. But it is important to acknowledge that I am not a hip-hop artist, executive, or insider. While I do dabble in spoken word poetry, I am nowhere near being seen as a spoken word artist or an emcee. I am not deeply connected to major hip-hop artists. In college, I interned in promotions at Capitol Records and Virgin Records but did not pursue a career in the industry. I chose to work in higher education. I started my career in higher education as an arts administrator planning hip-hop concerts and entertainment events on college campuses. Through my past work booking performers, I've met many hip-hop artists, but I don't know them personally. This is a book written by a fan who embraces the culture for other fans who also embrace the culture. Fans rarely get to speak on hip-hop as experts of their own experience.

Through the hip-hop–rich cultural programs that I created throughout my career, I saw very clearly that hip-hop is a culture that gifts its members the permission to believe in your own power, to claim your own brilliance, and to give yourself praise. Too often, in education, the power to praise rests with others. For students, the power is given to the teacher to praise and evaluate their performance. For educators, the power is given to their supervisors and school leaders to praise and evaluate their performance. For school and district leaders, the power is given to the school board. We are always waiting on someone else's voice to affirm our worth. Not in hip-hop.

Of course, the evaluation of others is still a factor in the music industry through music charts, ratings, awards, and media attention. Probably the most significant external evaluation comes from the consumer through record sales. The affirmation of others does matter across all industries. But what I most value about hip-hop is that hip-hop artists aren't waiting for a Grammy. They aren't waiting for Billboard to name them number one on the charts. They aren't even waiting for a platinum-selling album before they claim their greatness. They use their own voice to give themselves praise and value, and shine from the moment they open their mouths to rap. Imagine how that would feel for students to sit at a desk on the first day of school already claiming and believing in the honor roll, instead of having to prove to some doubtful other that they are worthy of it. Imagine what an educator might achieve if they could walk into the first day on the job already claiming a career achievement award in higher education or believing that they have a real shot at National Teacher of the Year in P–20, rather than having to jump hurdles to prove to colleagues, program coordinators, department chairs, and principals that their voice matters and they have something to contribute. By the time senior leaders are actually willing to listen, many new professionals have exhausted themselves to a point that they are too tired to even talk.

This project honors the life-giving, love-giving, permission-giving authority that hip-hop culture offers us—the authority to just take the mic and show the world what you've got. This means that in our work, we aren't striving to just "achieve." Achievement might simply mean graduating with the other hundreds of students at your school. Achievement might involve hitting your expected test scores and getting to keep your job. Sometimes our measures for achievement are pretty mediocre. Hip-hop artists and other professionals with a hip-hop mindset aren't just trying to achieve, they are striving to become superstars. This project is about that ethic: the mindset that creates superstars in any field.

# Acknowledgments

For my dad, who passed away in the process of my writing this book: Thank you for pouring absolutely everything you had into me so that I could become anything that I could imagine. Thank you for your love of music and your willingness to listen, enjoy, and appreciate it as it changed and moved in different directions. Hip-hop wasn't your jam, but you loved the way I loved it. I learned from you that what matters most is music's ability to bring people good times. My dearest memories of you involve records being played on our big, old-school stereo that looked like a piece of furniture in the living room. Please know that all that I do is for your honor. Rest well, dear spirit. There are no words for how much I miss you.

Many thanks to my husband William Henry and my mother Joyce Jenkins for the support and time given to me so that I could steal away and write in the midst of a pandemic, home schooling, and family loss. This was not an easy journey. Will, thanks for your positive belief that this project is something special. Love and thanks always to my sister Greta and brother-in-law Billy for their support since I was a kid. I will never forget those folks who poured love and invested in me as I started this journey in grad school and as a young professional—y'all sent checks in the mail, helped me move to various cities, and reminded me that I wasn't alone.

Thanks to my comrades in the struggle who participated and supported this project. Time is such a valuable thing and please know that your sharing it with me for these interviews is deeply appreciated.

Finally, thanks to my son Kai. Thanks for sharing me with my profession. Your grace and patience with having a mommy scholar is valued and appreciated. Please know that even when I am alone writing, you are always on my heart. At 9 years old, you remind me daily that hip-hop will feed the souls of generations to come. Thank you for sharing my love of dancing and music. You are always down to learn a new dance challenge or routine on YouTube. Thank you for your pretend play as a DJ with your little turntable and keyboard. Thank you for your loud, off-key singing and rapping. Your highly energetic, creative mind and your body that demands movement motivate me to do all I can to help create an educational system that can and will inspire you.

## CHAPTER 1

# Born to Rhyme, Destined to Shine
## The Hip-Hop Mindset Framework

Do you have a stage song? You know, the professional anthem that is play-ing in your head as you walk on stage (aka the conference room, the meeting room, the classroom). When entertainers or celebrities are introduced, there is usually music playing that serves as their secondary, artistic introduction. It fills the room with the spirit of that person. During her *Becoming* book tour, former First Lady Michelle Obama often walked out to "Girl on Fire" by Alicia Keys. What song plays in your imagination when you enter a room or sit down to start a work project? My stage song is Special Ed's "I Got it Made." The song is filled with nonchalant braggadocio. It makes me smile to hear the humor in the over-the-top, unrealistic brags in the song (e.g., that he has a "dog with a solid gold bone" and a waiter who made him "potato alligator soufflé"). It also makes me feel good. It is contagious as I listen to it. By mid-song, I also feel dope and audacious. Indeed, I got it made.

I am a professor. I am not an emcee, a dancer, or a DJ. But I *am* hip-hop. As an academic scholar, I also take words, ideas, facts, information, and cre-ate magic. It is a privilege and a pleasure to do this work. What's beautiful about the song "I Got It Made" is that Special Ed was only 16 years old when he wrote that rhyme 30 years ago—a song that still has the ability to boost the confidence of a 46-year-old professor. That's powerful. As we begin a journey to explore the ways of being, doing, and thinking that are hip-hop, you must first take a moment and appreciate what hip-hop youth did with language, because it all started with words. The youth that created hip-hop flipped the position of an entire cultural community. They took kids whom American society viewed as deviant, unimportant nobodies and turned them into superstars who were given a microphone to speak to the world. Hell yeah, I love hip-hop.

Hip-hop culture, born in the 1970s, has framed much of my cultural sense of self. As I was beginning to grow as a young woman and form a real identity, so was hip-hop. I align hip-hop with my cultural identity because it represents those of us who refuse to live our lives in the boundaries of so-cially constructed lanes and seek to bring all of ourselves into the work that we do. Hip-hop heads aren't just out-of-the-box thinkers. In fact, I contend that people who actually "think outside the box" typically don't use that

1

term. The box doesn't even exist in their mind. In hip-hop history, we see this proven by the youth who didn't need a canvas or a gallery to display their art. Instead, they reimagined subway and freight trains as mobile exhibit spaces. It was also illustrated in the ingenuity of the young people who recycled cardboard boxes into dancefloors and those who took three fingers, challenged the needle of the record player, and won. You really don't have to encourage or push creative thinkers to be different—they just are. No retreats, workshops, or motivational speakers were ever needed to inspire a generation of young people to build a cultural legacy that has sustained for almost 50 years.

But hip-hop culture is not about making great efforts to be different. It's about being unapologetically true. Being true and being different aren't the same thing, but in many societies around the world, one often leads to the other. My country, the United States, is a society that is steeped in both historic and contemporary oppression, racism, patriarchy, nationalism, and cultural imperialism, yet consistently refuses to acknowledge—and most often outright denies—the influence of any of these negative belief systems on U.S. policies, institutions, systems, or citizens.[1] That is why those systems continue. Denial serves to keep oppression alive. Denial maintains the status quo. Naming the history of oppression in our society is often viewed as a divergent act—unpatriotic and problematic.[2] In a society like ours, truth-telling is a revolutionary act. Truth-telling leads to change. While we often teach children that telling the truth is important, ethical, and even sacred, there are some truths that educators aren't ready to hear from their students. There are some stories and life experiences that don't seem to belong in the classroom or on the pristine stage of a school auditorium. In the American educational system, youth are allowed to speak publicly only when they have permission and approval from adults. So it was indeed quite different for a group of youth to grab the microphone and tell their own truths, in their own native tongue, and seek only the approval of their own community. It was innovative. And infectious. The young Black and Brown kids from New York who created hip-hop have given us all permission to be real.

Hip-hop culture is more than just the music that frames its foundation. It is not only the DJs, emcees, dancers, and graffiti artists who comprise the hip-hop community. Hip-hop habits of mind are also embedded in the professional approaches of educators, community leaders, politicians, doctors, lawyers, restaurateurs, and writers—multiple populations and multiple generations of people who identify with this culture. We are all hip-hop. And we bring a hip-hop mindfulness to how we work and show up in the world. I show up as a scholar who studies education, so this book is primarily focused on understanding what a hip-hop mindset looks like in the field of education. But the discussion is broad, and the insights are relevant across many industries and fields. A hip-hop mindset benefits any professional.

## CULTURE AS A POLITIC

A community often uses culture (cultural production, engagement, education) as a politic of social survival. A *politic* is a set of strategies that people use to advance themselves.[3] Undoubtedly, cultural folkways and heritage have taught us strategies of resourcefulness, resilience, language, navigation, and innovation.[4] Culture often serves as a life raft for those drowning in oppression. Our students need this life raft in the classroom. Community educator and activist Paulo Freire stressed how important raising critical consciousness is among the oppressed.[5] Resistant education helps traditionally oppressed communities to grow critical literacy and form their own strategies to resist oppressive systems and structures. Rarely do institutions built on frameworks of oppression do the necessary work of educating for freedom. And so, our communities use every means necessary to educate our people—porches, stoops, kitchen tables, churches, and cultural production. I learned from hip-hop things that I never learned in school.

Growing up in South Carolina, we rarely learned about any social experience beyond South Carolina. The South was all that mattered. So, I learned about the critical experiences of my racial and cultural peers in northern cities through hip-hop. I was exposed to international culture through the music that mixed in West Indian and Latinx culture. In school, we were never required to read books that helped us to better understand our own experiences and histories, much less the experiences of Black folx in other parts of the country. I want to stress here that I was born and raised in the South, which for many people is the geographical core of African American history. We were living on the land where this history was made and we never learned it in any real, deep, or nuanced way in school. If our schools didn't have us studying the major history that happened right here, they definitely weren't trying to reach all the way up to New York to teach us the northern Black experience. But outside of school, our music and the videos created to visually accompany that music were teaching us the similarities and differences between our southern experiences with oppression and those of our peers in the Northeast and on the West Coast.

Through hip-hop, I understood several things very clearly: (1) I was not alone; (2) Racism was a national issue, not a southern one; (3) Poverty happened everywhere, but looked different in different places; and (4) Young people could both say and do something about it. The first three issues are fairly obvious—witnessing life in other places expands your sense of connectedness to the world. But the last concept regarding youth agency was quite salient. In the South, generational hierarchy is real. There is a deep culture of showing respect by being quiet, being patient, waiting your turn, and knowing your place. And young people's place is typically the lowest in society. Adults were the doers in the South. Kids were to watch, listen, and do as they were told.

But it was very clear that there was no adult "telling" these young kids in New York City how to do hip-hop. They weren't following orders; they were creating culture. They were speaking independently. They were naming loudly who and what they wanted to be even if that seemed worlds away from the actual truth. A kid from the poorest projects brags about being super paid. A kid who might have been failing in school proclaims that they are talented, gifted, and Number One. What gave them this audacity to pick up the microphone and directly contest everything society was saying about them? In the South, old folx might say "Hush your foolishness" or "Stop telling stories." But these stories were exactly what all of us needed: Hope and possibility mixed with truth. Because the truth is those kids weren't just good, they were exceptional.

Generating a sense of greatness is important when you have lived a life on the margins of society. In their creative work, despite their life circumstances, hip-hop artists have always talked about their greatness, their skill, and their aim to be the best. At its core, hip-hop is about truth, nonconformity, excellence, and unapologetic love for communities of people that society has taught us don't even deserve love. At their best, the lyrics penned by hip-hop artists and the poems written by spoken-word artists are a valuable form of knowledge and social critique of the American experience. For me, hip-hop was my most culturally relevant form of social studies.

We knew so little about the North, so we often believed what we heard. And the word on the street was that New York City was a scary place, filled with young people who were all thugs. But then the young people of New York began to speak and rhyme and document their lives via music video. Special Ed didn't look like a thug to me, he looked dreamy. A Tribe Called Quest and De La Soul looked quirky and different, like some of my friends in my honors classes. MC Lyte wasn't like any girl I knew, but I wanted her swag in my crew. Hip-hop demystified the Black experience even for Black people who had become separated and culturally disconnected by the Great Migration. We could now share, exchange, and inspire. This was youth teaching youth to be more than their situation—to become whatever they dreamed, imagined, and spoke.

Whether art imitated life or life imitated art, it didn't matter. They had us believing that we could be whatever we speak. I'm sure many teachers told me this before, but hip-hop artists embodied a hardheaded determination to transcend their circumstances. They had us believing that we could fully acknowledge the poor neighborhood or housing project from which we came, show you images of our humble surroundings, denounce society for keeping its foot on our backs, and still proclaim ourselves King or Queen of the city—and then culturally become that very thing. As a southern kid, I had no clue who the mayor of New York City was in the 1980s. For me, New York City was Run-D.M.C., LL Cool J, Doug E. Fresh, Salt-N-Pepa, Eric B. & Rakim, MC Lyte, Heavy D, and KRS-One.

I argue that before an educator attempts to integrate hip-hop into their pedagogical practice, they must come to understand and value its essence first. As P. Thandi Hicks Harper notes:

> Hip-hop is an "all encompassing" culture for many of America's youth. It includes forces that affect and influence the choices these youth make in their everyday lives. Hip-hop represents a strong and unified youth consciousness; it is a powerful and pervasive movement among youth worldwide. Youth, regardless of who they are or where they come from, very likely will identify with at least some aspect of Hip-Hop culture.[6]

As a culture, hip-hop has always provided a physical space that brought marginalized communities into the center. This is what makes the hip-hop cypher so philosophically compelling. In hip-hop, a *cypher* is a circle of energy created by members of the community forming a physical circle and giving each person a turn to get in the middle and perform (rhyme or dance).[7] Each person gets their moment not only to shine, but to have the community literally centered and focused on their talents.

A cypher I witnessed in the unglamorous setting of a grocery store parking lot over 20 years ago motivated me to probe the value of hip-hop culture within people's lives. As I approached my car, I glanced at a group of really young boys. They had formed an informal cypher on one of the medians in the lot. As I shared earlier, I identify as a part of the hip-hop generation; at the time (the 1990s), I worked in student affairs on a college campus planning major events like hip-hop concerts, and I worked with undergraduate college student leaders (about half of whom wanted to be rappers). I share all of this to say that the concept of a cypher was not new to me. What struck me was how young these kids were. I walked over to the group because I wanted to hear what a bunch of 12-year-olds were talking about. Instead, I wound up critically analyzing the power of the cypher itself. It was something that I'd seen many times and had participated in as a poet, but I had never deeply dissected the cypher as a space of incredible knowledge production and personal development. One kid was in the center of the circle spitting a rhyme. The others were so intensely listening that they were physically bent over, leaning in to ensure that they didn't miss a word. Many of their heads and some of their whole bodies were bobbing to the rhythm being created by the emcee's words. The visual was striking; I thought that many teachers would love to have young boys listen that intensely in class. As I continued to observe the group, I grasped for the first time the level of self-confidence engineered within hip-hop culture. When the kid in the center finished, he was immediately applauded. He felt great. He felt listened to. He felt that his thoughts mattered. He felt that his talents were strong.

Then the next kid stepped up to take his place in the middle of the cypher. There was a clear sense of healthy competition. This new kid had genuinely applauded the boy before him, but he was also clearly determined to be better. Hip-hop culture shows us how to create genuine communities of excellence and a healthy competitive spirit rooted in kinship. This is what educators need to borrow from hip-hop, not to make young people rap to learn subject matter (schoolhouse rap). Educators who simply use rap or spoken word poetry as a memorization or rote-learning tool are missing the point of what hip-hop culture really contributes. These boys were free to be themselves—bright, playful, smart Black boys who aspired to be great at something. Participation in hip-hop cultural activities gives young people guts. The guts to take a chance. The guts to be vulnerable. And, most importantly, the guts to engage in important forms of truth-telling.[8] What I know for sure is that everyone of us standing in or near the circle that day felt great. We felt alive and a part of something good. Hip-hop culture, its community, its music, and its lyrics can do that for you. It gives you energy. It inspires.

Through the stories that they told in hip-hop music, young people countered the social narrative about themselves and their communities. The first thing that they creatively transformed was the meaning of words. They took words whose original meaning centered around deficit, negativity, and lack, and gave them new, positive meanings. They showed us that nothing has to be what we have always been taught it is. Anything and everything can be seen, viewed, and understood differently—whether it's words or people. Urban slang has taken the literal meaning of the word ill (to be in poor health, sick, deficient in quality) and made it mean the exact opposite. In hip-hop culture, to be ill is to be incredible, highly skilled, the very best. To "murder" something or "kill it" in hip-hop means to do so well that you end any possibility of competition. There is admittedly a lot of aggressive talk in hip-hop, but all mentions of murders, kills, and guns aren't literal. When you are hunting, no one can come back after you and re-kill that which you already shot. That kill was yours. It's done. Your name is on it. That's what emcees are seeking to do with words, with rhymes, with stages—kill it and stamp their name on it. Hip-hop lyrics remind me that I am dope and powerful. The culture gives me the language and the permission to own my aspirations to be great in life. Hip-hop culture affirms that it's okay to know and admit that I'm hot—I'm brilliant and talented at what I do.

Exploring hip-hop as a professional mindset in education is not about how you can use hip-hop as a classroom tool, but rather how you can embody it in your practice. Professor Christopher Emdin offered this call to the field of education: "I suggest that hip-hop educators move beyond the overly saturated and hyper defensive argument for rap in the classroom, and into a more active push for positioning hip-hop as a valid culture with positive attributes that can be built upon to make authentic connections to school."[9]

This book joins that realm of scholarship that moves beyond arguing the worth of hip-hop pedagogy or the content of rap lyrics. Instead, in this project, I deeply study hip-hop as a broader culture and its relevance to various professional disciplines. I dedicate my time to exploring what is good, valuable, and insightful in the culture. Enough has been documented on its problems. What haven't we considered? What are the things that we do not already know or understand about hip-hop? The research that informs this book falls into the category of what Petchauer labeled hip-hop aesthetic forms-scholarship that situates hip-hop as "a set of aesthetic practices containing and producing situated ways of doing (and being)."[10] To educators reading this book, you don't need to embrace a hip-hop mindset for your students; you need to do it for yourself. This book is for professionals. It is about the utility of the hip-hop mindset as an ethic of professional practice.

Following in the spirit of the canon first established by scholar Tricia Rose, I will acknowledge here what this project is and what it isn't. This is not a book about the history of hip-hop.[11] I am not exploring the artistic elements of the culture, but rather the spirit that is brought to the art—the mindset that creates it. I'm also looking at the habits of mind that the art inspires in those who don't even see themselves as artists. How does an educator embrace a hip-hop mindset? Can a person in business also adopt it? I am a cultural scholar, and this work paints a portrait of the culture that hip-hop creates. As Sean McCollom stresses in the article, "Hip-hop: A Culture of Vision and Voice," hip-hop is more than the artistic elements that form its practice.[12]

> Hip-Hop embraces these artistic elements, most definitely. But it also has blended and transcended them to become a means for seeing, celebrating, experiencing, understanding, confronting, and commenting on life and the world. Hip-Hop, in other words, is a way of living—a *culture*.

This is also not a book about teaching strategies or about those who integrate emceeing, spoken word, dance, or graffiti into their teaching or scholarship. Rather, I am trying to pen a portrait of what a hip-hop *ethic* looks like in professional practice outside of the art form. If you are a professional in any field who embraces hip-hop in how you show up in the world—how you think, act, and move—this book is definitely for you. But it is also for those who haven't even considered that they might have something to learn from hip-hop culture. Hip-hop culture is not simply a tool for you to "reach" students, nor is it a costume for you to put on to seem cool. Hip-hop is not something you can pretend to be. But it is a culture whose insights, wisdom, and inspiration some professionals need. In the book, I introduce readers to 15 educators who embrace a hip-hop mindset in their careers. I include insightful quotes from their interviews throughout all of the book chapters, and the remaining content of their interview is shared without analysis and framing in Chapter 6, "Can I Kick It?" The goal is to expose readers not only to the critical analysis of art, literature, and other forms of culture that helped develop the Hip-Hop Mindset Framework, but to also invite you into the hip-hop educational community—to hear their stories and learn from their reflections.

A cultural experience can inspire you to think differently or approach life differently, even if you never become a part of the culture. A conversation that I had with my dear friend Tony Keith Jr. (who is featured in this book) after he returned from time in Tanzania helps to illustrate my point here. One of the salient memories that Tony shared from his trip was from his visit with the Maasai. Maasai men are warriors, famous for being both fearless and intelligent in their approach.[13] What stood out for Tony was the open and unabashed show of affection, love, and friendship among the Maasai men. He commented that they held hands as they walked, embraced each other, and openly showed emotions of happiness, kindness, and joy. These warrior men were dispelling every stereotype that equated hypermasculinity with ideals of hardness, toughness, and lack of emotion. Tony departed East Africa forever impacted because that experience changed his mind about how he should show up in his relationships with male friends, colleagues, and students. It freed him to be human with his male peers. He did not leave East Africa as a Maasai member. He left with the inspiration to simply be his natural loving self. This is the cultural experience that I am suggesting all educators can have with hip-hop. You don't need to put down this book and go straight to the store to purchase a Kangol. You also don't need to claim to be a hip-hop head. You can simply just be inspired to change your mind about some things and try your hand at doing other things differently. I did this work because I am interested in illustrating a different type of hip-hop performance—how folx show off and show out beyond the stage.

## THE HIP-HOP MINDSET

Nine hip-hop–driven values, beliefs, attitudes, and behaviors emerged vividly from the research that informed this book. I refer to them as "practices." These professional practices, which form the Hip-Hop Mindset Framework, are organized below in Table 1.1.

The first mindset concerns Drive. Drive involves three practices: (1) *Hunger:* Hunger is about dreaming, grinding, and working to not just meet one's goals but to "slay" them. It is the act of craving and seeking an opportunity to be "put on." (2) *Competitiveness:* Competitiveness involves having high expectations and ambition to be the best. (3) *Honor and Kinship:* Kinship is about shining independently while maintaining communal connectedness (as in, "I'm dope, I'm #1; this is my life experience"

**Table 1.1. The Hip-Hop Mindset Framework**

| Mindset | Drive |
| --- | --- |
| Practice 1 | Hunger |
| Practice 2 | Competitiveness |
| Practice 3 | Honor and Kinship |

| Mindset | Approach |
| --- | --- |
| Practice 4 | Creativity |
| Practice 5 | Authenticity |
| Practice 6 | Ingenuity |

| Mindset | Posture |
| --- | --- |
| Practice 7 | Confidence |
| Practice 8 | Claiming Space |
| Practice 9 | Commanding Attention |

but also "My squad is dope, my crew is #1; this is *our* life experience in our community"). Honor concerns having gratitude for the ways that others have "put you on" and learning to do the same. It also concerns issues of respect—respecting the work of other artists, respecting the rules, respecting the community.

The second mindset is Approach. Approach involves three practices: (1) *Creativity:* Being unique, bringing something new to the existing corpus, is critical in hip-hop. There is a value in innovating—transforming or remixing something old into a fresh creation. Hip-hop artists are "seers" or visionaries who can see utility in what others may view as worthless; (2) *Authenticity/Integrity*: Representing oneself and/or community in a way that is real, clear, and true. Hip-hop is about accountability and showing up as your full, whole self (not a watered-down version to please others); and (3) *Ingenuity/Efficacy/Optimism*: Ingenuity concerns being clever and inventive. Cultural efficacy and optimism concern believing that you can do whatever you imagine. Before you invent anything, you must first believe that you can. Cultural efficacy is an optimistic belief in, appreciation for, and respect of one's culture and the people in it. Efficacy is driven by the question: Who are we waiting on to love us? We have to love ourselves.

The final mindset concerns Posture, or one's presence within their professional space. The three practices related to posture are: (1) *Confidence:* A strong belief in one's ability. Confidence concerns having the guts to be a non-conformist; to tell the truth; and to try something new. (2) *Claiming Space:* "Owning" any space that you occupy. To own it means to confidently enter, move through it, and transform it knowing that you have the right (the talent, the skills, the ability) to do so. To claim space is to reject ideas of imposter, renter, or borrower and claim the throne as your own. (3) *Commanding Attention*: Having a dynamic and engaging presence and knowing how to move the community. Speaking boldly and bravely (speaking loudly, in your language, and about the things that matter to your people). In hip-hop, microphones project your voice, they don't quiet it. Being heard is important. Listening is also a critical form of action (hip-hop's listeners do more than listen; they memorize, repeat, and internalize important words).

Figure 1.1 depicts the hip-hop mindset through three triangles or pyramids—an intentional nod to the great Ancient Egyptian pyramids of Giza. Why use pyramids? First, the pyramids of Ancient Egypt were grand tombs built to house the assets, gifts, and inheritances of the pharaohs. Ancient Egyptians were the first to believe in an afterlife and the wealthy desired to take their wealth with them after death.[14] These tombs were essentially storage houses for their wealth. Relating this to hip-hop, culture is a highly valuable inheritance[15] and asset.[16] And hip-hop is a community-built archive, a storage house of our cultural genius and community cultural wealth (documenting it through lyrics, music videos, murals, graffiti, movies, books, magazines, articles, and courses).

Additionally, the great pyramids are designated as "Wonders of the World." Scholars still debate how they were built with the mechanical and technological knowledge at the time. The fact that the pyramid complex is still standing is awe-inspiring.[17] As an artform, hip-hop has undoubtedly defied the odds in terms of its longevity. No one thought the music would last, and it is a social standard 50 years later. Beyond the music, as a culture, hip-hop's influence, impact, and global pervasiveness also stand as a "wonder," given that it was built by youth who had no access to the tools, privileges, or resources needed to build a multibillion-dollar industry. Yet they did.

When you understand hip-hop as a cultural mindset that has nothing to do with your ability to rhyme, breakdance, or spin records, you can appreciate that everyone can benefit from hip-hop mindfulness. You don't have to dress fly, talk slick, or know all the lyrics. In this book, I am encouraging an embrace of the hip-hop *mindset*—a more conscious understanding

**Figure 1.1. The Hip-Hop Mindset**

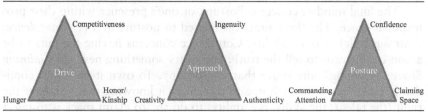

of the utility of hip-hop culture. To be mindful, you must be aware: aware of who you are, aware of the talent that you have to give, aware of how you work, and aware of why you work. Hip-hop mindfulness involves being keenly aware that what you are doing, how you are moving, the way that you are thinking, your practice, your pedagogy, your attitude, or your beliefs are invoking a hip-hop mindset and will help you to shine like a star in the process. Walking and moving through your life or your career with purposeful awareness gives you a bold kind of *swag*. An attitude of assuredness. Folx with swag don't just possess it, they know that they have it. They own it. Possession is simply to have something physically in your presence. Ownership is about having the legitimate right to it. Hip-hop mindfulness is about embracing your legitimate right to your kind of knowledge, your kind of scholarship, your kind of communication, your kind of brilliance, your kind of talent, and your kind of professional swag.

## CHAPTER 2

# Drive

While interviewing professionals for this book, I wrote a little comment on a notecard that captures why "drive" is such a critical aspect of the hip-hop mindset: "Chasing the GOAT gets you everything in the process." GOAT stands for "greatest of all time." If you are always striving to be the best, you wind up working so hard that you receive all kinds of growth opportunities, small wins, life experiences, setbacks (that create resilience), and affirmations (that keep you going). You may not start out as Number One, but the process of chasing that goal gets you much more than the title—it builds you into a superstar. Before there was Diana Ross, there was a group of young girls hungry for success called the Supremes. Before there was Beyoncé, there was Destiny's Child. Both groups were successful in their own right. They made money, they won awards, they slayed performances, they had an enormous fan base, and they influenced the culture. They were big. But for some people, even big isn't big enough. And while Beyoncé Knowles and Diana Ross may have had solo artist dreams, those past experiences (chasing the GOAT) shaped, molded, prepared, and built the two lead singers into the superstars that they would eventually become. Let's begin our exploration of drive by first exploring what it means to be hungry.

## HUNGER

Eminem opens the song, "Lose Yourself," with a question: What would you do if you had one shot to make all of your dreams come true—to have everything?[1] If we are likening professional ambition to the idea of being hungry, this question is essentially asking, "How hungry are you?" How large is your appetite? Success means different things to different people. Will an appetizer satiate you or are you out to ravish the buffet? Most hip-hop artists' answer would be they want it all—every course; or, as Jay-Z would say, they are trying to "scrape the plate." In other words, folx who are hungry sop up opportunity—they don't even leave crumbs of possibility uneaten. The difference between the appetizer and the market price prime rib signifies much more than just the size of your appetite, it is also a metaphor for the size of your dreams. It might also reveal a bit about the size of your personality.

I am pragmatic. I know exactly how much money I have in the bank and what I can afford on the menu. Even if finances are fine, I still might lean conservative out of respect—I don't want to bankrupt a friend who's just trying to be nice and treat me to lunch. I might only go crazy if it's a special occasion. But we all have that friend who goes all out regardless. It doesn't matter who is paying or if this is just a nothing-special dinner on a Tuesday night; they are ordering the prime rib. Why? Because they didn't come to a fancy restaurant to eat hot wings. They have dreams, and those dreams involve them using a fork and knife.

In the book *Decoded*, Jay-Z lays out many of the ways that he sees the culture of the streets and hustling influencing the mindset of hip-hop artists. One major influence is the culture of wanting the top spot. He explains that this culture of competitiveness is more than hip-hop attracting a bunch of alpha males (though he acknowledges that they are indeed mostly alphas). He also asserts that it is more than just wanting to get paid. According to Jay-Z, within both cultures (hip-hop and street hustling), a young kid is reaping rewards that surpass a good paycheck (even if that is something the kid desperately needs). Considering the odds one must beat to make it on the streets or in hip-hop, it is an incredible achievement to be the one who actually does. On the streets this might mean being the one who survives all the negative possibilities (death, prison, disability) to become the top dealer.[2] In hip-hop it might mean being the one who makes it through all of the obstacles, gatekeepers, setbacks, and challenges to become the top artist. When you consider that so many hip-hop artists have literally come from neighborhoods and housing projects that are so far on the social and political margins of their city that they don't have connections to anything outside of their surroundings, you have to ask, How in the world do socially and politically silenced, disconnected, disenfranchised young people get record deals? As Jay-Z asserts, they are willing to lay it all on the line and just go for it because "they think they're due for a miracle . . . The kid in McDonalds gets a check and that's it. There's no dream in fast food. Manager? That's a promotion, not a dream."[3] That's the critical difference with hunger in hip-hop. Folx aren't just trying to eat, they are holding out, grinding hard, believing they deserve that prime rib.

That doesn't mean that one expects to show up on day one and get the top spot. Even charge cards have limits; if you can't afford it, you can't afford it. What's most important is knowing very clearly that you want it and being willing to work passionately, purposefully, with love, dedication, and commitment to get it. Professionals who are hungry *care*. They care about being Number One. They care about achieving their goals. They care if someone else is in the spot that they desire. It matters. They feel it. A hip-hop mindset is not about being nonchalant and numb. It is about being very keenly aware of the opportunity that you want or that you just want an opportunity. Hunger is knowing that when you do get in the door of the restaurant and you are able to sit at the table, you will devour whatever op-portunity is served to you. The cry is, Just let me in, just let me eat!

We see these mindsets illustrated in the lyrics of various hip-hop songs. In Wale's "Ambition," he raps that the right time is always now when it comes to everything and that ambition can't be bought—it is in your veins. This means that our goals and professional desires are always ur-gent. The time is always now to make moves on your dreams. His reference to ambition being "in your veins" reiterates the point that I made earlier: People who are professionally hungry *feel* that hunger. It is a physical mani-festation of emotion similar to nervousness, anxiousness, and restlessness. Metaphorically, your stomach also growls with ambition.

What value does this metaphorical hunger have to professionals out-side of hip-hop? Tapping into the natural instincts that drive us when we are hungry keeps us on the move and ensures that we don't slow to a pace where we find ourselves sitting still. In the wild, animals that are full don't hunt. The only animals that you see out on the move and in the hunt (fo-cused, strategizing, seeking, and chasing goals) are hungry ones. The great thing about hunger is that regardless of how full you might be at the mo-ment (content in your career), hunger will always creep back up. Tonight's feelings of being stuffed and satisfied will soon subside and the pains will eventually come back, motivating you to get up, get moving, and reach for new bites to eat. It seems that those hip-hop artists who are able to sustain longevity in their careers are always hungry, always on the hunt. And that hunt often takes one of two forms: Either you are grazing or you are eating a five course meal.

Grazers amass a track record of constantly slaying goal after goal after goal. They are always on the hunt for the next great goal. As they achieve one accomplishment (a record deal), their eye is steady on the next-level accomplishment (a #1 song). In the realm of social activism, Cesar Chavez (the founder of the first successful union for farm workers) summed up this ethic with the mantra "*la lucha continua*" (the struggle continues).[4] As an activist, Chavez used this mantra to remind his comrades that there was no such thing as a stopping point or a final win. As soon as they achieved one victory, they began working on another cause. Why? Because the plight of the community reflected many different hurdles, and each required a similar work ethic from those who wanted to create social change. People can be hungry for a lot of things—hungry for job opportunities, hungry for social change, hungry to make a difference, hungry to make a mark in the world. When grazers accomplish a goal, they may definitely take time to celebrate and enjoy the moment, to relish in the space that they have worked hard to enter (this is hip-hop, and we do party). But they will soon be pushing themselves to beat their own best.

Hunger can also take the shape of a well-planned five-course meal. Many professionals move through life knowing that each opportunity is part of a greater life experience, a bigger life purpose. While they enjoy small wins in the process, they are in it for the big win, the throne. And so five-coursers approach everything they do with a Michelin star–type effort. Every new song is treated like it might win the Grammy because the artist is so certain that they are destined for the award. They are creating a catalogue, a professional reputation. This means that every day counts. If you are a teacher, every lesson plan matters. Every student does, too. Each course in a five-course meal must be on point, or the entire meal is ruined. It's a comprehensive experience. If we see our careers in this way, this means that no matter where I work at the moment (even if I know this isn't ultimately where I want to be); no matter the current position (even if this isn't my dream job); every experience contributes to the catalogue of my career. People will remember me here. I will create a legacy (good or bad) based on how I perform at each place. I can take an opportunity and use it to build myself up, or I can waste it.

What would have happened if someone like Dr. Dre or Ice Cube gave half an effort when they were with Ruthless, the small record company started by their neighborhood friend Eric "Eazy-E" Wright? Ruthless was established simply to release N.W.A records. It was not a major record company. At the time, Eric Wright was not well-connected or well-versed in the music industry. He was a hustler who had money that he could invest. Those members of N.W.A who were deeply in love with hip-hop and saw it as not only a passion but a life purpose could have easily worked the Ruthless angle only half-believing in the company's ability to launch them as major artists. They could have given Ruthless "good," holding their best for the "real" opportunity with a big company. But they were hungry. Actually, they were poor and living in South Central Los Angeles in the 1980s; they were starving. And that type of hunger makes you show out.

What Dr. Dre and Ice Cube laid down during their time at Ruthless Records, particularly on the "Straight Outta Compton" album, paved the way for them to chart their own path and blaze trails later on in their careers. That album sold 3.5 million units and it sealed Dre's reputation as a producer (creator) and Ice Cube's reputation as a lyricist (writer). These would become foundational skills for the later corporate (product development/creator) and Hollywood (movie script/writer) ventures outside of hip-hop that propelled both of them into true financial wealth.

Ruthless was simply the appetizer. It started it all. But I stress again that if they had shown up for work as anything other than a top chef, folx might have passed on the next course, or, in other words, not given them the next opportunity. In those initial hungry years, when they were seeking any opportunity available, they gave it their absolute best believing wholeheartedly that they could be great. Your institution might not be great, but you can be great within it. And you can promote your greatness outside of it, knowing that at the least, you can use its resources and platform to practice and grow your craft. Because on the real, another thing hungry folx don't do is turn down opportunities to eat. The hip-hop mindset teaches us to seize and slay opportunities to eat even if what we are holding is a burger. We eat because it will give us the fuel and energy to keep working and grinding until we are indeed sitting at the table holding that fork and knife, eating that prime rib.

## COMPETITIVENESS

Hunger relates to the first spark of ambition: the desire to just get in the door. But once you step into the arena, another critical component of drive is *competitiveness*. Winning is also a foundational ethic of hip-hop. Within the musical canon you see numerous songs that reference being a champion, being on top, or being number one. Kanye West has many of them including, "Touch the Sky," "Spaceship," "Celebration," "The Glory," and "Can't Tell Me Nothing." Why can't you tell him nothing? Because he is a 24-time Grammy winner with four No.1 Billboard Hot 100 hits and over 160 million records sold. As a producer, he holds the top spot for the most No.1 hip-hop songs.[5] He also sits on the throne of a sneaker empire that has solidified him as a billionaire. Politics and personality aside, West's importance in the hip-hop industry can't be denied. Competitiveness in hip-hop is not philosophical, it is real. Folx aren't just "embracing" a winning attitude or a "spirit" of competition. They are achieving on a grand scale. Jay-Z explains why competitiveness is valuable in the industry. "Competition pushes you to become your best self, and in the end it tells you where you stand."[6] This is a true statement about life in general. In any arena, once you step up to compete you are pushed to tap all your talents, all of your skills. And when it is all said and done, you will place somewhere: first or last, second or third, runner-up or champion. As a result, you come to know your weaknesses more clearly. You know where you currently rank and how far that is away from your goal. You also know who you need to beat to get that title, and you know their capabilities. But the point is that to discover all of this, you must get in the ring. To be an All-Star you have to play with them.

Within contemporary cultures of education, it seems that we are doing our best to erase competition from communities of learning. Of course, competition that is unfairly rooted in biased and racist forms of cultural hegemony and imperialism should not drive ideas of academic achievement, educational success, and intelligence measures. Unfairly tracking students into "winner" and "loser" courses based on racially biased standards is bad. Upholding certain types of students as the "good" and "model" students and assigning those labels based on conformity, compliance, socioeconomics, ability status, and race is bad. Even without issues of racial bias, pitting students against each other still isn't healthy. But competition itself isn't necessarily a bad thing for students or educators. There are some forms

of competition that are rooted in self-motivation, community encouragement, and shared passions.

In hip-hop, the "Top Five emcee list" is that type of competition. You
often hear the "Top Five" talked about in casual conversations in homes,
at social gatherings, in barbershops. Hip-hop fans *love* debating their list of
top five emcees of all time. This is not some official televised global award
nor is it a list published in a major media outlet. It is a list created personally
by hip-hop fans. Every fan has their own list—their own ideas about who is
the best. Yet all emcees want to make that list. If fans are naming their top
five, even if it's just a small group of folx gathered in their backyard, if you
are a famous emcee you want your name to be mentioned in that yard. You
want to be on that list.

We also see this in sports. Let's be real—all athletes are trying to top one
another. They may be best friends who practice together, dream together,
party together, and play on the same team. But each athlete still has an
individual reputation and a personal belief about their own talents. They
also most often have a healthy dose of self-confidence that tells them they
could probably take on their BFF and win if it ever came to that. Many team
sports players are keenly aware that they are always playing to keep their
spot, because there is another player on the bench waiting for the opportunity. Even if you do earn that top spot and come out as number one, your
title must be maintained. You work hard to get it, but you work even harder
to keep it, because you are now required to constantly work beyond your
last personal best. That's pressure. Makes you wonder how folx like LeBron
James or Jay-Z do it with such swagger and ease—with a smile. They have
adjusted to the flow of living life in overdrive and are now comfortable in
the seat of competition.

When you are competing to be the best at something that matters to
you, the heat of that competition feels good. It feels like a warm fire. We
want students to be warmed by the heat of ambition. Professionals also need
some fire lit under them, too. The spirit of competition in a hip-hop cypher
is intense, intimidating, nerve-racking, exciting, inspiring, and life-giving all
at the same time. Participants walk away from the space not bruised or de-
feated, but hyped, joyful, and happy. Even if you mess up, you walk away
determined to come back and shut it down the next time. That requires
practice and homework. You don't have to beg a dancer who missed a step
to go practice. You don't have to tell an emcee to go home and perfect their
free style if they were crushed in a battle. They will go home and get to work
without being asked.

Timothy David Jones, a community-based entrepreneur and scholar,
stresses that one of the most valuable assets that he inherited from hip-hop
was understanding that you can gain from losing. In a part of our interview
not included in Chapter 6, he says, "You learn so much from losing. I even
learned that you can also be inspired by the very person who beat you. You

almost use them as motivation to be better. Not in a way to try to copy them but you are trying to surpass them."

This comment immediately brought the rapper Meek Mill to mind. In the documentary *Free Meek*, he shares how losing a freestyle battle as a young emcee pushed him to be great because he never wanted to experience that feeling again.[7] "I watched my whole neighborhood turn on me in a second. When I walked off I was crying. It was a sad day for me, but it was one of the best days of my life because from here on out, I'm taking rap serious. Y'all gonna remember. You're gonna be playing my music one day."[8]

His work ethic was sealed in that moment of loss. The fact that he had such a visceral reaction to losing signified that he was always a champion. As I shared earlier, champions care. Winning matters to winners. If you can mess up and shrug it off, you might not be a winner. Even if they act nonchalant in public, people who are innately winners are secretly having stomach pains when they mess up. It matters. As the rapper Biggie Smalls once said, "No one gets into this game to be average."[9] That's facts.

Edmund Adjapong, a professor at Seton Hall University who is also featured in Chapter 6, explains that the pursuit of the win is never easy, even when you achieve it: "When you succeed there will always be people who test you—especially as an academic. Questioning your scholarship. But it's also an honor. Those are the moments when you solidify why you are the GOAT. Are you going to arrive in that moment and let it have a negative impact on you? Or are you going to navigate this gracefully as the GOAT?"

This comment also pulls me back to the Meek Mill documentary. What I thought was incredible about that street battle scene (which was taped by one of his friends) was that this very young 13-year-old Meek Mill does carry his defeat with grace. There is no acting out or lashing out. There is no minimizing or diminishing the other guy's win. He takes the loss that he has earned. He stays in the cypher and stands to face his opponent until the end. This is maturity that a lot of adults don't display. Many would run— quit the difficult job or quit the difficult student. A hip-hop mindset is about staying in the fight, taking the "L" (loss), going back to the lab to perfect the craft, and coming back into the cypher for the win. Giving up is not an option; remember, we're too hungry for that.

This idea of persisting through challenges and difficult situations can be difficult to put into practice because our careers should most definitely bring us joy. Work should feel like love, not labor. But in many workplaces the work can feel emotionally and physically exhausting. It is easy for me to say, "Stay the course," but what if the course leads you on a path to your own spiritual destruction? As a professor, I study issues of leadership, equity, and inclusion primarily in the field of education. P–12 school systems face a long list of challenges that form very real obstacles to creating dynamic, exciting, innovative, and impactful schools. Of course, there are schools with leaders who stifle invention and expression, and school cultures that aren't welcoming even for teachers.[10] But this isn't broadly the case. Instead, there are many talented educators working at all levels from teacher-assistant to principal who are committed to educational excellence and have viable ideas for educational change, but are so overpacked troubleshooting challenges that they have very little time to implement these new visions.

Navigating the continued increase in already large classroom sizes, social insecurity among students and their families, disparities in access to technology, the aftermath of failed high-stakes-testing policies like No Child Left Behind, the adoption of standards that allow very little flexible creativity in the classroom, the persistent decline in teacher salaries, and the decrease in funding for education makes the charge confronting educators much bigger than simply demonstrating a commitment to students.[11] Many would argue that teaching and learning is just one issue on a very long list of school priorities.

Within higher education, the plight also isn't easy. Colleges and universities can often appear to be too large a system to tackle. Cultures of rank and order among faculty can also serve to silence junior faculty who might have viable ideas for change. Higher education faces budget challenges, technology challenges, decreasing enrollment, racial justice issues, gender and sexuality disparities, increasing reliance on contingent faculty positions, and affordability issues. While typically these have been the concerns of university administrations, increasingly these conversations have made their way into faculty meetings, and the whole of the university is now being asked to think deeply and entrepreneurially about solving problems like enrollment, recruiting, and affordability. Professors don't just teach.

All of this changes the dynamics of the job. Educators who are genuinely passionate about engaging the act of teaching (not necessarily solving the problems of education), are rightfully exhausted by all that is required of them before they can do what they view as their job. I share all of this to acknowledge that simply saying "we don't quit" might come across as insensitive to the realities that educators face. Sometimes and in some institutions, the best decision is to leave (not to leave the profession, but to leave and join a new professional community). What I suggest that we can learn from hip-hop regarding the ethic of resilience is to not give up easily. A winning mindset requires us to embrace the reality that most competitions are not easy or quick. Whether it is in sports, business, arts, or education, competitions are often intense and require long hours of dedication and training—hard work. We must bring into our practice more than just a winning attitude. We must be willing to actively demonstrate tenacity and diligence.

In creating hip-hop, youth didn't immediately transform or change the world, they changed *their* world—*their* community experience. They literally watched the world burning around them and still played records, danced, and wrote poetry. If youth could do it, so can we. What marginalized communities of all kinds teach us is how to get up, move, create, and shine regardless of how dark the experience that you have inherited. Jay-Z explains:

> What you're looking at is a culture of people so in love with life that they can't stop fighting for it—people who've seen death up close, literal death, but also the kind of dormancy and stagnation that kills your spirit. They've seen it all around them and they don't want any part of that shit, not at all. They want to live like they want to live—they want to impose themselves on the world through their art, with their voices. This impulse is what saved us. It's what saved me. [12]

This does not mean that if you can't singlehandedly brave through a bad experience and transform a dysfunctional organization you have failed. Rather, this means that you can't let the dysfunctionality fail you—crush your spirits, talents, dreams, and joy. Whether you are a teacher in the classroom, an assistant principal, a student affairs practitioner, or professor at a college, be dedicated to the work and people who matter. Work hard for them and for yourself—build what brings all of you joy in the space that you can control. Don't be distracted by fighting with folks who aren't worth your time or energy. Do what you can to create a space where you and your students can thrive—even if you are laughing, learning, and leading only long enough to get you to the next opportunity. That is what we are doing for students at all levels of education: giving them what they need to get to the next. Educators can do the same.

## HONOR AND KINSHIP

*Honor* emerging as a hip-hop mindset made me feel proud as a fan of the culture. So often, anything hip-hop is painted as deviant and disrespectful. Honor and kinship emerged in hip-hop culture in the form of ethics like generosity, respect, love, and a welcoming community spirit. For these values to emerge as essential practices within hip-hop culture is refreshing to a cultural scholar like me. Telling the truth about cultures drives my work. And the truth is, hip-hop has become such a global phenomenon because it attracts people to it rather than repels people from it. Rather than making others outside the culture feel limited or less than (not fresh, not cool, not dope, not down), it actually makes people feel more of those things the closer they come to hip-hop culture. You feel fresh when you are listening to a song. The energy is contagious. I'd argue that's what schools should do. Instead of making students feel self-conscious and less than because of what they don't know or can't do, schools should act so that the more they engage with school, the better they feel about their abilities. It should make students brag about their academic abilities, not be ashamed and unsure.

In his book *Know Your Price: Valuing Black Lives and Black Property in America's Black Cities*, Andre M. Perry asserts that social and community advancement occur as a result of an investment in people who are trusted.[13] Social institutions, whether they are schools, health care facilities, or local governments, do not invest in people who they think don't matter. He explains that the racial profile that our society typically constructs of the deviant and hopeless often describes young Black and Brown people who have never been and will never be deviant or hopeless. Many of the ideas that society holds about what makes a person problematic are not criminal profiles, but rather a racial profile describing a particular type of life and cultural experience for which many White people have disdain. He gives the example of a 2016 incident that was named the "Wilkinsburg Massacre," in which two African American young men shot up a backyard party, killing five people. Perry says that a news anchor at a Pittsburgh TV station went on to make the following comments about the young men who committed the crime: "You needn't be a criminal profiler to draw a mental sketch of the killers who broke so many hearts two weeks ago Wednesday. They are young Black men, likely in their teens or in their early 20s. They have multiple siblings from multiple fathers and their mothers work multiple jobs."[14] Perry notes that "the mental sketch of the killer isn't dissimilar to a description of Black young people who had nothing to do with the murder."[15] Indeed. You can have brothers and sisters by multiple fathers and not be a criminal. Your mother can work three jobs and you can manage not to commit a crime. You most certainly can be a young Black man in his 20s and not be a criminal. This profile describes many of the students with whom I work as a college professor.

Considering that a Black or Brown child or young adult doesn't have to do anything major beyond showing up Black or Brown to be considered a delinquent, it makes sense that a teacher could easily walk into a classroom and mentally group the students into good and bad categories based on the limited information they know about them and their families. What then occurs is not just a tracking of students, but more so a tracking of educational resources and professional effort. The students' life circumstances make them undeserving of the educational investment. They are not among the trusted.

While hip-hop has been painted in larger society as aggressive, rude, and disrespectful, to those within the culture it is actually a space of welcome, generosity, love, honor, and respect. People come as they are within hip-hop culture, and they are accepted. One of the first lessons that you learn is honor. Most often, this comes through the concept of respecting the mic (and thus the person on it). Regardless of how rude and rowdy their lyrics might be, when participating in a cypher, an emcee will respectfully pass the mic and be quiet while others are rhyming. In fact, they will not only be quiet, but they will also actually listen to others. The audience in a cypher engages in an intense form of listening. They react to every slick phrase and showcase of skill, they are analyzing your words and can quickly identify street-level copyright infringement—they are listening to understand, not just to respond. As a professor, I have been in many faculty meetings where highly educated, so-called refined folx don't respect the mic. We watched the 2020 U.S. Vice Presidential debate where, in a very structured space (in which each person is given a specific amount of time and a moderator is designating the order), a candidate was still talking over the other candidate and disrespecting the mic to the point where Vice President candidate Harris had to remind the sitting Vice President Pence, "I'm speaking," repeatedly. Do you know where that doesn't happen? A hip-hop cypher. You wait your turn.

One of the hip-hop creative plays on language that I wholeheartedly embraced back in the day was the expression "GP," which stands for *general principle*. I wore that phrase out. "Yo, you owe me that just on GP." "But for real, I'll do it for you just on GP." Principle has always mattered in hip-hop. As an emcee, you want every eye on you and every ear listening when you are on stage, so you do the same thing when you are off the stage. You give what you hope to get. Even in very intense open mic venues this holds true. In the *Hip-Hop Evolution* documentary series (Dunn et al., 2016–2020), several open mic and emcee battle spaces were featured including the Lyricist Lounge in New York City and the Good Life Café in Los Angeles. The Good Life Café was a health food store turned open mic spot. The open mics were legend—always packed. Everyone that was a part of the community took honor seriously. Along with honoring the space, the microphone, you were expected to honor the craft and the work production of each artist. Snoop Dogg remembers you couldn't get on the mic and even sound like another rapper. As he says, audience members "were in there, bar watching . . . like . . . hold on . . . that ain't yours."[16]

While this open mic took place inside a health food store (think a serene, calming space), there was nothing gentle or calm about the open mic in the back of the store. It was the hip-hop version of Amateur Night at the Apollo and it was known for the community call, "Please pass the mic." The audience would begin to call out the phrase if an emcee wasn't performing well. It would grow from a slow simmer to an aggressive boil with folx standing, yelling, singing, and dancing, "Please pass the mic." As the rapper Murs explained, "That crowd was so vicious that something like 'Please pass the mic' sounded like 'shut the fuck up'" (*Hip-hop Evolution*, season 3, episode 3, 14:21). Even the rapper Fat Joe was booed off that stage early in his career. But ultimately this audience served as the most well-respected group of hip-hop critics and experts. If you could get them up dancing and cheering, you were indeed talented. It was the type of experience for which you spend hours practicing and preparing. As intimidating as the experience might have been, I still see the level of honor and respect demonstrated in the practice. No one was physically fighting and acting out, unable to take the criticism. The community members followed the rules they created. Whether you liked it or not, when the audience told you to pass the mic, you immediately got off the stage. And the audience, as rowdy and loud as they might get, were still only saying four simple words, "Please pass the mic." I mean, they were even saying "please." In other words, cultures of respect might look and sound differently across cultural communities. Yes, we do get loud and our "Pass the mic" might feel like "Shut up!" but it thickens your skin (which we could all use these days). After all, we do know that Fat Joe went on to make ten studio albums including one that was certified platinum.

In the Hip Hop Shop in Detroit (a clothing store with an open mic in the back room), everyone put their name in a hat, the host would pick two names, and that's who battled. No questions asked. The Hip Hop Shop was another intense and intimidating open mic space. What I mean by intense isn't that it was scary (as in, I may be in physical danger or there is a threat of violence). Rather, it was filled with such pressure and high expectations to be exceptional that it was intimidating for anyone who wanted to do well. And everyone wanted to do well. Detroit rapper Kuniva remembers battling with Eminem in the Hip Hop Shop. As he put it, he was "murdered" on the mic by Eminem, a then new emcee on the scene. "Yo, he said 'My face is white but you look like you've seen a ghost.' I don't even remember the rest of the rhymes after that. They were waking me up with smelling sauce. He fucked me up, he gave me a proper ass whupping. But I learned from it and it made me a better emcee. And I was taught by one of the best" (Kuniva, *Hip-hop Evolution*, season 3, episode 3, 32:41).

In all these spaces filled with aggressive, hypermasculine energy, there was no need for policing to force folx to follow the rules. These were spaces that people desperately wanted to be in and so they did what the community demanded of them: respect the process. Freedom doesn't mean that one is free from standards and expectations. If you want to eat, you can't mess up the garden. Folx will play by the rules and enjoy it because of how much they love the experience.

All the scholars interviewed for this project also mentioned the rich sense of community and spirit of welcome that they felt within their own hip-hop world. And these worlds were all very different. Some educators were hip-hop scholars who loved, studied, and used hip-hop as a pedagogical practice. Others weren't artists at all, but identified with hip-hop as a cultural and community experience. And yet others started their careers DJing, dancing, or emceeing and still integrate those sensibilities into their educational practice. Emery Petchauer, associate professor of English education, talked passionately about the spirit of generosity that he learned from hip-hop. For him, it was a space where folx were always willing to "put on" a young kid and give him an opportunity. That might be through allowing him to carry their crates and come with them to DJ a gig or vouching for a new emcee within an open mic or cypher scene.

This gets back to the point that I made earlier regarding how impossible it seemed for such marginalized communities to get access to record companies in the early days of hip-hop. A spirit of generosity, of doing what you can to help a hungry person eat, has always been a foundational ethic of hip-hop. It makes me recall the claims that Biggie Smalls used to make about his friendship with Tupac Shakur back when they were young, up-and-coming rappers, long before their notorious, bitter rivalry. According to Biggie, at various times when Tupac needed a place to stay, he would give him a couch to sleep on. Hip-hop is a space where intense competition and deep forms of community support can coexist.[17] Even though I'm out here still trying to hustle for my own big break, I'm going to invite you along and maybe you can get access too. Even though my aim is to beat you on the mic, I'm still going to do my thing and then pass it on so that you can have your time to shine. That's actually really beautiful living.

In my conversation with Michael Benitez, Jr., Vice President for Diversity and Inclusion at Metropolitan State University of Denver, we both kept coming back to the word grace. "There's a gratitude . . . that's grounded in a hip-hop mindset. How you share space. You can't allow a B-boy or B-girl to get on the mat and hug up the whole time. If y'all only have 40 minutes to kick it, do your thing for a few minutes, then get out the way and let the next peoples come in and do their thing. When you're rocking the mic or even in freestyle sessions, it's not some cat running with the mic, hugging up the whole time. You learn to share. I love that you used the word grace earlier. There is grace that comes with a hip-hop mindset. I think that's essential to who we are."

For Ian Levy, assistant professor of school counseling at Manhattan College, the sense of welcome and acceptance that he felt as a college student first trying his hand at hip-hop sealed the deal for him—he had found his cultural home. You will read in his interview in Chapter 6 how hip-hop emceeing became a form of therapy and personal growth. The love, welcome, acceptance, and embrace that he felt within the hip-hop cypher communities gave him the sense of confidence and belonging that educational institutions were not providing. Ian's raw and honest sharing of how hip-hop helped him to overcome educational self-doubt is so incredibly important because of the position that he now holds. Many young people would never think that a college professor would have had a rough time in high school. Many young people have no idea how common imposter phenomenon is among college and university academics. Regardless of how many degrees they hold, the beat-down that the education system can sometimes give to people's sense of self-esteem and cultural efficacy is real. Community or audience embrace within hip-hop feels like much needed life support. Within hip-hop, we are valued and embraced. We are among the trusted.

*Kinship.* Next to the community value of honor, I place *kinship*. While there is diversity of experience within any cultural or ethnic community, there are also many shared sociocultural and sociopolitical experiences that establish a commonality among groups. Often, the lyrics penned by the emcee speak to the larger community experience, even if their particular circumstances have changed. Several members of N.W.A are now multi-millionaires; in 1988, none were filthy rich. A rapper might give voice to poverty even if they are no longer living in it. Race is different, because it actually doesn't disappear with changes in social status, it just transforms. Regardless of any change in the routines of everyday life and despite their celebrity status, many rap artists still share past and sometimes current experiences with issues of racism, harassment, and prejudice. Many artists argue that they still experience racism even as A-list celebrities.[18]

There is also the familial and community ethic espoused by many rap artists indicating that we are all in this together. Outkast's classic song "Elevators" interprets individual success as being marked by everyone coming up. This means that I'm successful when all of us—me, you, your mama, and your cousin—are all living well. This lyric gives voice to the interconnectivity of the artist and the community. It equally illustrates the interconnectivity of any profession with its customers—educator to students, publisher to readers, restaurateur to diners, or doctor to patient. We depend on each other.

Additionally, there is the crew mindset that is such a major aspect of hip-hop culture. From the Wu Tang Clan (RZA, Ol' Dirty Bastard, Ghostface Killah, Method Man, Raekwon, GZA, Cappadonna, Inspectah Deck, Masta Killa, U-God), The Roc (Jay-Z, Memphis Bleek, Noreaga, DJ Clue), the Bad Boy crew (Biggie, Lil' Kim, Junior Mafia, P. Diddy), Death Row (Dr. Dre, Snoop Dog, Tupac), to more recent Young Money Entertainment (Lil Wayne, Nicki Minaj, Drake), T.R.U. (2 Chainz, Skooly, Sleepy Rose, Worl, Hott LockedN) and YSL (Young Thug, Gunna, Lil Keed, Lil Duke, Dolly, Strick, T-Shyne, Jerrika Karlae), association with a community of artists is critical. It is wise in any industry to associate yourself with colleagues that can both put you on to opportunity and make you better. In the hip-hop crew, each person is expected to shine individually and to have their own success. Their success makes the crew look good. Critically, the success of the whole crew typically starts with one person having some sort of initial success. That one person uses their access and their resources as a platform to launch the careers of others. So success begins as a solo endeavor but often becomes much more communal. This means that we should regularly ask ourselves, What colleagues have we "put on" or helped advance in their careers in important ways? How are you serving your peer community and not just your student community?

Finally, the last example of communalism in hip-hop reaches back to its first moments. Hip-hop began with young cultural conveners planning parties in rec rooms and gatherings at local parks. People coming together to share an experience is a quintessential component of hip-hop. While a song might elicit very specific and particular feelings in an individual, often the fond memories we hold of that song involve the parties, dance clubs, car rides with friends, or other social experiences that we had while listening to the music. When I asked my husband to name his favorite hip-hop song and tell me how it made him feel, he named Too Short's "Blow the Whistle." He actually played the song and described exactly what he was feeling as he listened to it—it made him feel young, invincible, bold, alive. But then he said this: "You know, what I really love about the song, though, is how whenever it came on, wherever we were, didn't matter the city or whoever we were with, if I was out partying with my teammates or my cousins at home—when it gets to the part where he says, 'What's my favorite word?!' all the dudes would yell the answer. I know some of the lyrics are disrespectful, but you feel like you are part of this community of dudes, dancing, yelling, feeling the same thing. I love seeing it."

I can't end a discussion on honor, kinship, and community without specifically discussing the role of women. The topic of women in hip-hop has always been a complicated issue. While the image of the industry has been intentionally painted as predominantly male, women have always been a part of hip-hop. From a cultural perspective, the "birth" of hip-hop is jointly credited to DJ Kool Herc and his sister Cindy Campbell, who worked together to host the infamous annual back to school jams that catapulted the culture into the community. As an industry, women were also at the forefront from one of the first record producers, Sylvia Robinson (who recorded "Rappers Delight" in 1979), to MC Sha-Rock (who is considered the first female rapper on wax), to Salt-N-Pepa (who were the first female hip-hop artists to go gold or platinum), to Da Brat (who was the first solo female rapper to go platinum), to Lauryn Hill (who holds the record for the highest selling hip-hop album by a woman), to Nicki Minaj (who holds the record as the highest selling woman rapper of all time), to Missy Elliott (who became the first female hip-hop artist to be inducted into the Rock & Roll Hall of Fame). Women are major players in hip-hop whether men like it or not. But the entry of women rappers into the industry has often been considered to express rather than subvert sexism, as they have often been "ushered in" or "hosted" by a male artist/producer (or as the lone woman within a predominantly male squad). The examples are endless: Nicki Minaj and Lil Wayne; Lil' Kim and Biggie; Foxxy Brown and Nas/Jay-Z; Eve and Ruff Ryders; Da Brat and Jermaine Dupri. I see this as family doing what family does. A tribe doesn't exist without women. Families don't exist without women. Even groups that were all male, like Tribe Called Quest and De la Soul, were still a part of a large kinship group called Native Tongues, which included women rappers Queen Latifah and Monie Love. There have also been several examples of mixed groups like the Fugees, Digable Planets, and Bran Nubian. I am not focusing on this particular debate about how women enter as rappers, but on the fact that if community is a critical value within the culture, you can't have a community without women.

While hip-hop is embraced by women globally, and particularly within African Diasporic, Latinx, Asian, and Pacific Islander communities, for this discussion I will largely focus on Black women because of their history, rank, and place as chart topping emcees. Hip-hop culture has always created space particularly for Black women to speak. Too often, the male voice and male lyrics dominate the critical focus of hip-hop studies. We love to interrogate what men say, what men rap, and that tends to lead us to misogyny and sexism. The lack of respect that our society at large holds for women, particularly Black women, most definitely plays out in song lyrics and even behind the scenes within the industry. But when looking at the topic of women in hip-hop, the true power lies in exploring what happens when women bless the mic. This is particularly salient because it seems that there is nothing our society detests more than the sound of a Black woman's voice. We have been taught that it is too loud, untamed, inarticulate, and rude.[19] While participation is paramount to educational success, many teachers must truthfully reconcile with the fact that they don't encourage or want Black and Latinx girls to speak up, speak out, question, or debate in class. They would prefer for them to be quiet. The student may be honestly asking a question; it still comes across to the teacher as a challenge. That might be hard to hear, but it is the truth. In a Karen Attiah article, "America Hates to Let Black Women Speak," she offers the following insight:

> Schools increasingly resemble prisons and students begin to look more like criminal suspects who need to be searched, tested, and observed under the watchful eye of administrators who appear to be less concerned with educating them than with policing their every move. Trust and respect now give way to fear, disdain, and suspicion.[20]

Valid educational transformation efforts discontinue the long tradition of viewing the student as the problem, and look at the instructional practices and administrative policies that create gaps in education opportunities, disproportionate rates of discipline, and greater educational pushout/departure among students who identify as African American, Latinx, or disabled. How is this collectively happening to the same groups of students everywhere in the country? That's no coincidence. That's racism.

Black girls are increasingly being targeted. In a panel discussion that I moderated on the 2019 documentary film *Pushout: The Criminalization of Black Girls in Schools* (based on Monique Morris's book of the same name), I shared how the ways that Black girls are often stereotyped as being aggressive, angry, loud, rude, grown girls with attitudes reminds me of how we have conceptualized the identity of the skunk.[21] More than any other characteristics, we tend to know a skunk for two things—the way it looks (black with a white stripe) and the smell it gives off. Skunks stink. That is the prevailing identity of the skunk. But the problem with this lies in the fact that the horrible scent skunks give off is just a defensive reaction. On an hourly basis, skunks don't walk around stinking. When they are threatened or fearful they give off this odor to protect themselves. Their defense response is so powerful and strong that the world has erased all other aspects and characteristics of the skunk and the animal is now only known as the animal that stinks. This is also the case with Black girls. The attitude that society perceives is a defense mechanism, a strong front and response meant to deal with the spirit murder, cultural and racial assault, sexual violence, microaggressions, poverty, and trauma that girls face in the world.[22] It makes sense that if you appear too hard to be broken, folx just might think twice about trying to break you. The defense response of some Black girls is so strong that this has come to dominate how people perceive all of them: They are their defense mechanism. In reality, on a daily basis, no Black girl is always exhibiting this behavior. They are walking around showing love, joy, silliness, intelligence, creativity, and care. But just like with the skunk, many educators see them and run. And when you are sitting in a position of power, the act of "running away" from these girls actually looks like you staying still, writing a referral, and pushing the student out of the classroom.

Let's be clear. Some children, whether in high school or college, do "act out," and seeds of bad behavior often take root outside of the school system. Even when it comes to those students who are guilty of wrongdoing, educational institutions need to transform their approach to judicial affairs. Professor Shaun Harper suggests a move from a stiff and procedural judicial process to a more developmental and educational process.[23] The truly disruptive student needs to be shown a new path. Changing the spirit and tone of school judicial policy and classroom culture hold potential benefit for everyone involved. Too often, educational spaces don't allow anyone to be vulnerable—students or teachers. Educators are sometimes grabbing to hold on to power instead of sitting in communion with ethics of love.

Though many students exhibit negative, disrespectful, and disruptive behavior in school, we know that not all students who are suspended have "acted out" and not all young Black and Latinx kids who find themselves permanently outside of the school system are out there because the stereotypes are true of them (they lack skill, come from a bad neighborhood, have uncaring parents, or suffer from psychological behavior disorders). Somewhere in the mix is a failed agreement between the student and school about what constitutes being a "good" student. Power lies in who gets to define what "good" means.

Passing Black girls the mic within hip-hop culture was a powerful form of resistance. And what those women rappers did when they got on the mic was something incredible. They took it and proceeded to talk about themselves—their histories, their beauty, their bodies, their sexuality, their spirituality, and their beliefs. Why is this critical? Because not only have Black women been denied adequate space for their voices to be widely heard in contemporary society, but even those who have been historic change agents have literally been written out of history (even when it is Black history being taught).

I live in South Carolina and one of the most important civil rights icons of our state was Septima Poinsette Clark. She was referred to as the "Queen Mother" of the civil rights movement by Reverend Martin Luther King, Jr.[24] Much of the civil rights knowledge and education that framed the Southern Christian Leadership Conference–led approach was informed by Septima Poinsette Clark's "Citizenship School" model. "The classes Clark established schooled thousands of students in basic literacy and civil rights, producing savvy new voters and changing the course of the Civil Rights movement."[25] Yet you could survey high school or even college students across the country (and probably within our own state of South Carolina) and most won't even know her name. Our society has shown us that no one is going to speak or teach about Black women in a real or meaningful way. Even our Black women history-makers are erased.

So what did women rappers do when they were given the microphone? In the late 1980s, Queen Latifah penned a song called "Ladies First," and proceeded to talk only about the greatness of Black women. In her machismo-slaying record, "Paper Thin," MC Lyte took the microphone and basically encouraged women to set relationship boundaries when it comes to their self-worth and self-respect. When Salt-N-Pepa seized control of their lyrics, the first song written and produced by Salt was "Expression," a song about not being afraid to be your true and authentic self. In the 1990s, Erykah Badu entered the scene with a neo-soul, Afrocentric, B-girl vibe that was spiritual, political, cultural, and outspoken. Erykah Badu emphasized "in performance and visual representation the possibilities for a multivocal black female experience."[26]

> At the forefront of Black creativity in the 1990s and still today, Erykah Badu has been referred to as "a bohemian B-Girl" whose interplay of jazz, soul, and Hip Hop is effortless and seamless. Badu embodies not only a new mode of black consciousness but she also melds an eclectic personal style—one part Afro-bohemian B-Girl, one part Afro-futuristic and one part old school Hip Hop.[27]

Badu embodied the ideals of being unique, original, and creative. In her lyrics, Badu has directly acknowledged that she makes a daily choice to "choose me"—to be her authentic self. She asserts, "I think a lot of people have lost respect for the individual, you know, the person who doesn't conform."[28] The act of being one's authentic self is essential to women in hiphop, really to women working in any field. It is a bold act to be fully and unapologetically a woman who centers herself—her mind, her experience, her knowledge, her brilliance—as a source of power.

The current success of Lizzo is another example. Noted as being a breath of fresh air and the self-love queen, her emergence as the 2019 *Time* Magazine Entertainer of the Year was significant because of what she represents as a person.[29] She is a Black, body-positive (full-bodied and loving it), woman who celebrates herself. In his BBC article, Nick Levine writes, "Over the past 12 months, Lizzo has become the inspiring, high-energy figurehead of the growing self-care movement—with its philosophy of actively nurturing and protecting your own mental and physical wellbeing—and a performer synonymous with unbridled joy and unapologetic self-confidence."[30] He goes on to note that Lizzo puts out music that celebrates women as powerful, joyful, authentic, and "salty" all at the same time. That isn't something our society is used to, particularly when it comes to Black women—we don't have a history of celebrating Black women and seeing them as multidimensional. In her concerts, I personally like that Lizzo isn't a full-bodied woman surrounded by super thin dancers on stage. Her stage shows include women dancers of all sizes. She is making space for young women who are just like her.

Of course, women rappers have a long history of addressing a range of issues from speaking on assault and respect (Salt-N-Pepa and Eve) to pushing women's sexual and erotic power (Lil' Kim, Trina, Cardi B, Megan Thee Stallion) to womanhood and motherhood (Lauryn Hill) to calling out society's double standards and hypocritical judgments of women (Nicki Minaj) to creatively contesting what representing women even looks and sounds like (Missy Elliott). The commonality lies in the lens from which they all speak; the gaze is always on their own Black feminine experience.

Women of color need this cultural permission to focus on ourselves— to take care of ourselves; to create programs for our cultural daughters and sisters; to read about ourselves; to speak our truths; to tell our stories, and to create our own interventions. In a recent study of the funding gaps between Black and White researchers, an NIH research team found that the research topic was a significant factor in the underfunding of Black researchers.[31] Black researchers were most often studying topics that focused on disparities, lifestyle, and race, which were found to be underappreciated in the proposal review process. In other words, there is a lack of professional value associated with doing work (research, scholarship, or interventions) focused on certain social issues and certain populations of people. The lack of funding enthusiasm, whether at the foundational level or the school level, encourages educational leaders and scholars to avoid focusing their work on these topics or populations. If Black and Latinx women can't help Black and Latinx girls for fear of being professionally ostracized, who is it that will actually step up and help our girls? Probably not the same society that hates them. In the entertainment community, I love the fact that nightclubs are pretty unapologetic—we play hip-hop here. This is literally how we get down. More and more, at least in the realm of educational research, it seems that researchers are now owning and claiming their space and selfishly studying the communities who need them most. But as demonstrated in the NIH study, this stance still has its funding consequences.

In her book *Hip Hop's Li'l Sistas Speak: Negotiating Hip Hop Identities and Politics in the New South*, Bettina L. Love (2012) shares the importance of building on the body of research that unapologetically centers Black women and girls:

> I think it is critical that research in the field of Hip Hop Studies begins to focus on the lives of Black girls, as Black girls' lives are linked to inequalities. According to Collins (2000), Black girls have little protection from social, political, and economic injustices. This is why it is fundamental to interrogate Black girlhood. Black girls have to negotiate and navigate not only communities raided by crime, sexual assault and harassment, and poor schools but also liberating, counter-cultural, misogynist, and sexist genre of Hip Hop music and culture, which is empowering and disempowering within the same beat.[32]

She goes on to name researchers who are doing the work of centering Black girls: Elaine Richardson's work on how Black women navigate stereotypical images in rap videos and Ruth Nicole Brown's work focused on Black Girlhood Celebration. Monique W. Morris has also been a champion of Black girls, leading the research-driven attack on gender- and race-biased school discipline policies. There are numerous other scholars, like Charlotte Jacobs, who has written books on gender-conscious schooling; Gholdy Muhammad, who has explored issues of language, identity, protest, and criticality among Black women and girls; Crystal Leigh Endsley, who focuses on the intersections of art, activism, and girlhood. I say their names not for you to simply read, but for you to note. Seek out their books and articles as you continue to dive into this topic. What makes their scholarship magical is that it is rooted in love—it is soul work. That's what promising practice looks like to me: Following your passions and fulfilling your purpose. Bettina L. Love's own scholarship has also centered the experiences of Black girls by seeking to understand their lives in their community, in their schools, and in hip-hop culture.[33] In discussing the goals of her work, Love states: "I hope to pay back a small portion of my debt to Hip Hop. I feel I owe it to Hip Hop to explain its significance and the way it shapes the lives of urban Black young girls who, like me, learned more from Hip Hop and

Black popular culture than from twelve years of attending America's public schools."[34]

Toni Blackman's Rhyme Like a Girl (RLAG) organization is a practice-based initiative that engages young women and girls in cultivating their craft as emcees from songwriting to relationship building to harnessing the power of their energy both on and offstage. Toni's full interview in this book is powerful and important in understanding the cultural strengths of hip-hop. One of the many nuggets of wisdom that she offers in the conversation is the value of commanding attention and claiming space. She relates how the best emcee doesn't simply *instruct* the audience to move, rather they use their voice and their presence to *inspire* movement. The audience will follow the rhythm and power of your voice—they will come closer to the stage, they will complete your verse, their bodies will sway in whatever direction you are swaying. You don't have to force it—they move because they feel your energy. The work RLAG is doing is critical. Who else is taking time to teach young people how to understand the power of their own voice? Most people scream simply because they don't feel heard. And on that note (because students aren't the only ones screaming in the classroom), who is teaching future teachers this skill—to harness the power of their own voice and energy?

All this scholarship serves as an example of what passing Black girls the mic looks like in educational practice. Passing girls the mic in education means doing research that allows them to tell their truths and to participate as partners in the educational experience; teaching histories that help Black girls to know about more Black women; creating assignments that encourage girls to investigate, interrogate, write, speak, draw, and create work that illuminates their life experiences. We need to actually let Black girls in. I don't mean let them in the classroom to sit at a desk and watch other students grow and develop. Philosophically, we need to put them on stage (in the spotlight, in the center) and allow them to claim their space in the institution.

What the history and culture of hip-hop contributes here is an example of an experience created based on the very idea of full, embodied participation. Youth used their minds, voices, language, values, belief systems, bodies, rhythm, hands, artistic sensibilities, style, and imagination in creating the culture. For decades, hip-hop youth have told their own stories about their own lives and the world actually listened. Too many educators are turning down the volume on both the music and the young people. The field of education can learn from the ways that hip-hop culture has created unedited, unfiltered, unsurveilled space for Black, Latinx, and Asian women to speak, move, and fully participate.

But educators must also wrestle with the contradictions of being called to teach a group of people whom your field's policies disregard and disrespect (just as hip-hop culture is not off the hook regarding the patriarchal, misogynist, and sexist treatment of women within the culture). We can't have that discussion without referencing one of the current heavyweight champs of women rappers. Nicki Minaj has both accepted and defied the oversexualization of women in hip-hop. Her track record as one of the top five highest selling female artists of the century, across all genres of music, has earned her the right to claim being a top artist. She has sold 100 million units in the United States alone.[35] Yes, she moves in and out of pop and hip-hop (as do Lizzo and many other artists nowadays). My focus here is what we can glean from how Minaj has moved on the mic.

She entered hip-hop during an era that had all but eliminated the idea of complex, multi-vocal, socially, or politically conscious women emcees. Within the last two decades we have seen women being allowed to enter the hip-hop industry only body first. There has been much debate and voice given to championing women's rights to show up sexual, to embrace and use their bodies, and to own their erotic power.[36] These arguments are all valid. But we probably need to ask the question, Who is really demanding this? Is it the women or is it the industry? Or both?

> During [hip-hop's] '80s-'90s independent heyday, there was space for fly girls, b-girls, sisters with attitude, and regal queen mothers. Corporate conglomerates achieved increasing dominance, then piled investment behind certain clichéd images and—against a backdrop of massive female under-representation and straight-up abuse in the business—ended the era of respect for female hip-hop artists. For the past two decades, only women who accepted a strictly circumscribed role as commoditized sex objects received opportunities, female identity was defined by pornification, and the 'video ho' became the omnipresent role for women in rap. Nicki Minaj came up in an industry where women were to be seen—semi-nude—and not heard.[37]

As an emcee, Minaj entered body first and half-naked, which was the only space permitted to women hip-hop artists. But what she did was rap the hell out of some lyrics in her two-piece. Her skill is undeniable and her sustainability as a top artist over a 10-year period (as music changes and flows in new directions) makes her a testimony to the power of skill. What I get from her approach is that regardless of what limiting parameters might exist in your position, don't let that diminish your ambition. The sheer strength of your skills, ability, and talents can still propel you to greatness.

> The fundamental underpinning of G.O.A.T. status is talent and, in this regard, Minaj is a singularity: she can rap at pace or in a dozen flows; she binds her tone and delivery perfectly to the sentiment expressed; her acrobatic change-ups rely on an underrated level of athleticism to ensure total control over her breath. As a lyricist, her words are a firework display of sharp metaphors, humorous comebacks and putdowns, a rainbow of emotion backed up by a talent for wordplay.[38]

Whether or not you're "Team Barbie," you have to admit there aren't many people who can do what she does, animating her voice while keeping steady pace with a lyrical flow and cadence. She doesn't miss a beat. Athleticism is a perfect word. She could easily have become deflated and shrunk in stature based on the limiting parameters offered to women in the industry. But she was hungry, so she ate that stripped-down burger. And rather than allow industry limitations to restrict how she showed up in the studio or on the stage, she went in the opposite direction—making her voice, her style, and her bodied presence all big. What she didn't strip down was her talent. Black folx have been doing this for centuries—being excellent in the face of oppression.

In the field of education (and other corporate fields), her example makes me think of the chief diversity officer role. Opinions on whether institutions have a true commitment to and investment in these roles to create real change varies widely. For many CDOs, the job can be extremely frustrating, particularly if creating the position is the only plan of action by the institution (not establishing a functioning office with human and fiscal resources). Many institutions hire CDOs and then proceed to strip them naked. And even with a full office, equity and inclusion transformation can only happen in organizations that want to change. Too often institutional resistance to ideas for policy change start almost immediately after the campus welcome party. What we can gain from a study of hip-hop artists like Nicki Minaj is remembering who we are and what we can do: use our sheer talents and skills to create something big and brilliant, despite the odds. As an educator, I can absolutely understand what it's like to perform and excel in an industry that gives you a deal, and then treats you with contempt and disrespect. Don't kill yourself trying to create miracles out of inequitable lack, but absolutely use the skill that you already possess to bless the mic.

Creating space for women is important (thanks for the record deal, thanks for the job). But respecting, loving, and honoring women is also important. That's what community does. That is what kinship is about. Neither industry—entertainment or education—has mastered the art of fully loving Black, Latinx, or Asian women and girls. But it is possible. It is actually owed. I am speaking here as a Black woman—Black women and girls have poured so much love into the field of education (Black teachers) and hip-hop (Black women rappers, dancers, executives, and models). They have helped build the foundations of both fields. They have shown up as hungry, driven, skillful, and successful masters of their craft. Their outcomes have been outstanding. So, to reference Ms. Lauryn Hill, it's time for some reciprocity.

# Approach

*Approach*, as a mindset, concerns *how* we do what we do. Within hip-hop communities, ingenuity, creativity, and authenticity are essential to how they approach the work that they produce.

## INGENUITY AND CULTURAL EFFICACY

The Universal Zulu Nation, a foundational hip-hop group established by Afrika Bambaataa, offers one example of how a hip-hop mindset has always been about having the guts to try the impossible. In his book, *Can't Stop Won't Stop: A History of the Hip-Hop Generation*, Jeff Chang begins the history of hip-hop with the history of African American gangs in New York City and this history of the Zulu Nation.[1]

Bambaataa grew up in a family that was actively engaged in the global Black liberation movement. In his own reflections, Bambaataa points to a self-education through popular culture, which informed his perspective on Black solidarity and unity. From his mother's politically charged record collection, which included Miriam Makeba and James Brown, to his viewing of movies like the 1964 film *Zulu*, Bambaataa understood from personal experience that popular culture could create a transformative and socially critical space for Black people.

Seeking a space of Black male embrace, he joined the Black Spades gang. By 1971, the Black gangs in New York had called a truce to violence against each other. However, the violent anti-Black reaction to school desegregation made membership in gangs difficult to give up. It was needed for protection. For Bambaataa, several life-changing experiences would eventually motivate him to leave the gangs in order to form the Zulu Nation and ultimately change his name from Lance Taylor to Afrika Bambaataa. A shoot out with the police that killed his cousin left the gangs wanting to declare war against the police. It seems that Bambaataa saw no way to win such a war. After his cousin passed, he won a housing authority essay contest that sent him to Africa and Europe as a prize. This trip changed his life. His understanding of community and solidarity transformed after personally observing and experiencing community life in an African country.

He came back sure that he could organize former gang members into the "Zulu Nation" with an explicit focus on Black unity and stopping violence. Music was always a backdrop in gang culture. (Honestly, isn't music a backdrop of all our life experiences? We listen to it through all that we do and feel.) The Universal Zulu Nation believed that music and dance could be a tool to stop gang violence. The Zulu Nation offered youth an alternative space focused on peace, unity, love, and having fun. They believed that they could draw kids out of gangs and offer those that had already left the life a more culturally meaningful space. The youth involved in gangs were essentially seeking a space of belonging and the Zulu Nation believed music and dance could offer them options. They set out to create a culture movement and they called it hip-hop. They spread hip-hop through basement parties, block parties, and social gatherings largely attended by former gang members. Former NYC gang members who witnessed the evolution of the Zulu Nation affirm that their efforts did get results. Chang summarizes it beautifully:

> If you are Gods, Bambaataa seemed to say, then it follows that you are as capable as I am to make this new world. Zulus celebrated the instinct for survival and creation. Living young and free in the Bronx was a revolutionary act of art. To unleash on a social level these vital urges was the surest way to ward off mass death. Bambaataa's message was: We're moving. There's room for you if you get yourself right. Perhaps this is why, of all the utopias offered to the rabbles of outcast youth, Bambaataa's spread through the streets of the Bronx and then into the world like a flaming wick.[2]

Hip-hop as a culture movement was about believing in youth, and giving them a platform to be great. It was a phenomenon based on cultural optimism. While gang culture offered youth personal acceptance (even of their rage and rambunctiousness), hip-hop tapped into their cultural ways of being, knowing, expressing, and doing. This is important. A hip-hop mindset is about believing that culture is powerful and important. It's about believing in the people and respecting the community. This optimistic belief in the culture is the foundation of cultural efficacy. Considering youth experiences within present-day educational institutions, we can clearly see and understand that students will probably always "act out" or "rage against the machine" that is murdering their cultural spirit, if there is no alternative. Young people who actually want to be playful, loud, crazy, cool, and joyful express rage, upset, and frustration simply because that is a natural response to oppression. Give them something delicious to chew on and they will eat. Respect and honor their culture and they will create. Encourage them to believe in themselves and they will invent something incredible.

I will share an example from my time working at Penn State University. The university had a thick history of Black student protest and rage against administration. When the first major protest occurred during my tenure there, I spoke frankly to our university's vice president of student affairs, vice provost for educational equity, and president. I said that White students on that campus were given significant resources (human, physical, and financial) to sustain their traditions. What traditions did Black students have? Protesting was their college memory. When they would gather as alumni in 10 years, they would probably remember fondly and tell stories of their times protesting in college. I argued that the institution was not giving them anything else to remember about their college experience. If administration wanted Black students to stop raging against the machine, then we needed to create, transform, and build an amazing college experience for them. This required us to face the fact that as amazing as Penn State was for thousands of people (including the leaders in this meeting who were making a lot of money doing what they love), it was not an amazing college experience for many ethnically diverse students. Being admitted to college was an accomplishment, and they were proud to be there. They needed to be there to achieve their goals. But at that time, I didn't know any student of color who would call it "amazing." I shared that an "amazing" experience isn't built by throwing the students crumbs. They didn't need one or two seats on the White-centered homecoming committee. The university needed to build entirely new, large-scale experiences that centered ethnically diverse students and championed what mattered to them. These needed to be major initiatives, the type that are important enough to take place on the main university lawn (a highly coveted, protected, and unavoidable space). I suggested that our efforts not only be large and varied, but that they should also be ongoing. This meant that we would keep giving it and giving it until those experiences became campus traditions. When I look back on two of the university cultural centers that I led, both are still running programs that I developed there. One initiative has been running for over 24 years at the University of Maryland and the other for almost 18 at Penn State. That's called tradition. The University of Maryland lists my program, The Juke Joint, as an official homecoming tradition. It has become a longstanding institutional program.

This takes imagination. When I first arrived at the University of Maryland, the Black student population was protesting both the Black Cultural Center and the university at large for failing them. They had nothing until we imagined it. We must have the creative vision to imagine what a culturally rich and dynamic school looks like because we haven't had many concrete models to follow. On our campus, this meant imagining a major new campus tradition that centered ethnically diverse students. That simply did not exist on our campus. Our campus, our students needed educators who would do more than theorize, more even than stand and teach; they needed at least some leaders who would help them create new opportunities. We needed seers and inventors, leaders who could look at a blank slate and see possibilities. We needed educational administrators and teaching faculty with the audacity to shock even themselves by what they can create.

Hip-hop gave young, educationally discarded kids a cultural seed that kept growing until it surpassed even their own expectations. Even if their goal was to in fact start a cultural revolution (a revolution is a fundamental and sudden change),[3] hip-hop stopped being a revolution a long time ago. It is now everyday life. Hip-hop beats are embedded in almost every commercial on television; its linguistic approach is now mixed into American English; its artists are beloved icons; it is embraced across almost every ethnic and racial community; and it reaches all corners of the globe. It is as essential to American culture as the concept of apple pie. As a matter of fact, I'm not even sure if all members of Gen Z are familiar with the apple pie metaphor. But everyone probably knows hip-hop. The growth and evolution of hip-hop is a perfect example of the power of culture to change lives.

## TURNING THE TABLES: CREATIVITY AND ORIGINALITY

At its core, hip-hop embodies the spirit of innovation, creativity, and the guts to be different. Toni Blackman, a hip-hop educational pioneer and the first Hip-Hop Ambassador for the U.S. State Department, stresses that hip-hop culture gave her the unshakeable belief in the power of her own creative mind—that if something didn't exist, she could build it; if something hadn't been said, she could say it; if something needed to be created, she could create it. As we trace the history and development of hip-hop culture, one thing that remains consistent is the audacious belief that if you try something new, it might actually turn out dope. What would make a kid think that moving a record in the opposite direction could create something magical? Creativity is at the core of a hip-hop mindset. Whether it is an emcee creatively playing with the flow of words, dancers pushing the creative boundaries of what their bodies can do, or graffiti artists re-imagining buildings and train cars as public art galleries, teachers reimagining the art of instruction or educational leaders getting creative with the culture of their school, the ability to stand out as original and unique is an essential ethic of hip-hop. So let's unpack creativity.

What does it mean to be creative? What does it involve? A foundational component of creativity involves the art of reimagining—the ability to take a thing and use it differently. A record player is simply a sound unit (it is actually an all-in-one record-playing unit). It plays the record and projects the sound. But hip-hop culture reimagined the turntable component of the record player and established it as a musical *instrument* that could be manipulated and played by a DJ just as a musician might play the guitar, drums, or horn. There is now a technique to it—a way to "read" the record just as you read music. Hip-hop artists created the ability to make new music and sounds simply by rethinking the direction that the record was played.

Beyond the music, hip-hop culture is broadly all about reimagining. Disenfranchised people are reimagined as neighborhood kings and queens; housing projects are reimagined as sacred places; words are given completely new meanings; struggle is interpreted as a badge of honor; and a microphone is reimagined as one of the most powerful objects on earth (with the strength to lift folx out of poverty, a reach that spans the globe, and the power to change everything about your life). Why can't this be the case with schools? Why can't disenfranchised students be reimagined as brilliant scholars, struggling schools be transformed into sites of powerful learning, and education itself be the life-changing experience that was its original promise?

Hip-hop youth didn't look at their lives—their communities, their families, themselves—and see useless junk. They were imaginitive, ingenious. Hip-hop culture is one of the most organic forms of asset mapping—mining the culture, the community, and ourselves for viable and useful assets.[4] As in, "We may not have a beautiful shiny stage, but we have this concrete to dance on." Or, "I may not write and speak the way that they want me to in school, but I've got something to say and I talk slick. So pass me the mic." There is an optimistic possibility that is essential to the creative mind. You are not limited by what is immediately before you. Creative minds are seers. They can see and imagine something different. It's the chef who can turn your kitchen scraps into a gourmet meal. It's the writer who can transform a blank page into a story that will change your life. It's the educator who sees talent and possibility in the kids that others see as worthless.[5] It's the professor who sees a college classroom as a community command center for social change. We need all of this in the American education system. What could our schools be if we, the leaders, could be more creative?

For the hip-hop mind, creativity involves several critical values and practices. First, there is a value for being original or unique. One of the most vivid examples of the efforts that hip-hop artists once took in their quest to stand out and be unique is the older practice of *crate digging*. In the documentary *Hip-hop Evolution*, emcees like Q-Tip and Busta Rhymes shared their memories of the Roosevelt Hotel Record Convention and chronicled the labor artists were willing to put in just to discover a rare and unusual song to sample. Kathy Iandoli (2014) offers some history in her article "The Lost Art of Crate Digging."

> There is a utility for crate digging that dates back decades to the earliest days of hip-hop production, because records were the raw materials for hip-hop tracks . . . To acquire the vinyl, they would hunt. They raided record stores and hit record fairs in the early morning hours to scour through crates and crates of wax.[6]

The effort behind classic crate digging was the hunt for originality and uniqueness—a song or sound from the records in the crates that would stand out or set an emcee apart from the crowd. An artist wants to be "different," "unique," or "special," but these labels can only be given or affirmed by the community. You need the crowd to react to your uniqueness, to applaud it and admire it. Individuality in hip-hop has nothing to do with being independently successful (a lone ranger hoarding your ability and success). Instead, it is about being fully submerged in a community and having the talent and skills to not only be seen, but to also be uplifted by your people. The people you serve have the power to make you a success. For the artist, that means the concert audience and the consumers who buy the music. For the educator, that means the students and their families. Your success is inextricably bound to what students do—how they behave, how they perform, how they react to you, and how they move as "one of your students" in the school. Your principal loving you won't win you teacher of the year. Student outcomes earn you that honor. Getting close to and creative with our students is required. Every educator interviewed for this project named creativity as one of the most critical aspects of a hip-hop mindset. And they specifically saw their own creative abilities as the primary reason for how and why they stand out professionally.

But it is important to note that each professional did not take their creative abilities for granted as being innate or a characteristic that they "just happen" to have. Creativity and uniqueness was a goal that they actively pursued. In their work, they *sought* to be creative. They *wanted* to be unique—to approach education in new and interesting ways, to develop initiatives that had never been done before, to come up with solutions that might seem impossible. And so in their professional lives and training, they were crate digging—searching for and seeking out concepts, ideologies, scholars, thinkers, and experiences that would elevate their work to a new level. This moves the "researching" work of crate digging into the "producing" realm of remixing. Researching songs and producing music in hip-hop are akin to theory and practice in other fields. Do you have the creative capacity to take the research (old records) and develop dope interventions, curricula, or policies (new music/remixes)? It is not enough to "know" music. Successful artists can also "do" music—rhyme, spin, or make beats. They produce outcomes.

The art of remixing taps the creative capacity to take what is seen as a complete and finished product and breathe new life into it, give it a new sound, take it in a different direction. Sampling and remixing a song is not about simply extending the life of a song (life support). Rather, remixing is about resurrection: Digging through a crate, finding a long-forgotten record, and bringing it back in a funkier, slicker form. Hip-hop–minded professionals apply this mindset to their work. Some folx are lucky to have jobs that allow them blank slates to create new things and innovate new ideas.

But most folx inherit their work. The new principal inherits a school that someone else used to lead. The new teacher is assigned to teach a grade level or class that their colleague taught the year before. The multicultural affairs director at the college often inherits the leadership of the department from the previous director. These are all organizations and communities that already existed. They have histories, ways of being and doing, and longstanding cultures already in place. If the newly hired leader comes in, changes nothing, and continues to let the same song play on repeat, it will probably be said that they didn't contribute much. Nothing changed. But if this new leader can tease out the very best of what already existed, take those initiatives and enhance them, and then add on completely new programs, practices or approaches, their legacy will be that of a visionary and innovator.

Remix culture in hip-hop is grounded in love and appreciation for the original song being sampled. Remixing in the spirit of hip-hop requires you to have respect for the craft. For emcees, the craft was music. Veteran producers of hip-hop were scientists dissecting tracks, librarians of musical culture, mathematicians of the BPM, and above all music historians. I recall thinking this about Sean Combs (Diddy) as he built up Bad Boy Entertainment through a catalogue comprised heavily of sampling and remixes. At one point he actually claimed to have invented the remix.[7] He may not have invented it, but he was definitely the king of it in the 1990s. As a music lover, I viewed Diddy as a kindred spirit. I could tell by his repertoire that he absolutely loved music. Remixing is not simply borrowing or copying, it is about admiring and elevating.

As I reflect on my own practice, one of the best examples I can offer of how to interpret this mindset within educational practice comes from my time serving as director of the Paul Robeson Cultural Center at Penn State University. When I accepted the job, I was replacing a director who had retired after leading the cultural center for 30 years. I spent my first semester in conversation with everyone on campus. I met with students, faculty, staff, community members, and alumni. I wanted to hear their thoughts and opinions of the center. I asked two questions: What must absolutely stay in place? And what is something new that you wish or dream the center could do? Overwhelmingly, most of the faculty, staff, and alumni who had longer histories with the cultural center mentioned that they wished the center could bring back a program that had been gone for some time.

Apparently, back in the day, the "Robe," as it was called, used to serve lunch for faculty, staff, and students as a student organization fundraiser. They would sell plated lunches of soul food. Many folx on campus shared how important that fellowship time was during the day and how it organically brought the campus community together. In the past, the cultural center was located in a small, modular building tucked away in a location that offered privacy when it came to the activities of the center. In other words, it was far off in a corner of campus where no one paid them any attention. The center's multimillion-dollar renovation and move to a central location on campus now connected it to the student union and all of the food vendors in that building. New changes in catering policies prohibited students and staff from cooking and selling food. Only approved professional caterers were allowed at all university events. The old lunch program didn't make the move to the new location.

But as my husband loves to say, multiple people don't tell the same lie. This was clearly an important historical program. It was actually the answer to both of my questions. There was no current program that folx demanded to remain. Almost no one had ideas for new programs and initiatives. What they wanted was for us to bring back an old program and for me to do my job and come up with other fresh, new ideas to establish a full, robust portfolio. And here enters the remix. I saw my charge as developing a contemporary play on this old program that would give the campus back its cultural lunch hour. We created a new initiative called "Taste of the Diaspora" (whose name I sampled from a student program that had been hosted at my previous institution). It was a free noontime lunch hour that featured a different diasporic culture each month (African Diaspora, Asian Diaspora, Latin Diaspora, etc.).

I started the process by crate digging. One of my favorite events hosted by the Smithsonian Institution in Washington, D.C., was the Folklife Festival. The festival transformed the National Mall into a vibrant cultural space with tents, artifacts, demonstrations, and research exhibitions. In the spirit of that festival, we turned our ballroom into an educative cultural space with historic and contemporary facts and information about the featured cultural community. These research exhibits were placed throughout the room to allow attendees to walk around at their own pace and learn. I located a caterer who was willing to custom-make food based on the menu and recipes that I provided each month (the school is located in a part of central Pennsylvania where ethnic restaurants were limited). In the end, we were able to offer a free, mega buffet of ethnic cuisine each month. And we honored what folx most loved about the program—that there was no agenda, lecture, or performance. Folx just gathered, talked, laughed, let loose, and created a community on campus. Beyond the research exhibitions and some conversational cards placed on dining tables, there was no main event. We took the spirit of the old beloved program and remixed it—made it free, expanded the food, added music, hosted it in a larger space that could accommodate more people, and included an educational exhibition. This was a huge success that gave our stakeholders back an experience that they loved while also pulling in several hundred more folx who had never experienced the cultural center.

Thinking back on this initiative now, in the current realities of increasing food insecurity among college students, the value of the cultural lunch hour takes on new meaning. But always at the foundation of our work building this initiative was a black and white picture from one of the old lunches in the original cultural center. It was a picture of a group of faculty and students laughing and eating. What we sought to honor from that image was not simply serving some cultural food, but rather creating a space for ethnically diverse Penn Staters to be culturally free and culturally safe—a space of joy and communion. A space where ethnically diverse students, faculty, and staff could be seen, introduced, known, and protected. Because we all need to be cared for in these educational spaces. That's what honoring the craft means. In the brief 5 years that I spent as director, I wasn't trying to outshine my elder who ran that center for three decades. My goal was to honor, remix, and elevate the legacy that he created.

## REPRESENTING: AUTHENTICITY AND CLARITY

The final aspect of approach concerns the authenticity of what is created. Within hip-hop culture, it is not enough to just be unique and different. Anyone can choose to be divergent—to intentionally distance themselves from the way everyone else thinks or acts to seem special or to gain attention. Within hip-hop culture, the ethic that puts ego in check is *authenticity*. Your brand of different must be authentic—it must be real and meaningful. You don't make a bold statement simply to get others to react. You make that statement because it is a truth that must be told. You say what you said because it needed to be said, because someone had to say it and you have a microphone (power). You use your voice to move the crowd, not just to hear yourself speak. The age-old ideal of "representing" continues to hold sway. Back in the day, this might have been a question of how authentically you are representing your neighborhood or friendship circle. Today, it also means how authentically you are representing yourself. Are you who you say (or think) you are? As Lauryn Hill said, "Don't be a hard rock when you really are a gem."[8] In other words, don't try to be that which you are not. This is one of the most freeing aspects of hip-hop culture. Representing poses the question, Do your subjects and verbs agree? In other words, do your principles and actions meet?

As I was growing up with hip-hop, I remember feeling that the pressure to "represent" was so heavy back in the day. In the late 1980s and early 1990s it was such a serious thing. Folx were not playing games about checking your authenticity. From threatening to "pull your Black card" if you came off like a racial assimilationist to feeling the pressure to be able to prove or validate any claim you make regarding who you are, what you are about, or where you are from (e.g., "You from the projects? Let me see your license"). Representing was real. I now look back on it and laugh because it was such a raw form of accountability. Being held accountable to be your authentic self is an important act of racial liberation. In so many social and institutional spaces, ethnically diverse communities are pushed, harassed, and bullied into being something other than themselves.[9] From the Indian Acculturation Schools to the Missionary Freedmen Schools to the hundreds of contemporary schools and colleges that are still actively teaching students to speak, think, and act differently from their own cultures, school has been the primary venue through which ethnically diverse youth and young adults learn to hate and look down upon their own cultures, communities, and by extension, their own families. In his classic text, *The Mis-Education of the Negro*, Carter G. Woodson offers an explanation that remains relevant today:

> The same educational process which inspires and stimulates the oppressor with the thought that he is everything and has accomplished everything worthwhile, depresses and crushes, at the same time, the spark of genius in the Negro by making him feel that his race does not amount to much and never will measure up to the standards of other peoples. . . . As another has well said, to handicap a student by teaching him that his black face is a curse and that his struggle to change his condition is hopeless is the worst sort of lynching. . . . It may be of no importance to the race to be able to boast today of many times as many "educated" members as it had in 1865. . . . The only question which concerns us here is whether these "educated" persons are actually equipped to face the ordeal before them or unconsciously contribute to their own undoing by per-petuating the regime of the oppressor. . . . No systematic effort toward change has been possible, for, taught the same economics, history, philosophy, litera-ture and religion which have established the present code of morals, the Negro's mind has been brought under the control of his oppressor. The problem of holding the Negro down, therefore, is easily solved. When you control a man's thinking you do not have to worry about his actions. You do not have to tell him not to stand here or go yonder. He will find his 'proper place' and will stay in it. You do not need to send him to the back door. He will go without being told. In fact, if there is no back door, he will cut one for his special benefit. His education makes it necessary.[10]

Considering this history, the culture of authenticity within hip-hop can be appreciated not so much as a *pressure* to keep it real, but rather a *permission* to keep it real. A permission to claim your community, to honor your mother tongue, to be loyal to your crew, to name your experi-ence, and to speak your truth. It gives you the green light to challenge the status quo. Hip-hop situates itself on the other side of cultural hegemony and racial assimilation. It doesn't just lovingly encourage or gently nudge you to be yourself; instead, it projects an urgent sense that the commu-nity is holding you accountable. "Don't fake the funk." "The streets are watching." "Yo, you better represent." In her interview within Chapter 6, Crystal Leigh Endsley, an associate professor of Africana Studies at John Jay

College of Criminal Justice, explains that the very relationships that are so critical within hip-hop culture—the squad, the crew, even the audience—are all integrity measures. Your relationships are cultural devices that hold you accountable.

In many ways, hip-hop gives you permission to see yourself as not just enough, but actually dope. You don't have to be flawless. You don't have to please everyone. Everyone who dances to your beat won't necessarily be your fan. But they will bob their head. You don't have to say all the right things or make all the right moves. You will stumble over words and steps; superstars know how to keep going in those moments. The art of recovery. The only thing that is absolutely expected of you is for you to be your authentic self; to actually be who you say you are and own it. This is a mindset that is valuable in any field.

Hip-hop shows us all of ourselves—the beautiful mess of it all. And let's be real, you cannot encounter the ugly chaos of oppression and not be a little messy. Isn't that what oppression is intended to do? We shouldn't be shocked when we see the outcomes. Black folx, in particular, haven't just had it rough. To put it that lightly is insulting. We have survived sheer terrorism and lived to talk, scream, write, and rap about it. So, yes, we are everything from Uncle Luke parties to Dead Prez radical activism. Hip-hop artists like Nas have shown us through their art that there is no shame in revealing all sides of yourself. Nas can be an incredibly conscious, knowledge-rich emcee. But he can also show up as a playboy, street hustler, and womanizer. He's not perfect and he shows up with all his contradictions. That's authentic. What would be fake is for him to *only* present as this African-centered, activist-oriented, wise man. He is clearly self-taught and extremely knowledgeable about African American history and culture. But he is also from the streets and has that knowledge base too. He is also from a good family and loved his parents and so he also shows us that side of himself. "Love you daddy" is in his lyrics on the *God's Son* album. He doesn't try to be just one thing all the time because that is not who he is. We can all learn from this, particularly educators. We need to allow teachers and educational leaders to be human, to feel, to express, to have a culture, a history, and a life experience.

Another aspect of authenticity is clarity. Several of the elite educators mentioned that, for them, a hip-hop mindset also concerned writing, speaking, or working so that the audience whom they represent will fully see themselves. Particularly as educational researchers and writers, many educators felt that their authenticity was tied to the ability to get it right. Getting it right might take the shape of skillful writing that paints an accurate and authentic portrait of social experiences or a teaching practice that is comprehensive and clear so that learners come away from a course more informed, inspired, and engaged in a subject. Andre M. Perry, senior fellow at the Brookings Institution, argues that the goal of an academic (researcher and writer) is essentially the same goal of an emcee—to communicate in a way that will allow people to feel it.

Bettina L. Love, professor of Educational Studies at Teachers College, Columbia University, says that hip-hop has been a major influence on how she writes as a scholar. According to Love, a hip-hop mindset doesn't just help her to write well (creatively using words, forming sentences that flow well), but more importantly, it pushes her to be clear and accurate. Because accuracy matters in hip-hop. Representing the experience and telling a story that is vivid, raw, clear, and accurate is deeply valued within the culture. In his book *Decoded*, Jay-Z shares how the group Run-D.M.C.'s approach to lyric writing and storytelling heavily influenced him as a then fan and aspiring rapper. "Their voices were big, like their beats, but naturally slick, like hustlers. The rhymes were crisp and aggressive. When he rapped about having a 'big Caddy, not like a Seville,' he was being descriptive and precise. Run didn't just say a car, he said a Caddy. He didn't just say a Caddy, he said a Seville. He painted a picture and then gave it emotional life. I completely related."[11] Detail matters. And it matters not only in writing rhymes but also in creating any type of experience for others. Whether you are telling stories or planning lessons or planning educational programs and events, detail matters.

As I reflect on my past experiences as an educational practitioner leading university cultural centers, I see clearly how I embraced this ethic in the programs that we planned. We didn't just simply book artists, order A/V, send out bland flyers, and set up seats. We created experiences that were culturally authentic and accurate. We transformed environments and paid attention to the décor we used, the music that played as folx entered, the catering that was offered. We didn't just read a bio and bring a speaker on stage; we culturally celebrated and loved them up to the mic. Every aspect of what we do is a learning experience. Even in the way we introduce our speakers we are showing our students how to honor and appreciate someone. This attention to detail is something that we can adopt in all aspects of the work we do—how we write, how we plan, and how we lead.

Beyond the ability to "get it right" and to be accurate, there is also this beautiful acknowledgment by the hip-hop artist, scholar, educator, or leader that the story or experience is worth telling in the first place. Our communities and neighborhoods are worth claiming. Our people are worth the extra time it takes to be accurate and precise. This was a mantra when I was a department head: All over campus, people give Black and Brown students a mediocre effort. They throw a pizza at them and say they should be grateful. That won't happen in a department that I run. We respect our people. These students deserve to walk into a beautiful room or a beautiful experience just like the president of the university. We take care of every detail and we honor them. Hip-hop culture communicates that we are worthy. The familial, navigational, and resistant capital found in our culture is worth talking about, rapping about and speaking on poetically.[12]

And our struggles must also be known. We must testify to the discrimination that we experience in our streets because our lives and our rights matter. Writing with clarity means making space to clearly communicate the legitimate rage that is felt by oppressed communities. Often academic environments are pushed to be soulless spaces, void of honest, real reactions to the incredibly hostile, violent, and even horrific topics that we teach or research. Instructors are pushed to teach from a neutral stance. Researchers are directed to write objectively, distancing their personal perspectives to prevent bias in the analysis. We are literally expected to interact with violence in very intimate ways—we touch it with our fingers (type); we view it with our eyes (read) and we speak it from our mouths (lecture)—and yet our presentation should be void of emotion. This is absolutely ridiculous. As another brilliant hip-hop group, the Geto Boys, expressed, fuck that shit, people are killing us. There's no neutrality around terrorism and murder, hate, and racism. Chuck D asserts, "Hip hop with its use of words can be a vehicle for any voice . . . but hip hop as a vehicle for the angry voice could fight the malfeasance taking place in society."[13] One of the primary gifts hip-hop gives us is the permission to write what is real. To speak boldly and unapologetically. To tell the truth in our own way and in our own voice. That's why the phrase "I said what I said" is so popular right now. We just need to own our words and thoughts. Jay-Z explains how this honest truth-telling about issues of internalized racism and colorism has been therapeutic in many ways:

> Even when hip-hop aired some of the ongoing colorism among black people—like Biggie rapping that he was black and ugly as ever—the point is that we were airing out, not sweeping it under the rug and letting it drive us crazy trying to pretend it didn't exist. Just one more way that hip-hop kept us sane.[14]

One of my first pieces of writing that explored the merits of hip-hop in education was the article "Mr. Nigger: The Challenges of Educating Black Males in American Society."[15] The title was a play on the song "Mr. Nigga," by Mos Def.[16] The message in the song is that regardless of what a Black person does to please white dominant culture in their attempt to achieve the American Dream, they will still be seen as a nigger. Society will simply stick the prefix "Mr." in front of their names as a nod to their effort at respectability politics. Now you are basically "Mr. Nigger." The song is brilliant, as is most of Mos Def's work. I thought the article was also brilliant in its truly interdisciplinary approach to the issue. I labored on that one and pulled on history, sociology, psychology, and media studies to wrestle with the full scope of the Black male experience. But the article was hard to get published because of the title. Several journals urged me to change the name. I refused. *I said what I said.* The title made the strongest point on the page. Eventually, *The Journal of Black Studies* published the article, and I received a personal note of praise from Dr. Molefi Kete Asante, the scholar who coined the term *Afrocentricity* and who served as editor-in-chief of the journal. Needless to say, I felt affirmed. The article went on to be one of the most accessed articles in the journal for a few years (I suspect because of the title). It is another example of why we can't be weak with our words. In the article, I discuss hip-hop as an inclusive space for Black male thought, rage, and expression. It is one of only a few spaces in society where Black and Brown people have permission to just be Black and Brown: to speak Black and Brown language, to think Black and Brown thoughts, to express Black and Brown culture, to embrace Black and Brown rage, and to adore and adorn Black and Brown bodies.

This is the beauty of the Black and Latinx genius that created hip-hop. From schools to churches, all of society's cultural institutions teach us that we are racially not enough. The hip-hop community's response is brilliant: Your books and media socialize us to devalue our looks, words, and voice, so we will create our own cultural institution that demands we be all of those things that you hate in us. You oppress and destroy the economic infrastructure of our neighborhoods; we will claim our housing projects and make them famous. You hate our voice; we will take a microphone and yell at the top of our lungs. You want us to be invisible; we will wear jewelry that blings and shines bright. You portray us as unintelligent; we will get paid to write and speak. We won't deplete ourselves of our cultural joy just to avoid your stereotypes. Yes, we will dance, rap, sing, yell, curse, and then brag about it. You write us out of educational texts, so we will research and write about our own communities and seek their approval as the marker of success. The culture knows exactly what the culture needs: The freedom to be our real, true selves.

Hip-hop culture confronts cultural oppression and racism by speaking directly to them in lyrics; behaving boldly (loud, ratchet, bodacious, aggressive) in an effort to spite them; and creating counterculture environments that establish community-derived sources of power. When I use the term "confrontation" I am not talking about altercations or hypermasculine aggression. Rather, I am talking about hip-hop confrontation as a strategy of change. If you cannot embrace confrontation, you cannot create change, because in order to create something new, you must confront the problems in what already exists. In an interview for an AMNY newsletter article that chronicled the 1977 New York City blackout and its impact on hip-hop culture, scholar Joseph Schloss offers the following insight: "So much of hip-hop is about not playing by the rules of the rest of society. And part of justifying that is saying, 'If we're not going to be treated fairly under those rules, what do we owe them? Why shouldn't we come up with our own system?'"[17] For educators, an embrace of hip-hop mindfulness is the permission to not ask for permission, particularly when it comes to affirming students' cultural identities and histories in the educational experience. Why are we asking permission to confront racism in education?

We have had way too many years of cultural exclusion and oppression in education, so this book isn't a gentle nudge or loving encouragement for educators to keep it real. In the spirit of hip-hop, this is a strong push to hold yourself accountable. How are you curating educational spaces that show up culturally different in students' lives? If you are a school principal, how is your school showing up culturally different—creative, authentic, and true? If you are an instructor, how is your classroom showing up culturally different from the past—representative, inclusive, flexible, and open to the diverse ways that students live in the world? As bell hooks urged so many years ago, how are you teaching to transgress and to build a better community?[18] If anything, not only does hip-hop give us the permission that we need to be innovative, but it also serves as clear proof of the incredible outcomes that occur when we honor and embrace the cultures of the people that we serve. Rather than trying to change and refine our students, we should be focused on trying to understand and integrate their cultural genius into our institutions. Help them help you, or, as Rakim shared, when youth are taught to speak the truth, watch all that they create and do.[19] The bottom line is if teachers, students, principals, faculty, and college administrators take the leap to just culturally be yourself, what happens just might blow your mind.

## CHAPTER 4

# Posture

Style has a profound meaning to Black Americans. If we can't drive, we will invent walks and the world will envy the dexterity of our feet. If we can't have ham, we will boil chitterlings; if we are given rotten peaches, we will make cobblers; if given scraps, we will make quilts; take away our drums, and we will clap our hands. We prove the human spirit will prevail. We will take what we have to make what we need. We need confidence in our knowledge of who we are.

—Nikki Giovanni [1]

## ON BEING A BADASS

The goal of this book is to lay a theoretical foundation and knowledge base for understanding the concept of a hip-hop mindset. But as I approached writing it, I couldn't help thinking that folx deep in hip-hop communities probably wouldn't use the words "mindset" or "mindfulness." (Well, maybe Russell Simmons and RZA are exceptions since they are so deep into meditative and mindfulness practices.) But generally, I can't say that the term mindfulness is indigenous to the culture. So what is another word, using hip-hop's mother tongue, that best exemplifies the overall aura of hip-hop? Maybe *swag*. Within hip-hop culture, swag has come to mean a state of being, a way of representing, an aura, a vibe. The standard definition of swag defines it as goods, money, valuable items, or fabric that can be adorned or used to decorate.[2] In hip-hop culture, swag is traditionally seen as any item that holds value. That item then transfers its value to the person in possession of it. In marketing, swag is the name for promotional items that are given away to promote something. The acronym is "stuff we all get." Stuff. Things. Value. Wealth. But in hip-hop, swag is free. While hip-hop artists may boast of having money and being paid, they actually don't need money to have swag. It's not a requirement. Swag is simply how you carry yourself. It is an expression of confidence.

In hip-hop, swag is a philosophical mindset that gives you color and flavor. It is an attitude of assuredness. Merriam-Webster cites a "US slang" meaning of swag as "bold or brash self-confidence." *Cockiness* and *swagger* are listed as related terms.[3] This personifies the absolute cultural magic of hip-hop. A broke kid who lives in the projects and has been kicked out of school can take the microphone and tell the world how dope he is. He possesses nothing. He has not one item or thing to associate with or prove his claims. He is not bad, brilliant, or dope because of what he owns. In a community where you own nothing, you are bad, brilliant, or dope simply because of who you are. Don't be mistaken—clothes, shoes, fashion, and style do contribute, but it is absolutely possible to have swag as a trait without actually having swag as an item. Interpreted outside of hip-hop, this is also empowering because it means that exceptionality is not determined by the credentials or titles that you possess.

How do you show up as national teacher of the year without receiving the award? How do you demonstrate your ability as an outstanding leader without your doctorate or the title of Principal or Director? One of my favorite examples of this is portrayed in the movie *Boiler Room*.[4] As a movie genre, *Boiler Room* is a vivid example of White cultural appropriation of the hip-hop aesthetic. It is also an excellent case study of the power of swag. The movie was conceived after its creator, Ben Younger, interviewed for a position at the firm Sterling Foster & Company in Long Island. The firm would actually later be shut down on a stock-manipulation boiler room case similar to what is depicted in the movie. The movie follows the life of Seth, played by Giovanni Ribisi. Seth is a young, White male college dropout who is brilliant at facilitating underground gambling games and who then takes those skills to Wall Street. In the movie, Seth meets a broker at one of his illegal gambling nights. The broker is impressed with Seth's ingenuity, skills, and professionalism and recruits him to work at his firm, J.T. Marlin.

I'll pause here to acknowledge the White privilege present in this story line. Although there is a lot of hip-hop played in the background of every scene, make no mistake that this is a story of White male culture. The business acumen that some African American and Latinx men demonstrate in street hustling could make the small group of young men who engage in those activities filthy rich, in legitimate ways, if they had the opportunity and weren't facing issues of racial injustice, prison industry, economic exclusion, and community isolation.

Back to Seth. Seth's cousin comes to one of the poker games and introduces him to his friend from J.T. Marlin. They hit it off and the friend extends an invitation for Seth to explore becoming a junior broker. Seth doesn't know that the company is engaged in illegal boiler room practices. He takes the leap to become a broker. In the orientation scene, the character Jim Young, played by Ben Affleck, gives advice to his young recruits in a dynamic motivational welcome speech. He shares that the company's mantra is simply, "Act as if." Act as if you already are who you want to be. Act as if you are the president of the firm.[5] This advice is undeniably and fundamentally a hip-hop ethic and mindset.

The movie includes a lot of hip-hop music in its soundtrack (Rakim, Notorious B.I.G, A Tribe Called Quest, Lords of the Underground, Slick Rick, De La Soul) and directly references hip-hop artists in its narration. By doing so, they acknowledge that this audacious swag that you are witnessing among these characters is a hip-hop cultural mindset applied to White men working the stock market. Of the 15 songs on the *Boiler Room* soundtrack, 13 are hip-hop songs. There are a lot of music genres that could have been a perfect backdrop for a story about young White men hustling for their dreams, living it up, and building up their confidence and audaciousness. Rock and heavy metal would have been just fine. But to truly bring home the concept of possessing swag even if you actually possess no collateral, to personify the idea of turning nothing into something, and to underscore the brilliant potential and capacity of young people who have been pushed out of traditional school environments, you need hip-hop. There is an edge to the music that underscores the edge to the mindset. I share this film, out of the long list of other films with hip-hop soundtracks, because it also reiterates the point that I make in this book about hip-hop mindfulness being relevant to those who are not artists. If you can truly understand, appreciate, and embody the essence of hip-hop culture, there is much that it can offer to any professional with ambition and a desire to be great.

The word *posture* can help us to understand the hip-hop mindset. In this case, I'm not thinking of the typical negative use of posturing as pretending to know more, have more, or be more than you really are. Rather, I am talking about the foundational sense of posture as it relates to taking a stance or asserting a position. The standard definition of posture is the position in which someone holds their body.[6] Relating this to hip-hop professional identity, posture then becomes the position you take in your work. It is very much connected to the idea of positionality: how your hip-hop identity influences your understanding and interaction with the world. This concept of a hip-hop mindset is not a list of "best practices" for professionals nor is it an outline of "classroom strategies" for educators. It is a mindset, an aura, a personal quality that ultimately starts with this sense of swag that you bring into your work, whatever that work might be. In education this means it is useful whether you are a teacher, administrator, school counselor, or coach.

*Mindfulness* is simply the state of being conscious or aware of something. Hip-hop mindfulness means that you can vividly see and understand your actions and attitude as culturally being hip-hop. Once you free yourself to embrace and become a part of a community whose values are rooted in aspirations to be great, to innovate, to create, to elevate, and to mix things up, you might also find yourself achieving more than you could ever imagine. By advancing the concept of a hip-hop mindset, I am simply suggesting that we walk purposefully in the spirit of hip-hop—in other words that we locate, own, and embrace our swag.

## SHINE BRIGHT LIKE A DIAMOND

While hip-hop swag is most often seen as a character or personal quality, material culture is still very important in hip-hop. Over the years, the materials that have mattered in hip-hop have included shoes, clothes, cars, homes, and jewelry. These objects all visually transfer literal value to the artist—importance is determined by the wealth that these objects represent. Of all the material forms of swag, jewelry has been one of the most sustaining forms of material culture in hip-hop. This is particularly salient, because a deep analysis of the history and metaphorical uses of jewelry reveal mindsets and cultural interpretations that hold significant meaning. If you step back and listen intently and look broadly at the social context of the lives of hip-hop cultural group members (classism, neoliberal racism, educational exclusion, and racial disparities across school discipline, criminal justice, health care, and unemployment), then you might better understand what would make a kid who is living in severe poverty rhyme about having all the cash, cars, and jewelry in the world. It is another form of dreaming. I personally challenge the idea that braggadocio is inherently bad. In fact, I see it as a viable tool of self and cultural efficacy building among youth and young adults. The desire to shine bright, to stand out, and to be seen holds value for us all.

What does *bling* have to do with education? "Bling" is the imaginary sound made by light reflecting from a large diamond.[7] The metaphor is used to exaggerate how much expensive jewelry a person is wearing. Through the years, the jewelry of choice within hip-hop has ranged from solid gold to platinum to diamonds. Regardless of what metal or stone might currently be the popular choice, the concept of "bling" is about how much of it you can afford. The creative imagination associated with the word "bling" is a quintessential ethic of hip-hop culture. Beyond status claiming and power yielding, "bling" and the long history of audacious jewelry in hip-hop culture is about the ability of artists who often came from minimal economic backgrounds to imagine bright lives full of power, abundance, worth, and wealth—literally living large.

A quick hip-hop history lesson illustrates what it looks like to dream something into reality. One of the first images of a rapper being adorned with gold jewelry was the cover of Kurtis Blow's self-titled debut album released in 1980. Blow is pictured shirtless wearing six thin gold chains. By the mid-1980s hip-hop artists like Run-D.M.C., Eric B. & Rakim, Slick Rick, and Big Daddy Kane popularized the thick "Dookie" rope chain. LL Cool J not only sported a 27mm long chain but went so far as to adorn an actual black panther with a dookie chain on his *Walking with a Panther* album cover. On his *Long Live the Kane* album cover, Big Daddy Kane is pictured adorned in gold and seated in a way that mirrors historic images of African kings and Greek gods. This imaging is important because the history of being adorned with gold jewelry traces back to ancient Egypt and connects hip-hop culture to its African roots.

The color yellow had special meaning in ancient Egypt. Yellow was a symbol of something being indestructible and eternal.[8] The objects associated with the color yellow, the sun and gold, were adored and respected. Statues were often built in gold; kings and queens were fully adorned in gold; and nobility were buried in solid gold coffins.[9] African king Mansa Musa, who ruled the Mali empire in the 14th century, was the richest person in human history and known for his love of gold—his caravan consisted of 500 heralds all carrying gold staffs and his entourage traveled with a large amount of gold bars.[10] The association of gold with power and status predates hip-hop by several thousand years. The concept of showing the world what you've got is an African cultural legacy. Hip-hop artists in the 1980s brought into the contemporary world a very long African tradition of using jewelry as a symbol of status and importance. What was different within hip-hop culture was the spirit of competition. Because there were no official kings and queens of hip-hop, rappers were often self-proclaimed royalty. The title "king" or "queen" could be taken at any time, which meant everything was a competition—lyrics, record sales, clothes, and especially jewelry. Artists often bragged about such things very early in their careers when they probably couldn't afford any of it. While hip-hop artists often talk about wealth, they demonstrate that their true wealth lies in their talent. When all you've got is your natural born talent, then you must show off that talent. In some ways, early hip-hop artists were given street passes for claiming wealth that they didn't have. No one believed that Special Ed had a butler or a dog with a solid gold bone. This was just creative writing. But where expectation becomes real was your talent. You couldn't fake the funk with your talent or your skills. Those have always been the real assets that matter in hip-hop. As the industry grew and hip-hop artists became millionaires and eventually billionaires, the material wealth became icing on the cake. But understand, hip-hop artists always knew they were fly.

The term "Bling Bling" was made famous by the Cash Money Millionaires in the 1990s. It is the ultimate catch phrase to personify the audaciousness and extravagance that has been associated with the status claiming, place-making, and braggadocio that is central in the history of hip-hop music. Minya Oh sums it up best in an interview about her book, *Bling Bling: Hip-hop's Crown Jewels*:

> Hip-hop artists were the ones who were leading the way to have this amazing, beautiful fantasylike view where there is no such thing as too much. There's no

such thing as being overdressed—these are guys who wear fur coats to a picnic or diamonds to go play basketball.[11]

The entrance of the term "Bling Bling" into the world finally gave a name to this culture of enormous dreams, possibility, celebration, and the whole notion of the "come-up" (coming into money and stature). The language has changed through the years and many within the culture now refer to "bling" as "drip." Regardless of the words used, the message is still the same—look at how I shine. In 15 years, hip-hop went from six thin gold chains to platinum and diamonds. How did they do this? They simply spoke it, acted it, and made it so. They turned ideas into reality. Because of this, I firmly believe there are benefits to braggadocio. In the Tao of Wu, RZA states that "Jewels are minerals, compressed pieces of earth, stacks of crystalline carbon. What gives them shine is their history. It's the same with man."[12]

Many spiritual faiths believe that there is power in the tongue.[13] Some followers (like my mom) take it so literally that they refuse to speak out loud phrases such as "I am sick" even when they are actually sick. They believe you must speak only what you want to exist. You don't claim that which is negative. I believe the mind, tongue, and body have an undeniable relationship. When we speak, we begin to believe or talk ourselves into it and once we believe it, we act on it and make it happen. If I say that I feel strong and healthy, what might happen is that I first feel motivated to exercise. Once I work out, I feel energized to cook a healthy meal. Eventually, I become healthy. I talked myself into action that transformed my health. But it started with me saying that I felt strong and healthy even when I was unhealthy and overweight. I spoke my dreams. In The Gospel of Hip Hop, KRS One writes:

> Know this. Words are truth's physical image, and we are made into the image of the words that we think and intend . . . We are that word, and the abilities we give that word are the abilities we give to ourselves and to our children forever. [14]

Hip-hop artists always speak the future as if it's happening now. They share their goals as current realities. That's powerful. But is bragging necessary? No doubt you can be a positive thinker without being a braggart. I am a confident person, but I am not cocky. In fact, I place an extreme amount of value on humility. You can talk to me for hours and leave not knowing what I do for a living or how many degrees I have earned. I don't brag about who I know, what I own, or what I've done (except on social media, which I use as a platform for professional promotion). That is what makes my appreciation for hip-hop braggadocio so interesting. I don't just appreciate it. I *love* it. Many years ago, I consciously asked myself: What exactly do you love about hip-hop? I wasn't a serious hip-hop head like some of my friends who were deep in the underground, or who knew EVERY lyric ever written by every artist, or who had collections of records and CDs that they protected like antiques. I liked hip-hop but I was also a huge Whitney Houston fan. So there's that. In that contemplative time that I spent in communion with some of my favorite hip-hop music, I realized that what I loved most about hip-hop was braggadocio. But I call it an ethic of excellence. I love hearing artists speak their worth, give voice to their goals, and acknowledge their talent.

The reality is, I truly believe and know that I am as dope as most hip-hop artists described themselves. Hot, fresh, def, dope, ill, sick; I silently claim all of it. Tony Keith Jr., one of the elite educators interviewed for this project, often calls me the GOAT (greatest of all time) of educational programming. I'll take that, too. I think these things on a daily basis. These beliefs walk with me into meetings and light my fire as I work. I contribute because I know that I have something to contribute. I speak because I know that what I have to say is important. I excel in my work because I'm not just trying to accomplish the task and cross it off, I'm trying to slay it. I'm always going for Number One. It's a professional lifestyle. When I slay something professionally (a presentation, speech, project) my husband calls me Michael Jordan '98. This means that you come in, show out, and finish it in a way that reminds everybody exactly who you are (in case they forgot). In the song "Ni**as in Paris," Jay-Z threatens to go "Michael," then tells the audience to take their pick among the great men that carried the name: "Jackson, Tyson, Jordan, Game 6."[15] It is the same idea said differently. What do all those Michaels have in common? Greatness. And game 6 of the 1998 NBA Finals solidified for everyone, at that time, that Michael Jordan was truly the GOAT.

Just as hip-hop's brash form of confidence inspires (and even hypes) me to claim my own excellence, it can also inspire a generation of new professionals who have been taught to celebrate everyone other than themselves. On the other end, it can also inspire a healthy dose of self-mattering to populations of students who have been made to believe that the best thing they can do to succeed is change all of who they culturally are. In my article, "A Beautiful Mind: Black Male Intellectual Identity and Hip-hop Culture," I share the following insight:

> Identity in hip-hop culture has been and in small pockets continues to be about absolute excellence, a strong sense of self-efficacy, and a pursuit to be the best . . . In their music, artists from KRS-One to the Roots to Jay-Z have always talked about their greatness, their skill, and their aim to be the best. It is questionable whether this ethic of excellence has been clearly seen through the smog of stereotypes obstructing our view.[16]

When I use the term "ethic of excellence," I mean that artists often brag about all of who they are, not just their appearance or performance. They aren't solely talking about jewelry or cars or clothes. They are saying much bigger things like: "I am good at what I do," "I am paid well because I'm the best," "I am creative," "I am talented," and "I am the greatest." Hip-hop has organically shown us for decades what "Black mattering" looks like. During a time when young adults are screaming for the world to care about Black lives, we need this type of audacity—to have the nerve to love ourselves and talk about it. Braggadocio goes beyond simply engaging the act of mattering. It is about demonstrating what it is to adore, admire, and love Black minds, bodies, talents, skills, and voices—to brag on it all. I know from personal experience having a father who always bragged on his girls that bragging is an act of love. And sometimes you just have to love yourself. You can't wait for other people to give you shine. That's beautiful and necessary for both students and educators. Instructors, administrators, and parents all need love and appreciation poured into them so that we can confidently and even brilliantly live our purpose and claim our space as transformational leaders.

## WATCH THE THRONE

To command attention and claim space, you must first own your greatness. How does it feel to walk into any space (a job, a school, a committee) and know that because of your talent and brilliance you will ultimately "own" this space, or in other words, you will transform it, lead it, mold it, and shape it by the time you leave? It's your castle—your throne to claim. Jay-Z and Kanye West named their 2011 collaborative studio album *Watch the Throne*. The word *watch* is worth stressing here. To watch something is to protect it, keep your eye on it, not lose it. In both hip-hop and in life, someone is always vying for the throne. They are coming for it from all directions. The popular HBO television series *Game of Thrones* depicted this truth perfectly by chronicling several ruling families from various corners of the world who eventually meet to battle for the Iron Throne and control of the Seven Kingdoms of Westeros.[17] Throughout this long-running series and the book that inspired it, these families are always working, plotting, training, and scheming for the throne, to claim the leadership, the land, the space. But royal families are not the only ones who claim space. Jay-Z explains the motivation behind the "Watch the Throne" title as it relates to the music industry:

> Watch the throne, you protect it. You just watch how popular music shift, and just how hip-hop basically replaced rock and roll as the youth music. The same

thing can happen to hip-hop. It can be replaced by other forms of music. So it's making sure that we put the effort into making the best product.[18]

In this case, he is referring to watching the throne to ensure that it doesn't die. You are watching for signs of aging, paying attention to areas that need some sprucing up. It's about keeping it fresh and relevant. Even a mansion will crumble if you don't take care of it. In the field of education, we can take a lot from this perspective. There are many educational practices, lesson plans, programs, and traditions that need some sprucing up. The culture of comfortability in education, where we create one great idea and never innovate beyond it, must stop. Even if a program does have staying power, it must always evolve, grow, develop, and transform in meaningful ways to keep up with the current culture of students. To watch the throne is to keep a self-critical eye on your own practice. How are you doing? What are you doing? How are you evolving?

Watching the throne is also about securing your place. If you have enjoyed success and some professional acclaim (at your school, on your campus, in your field), what are you doing to protect that status? There are always others out working hard to become the next great name. And that's a good thing. This is education. There is room for all of us to be great, and students are overwhelmingly the winners when everyone who serves them (teachers, administrators, counselors, advisors) is working hard for the "Grammy," the Number One spot, the title, the throne. If you want to keep your top spot, you've got to stay fresh, be excellent, and be confident. You must also be seen. You have got to claim space and show off so that folx see you, tell your story and acknowledge your greatness. Because being seen isn't just about you. If the kids who created hip-hop kept it in basement rec rooms and didn't have the guts to show off in the middle of a public park, or take the journey to Manhattan nightclubs, or say yes to being on camera when television shows started coming around, the world would not have known about hip-hop. Showing off tells the story and helps to set new standards of practice. When we shine a spotlight on culturally dynamic educators and educational practices, when students become your ambassadors and champion your work, when colleagues become your advocates and refer to your work, when media outlets become your conduit and publish your work, that all contributes to changing the field of education. In my recent book, *Reshaping Graduate Education Through Experiential Learning and Innovation* (2020), I compare the mechanized, mass-produced feel of education to the restaurant industry:

Could McDonalds ever receive a Michelin star? . . . There is comfort in generally knowing what you are going to get—no mystery, no surprises, or disappointments. But some might argue that it is actually the unfamiliarity that makes eating at a highly rated, unfamiliar restaurant so incredibly exciting . . . The critical question isn't how to dismantle the McDonalds franchise. The speed, efficiency, affordability, and comfort of standard mass production isn't going away in any industry. Instead, my question is what are the creative chefs doing over at the non-chain restaurants? Everyone knows about McDonalds, but how do we help spread the word about the fantastic local spots or the incredible five-star establishments? What does a fresh, inspiring, gourmet meal look like as a metaphor for teaching and learning in graduate school? Like McDonalds, we are already familiar with the usual structure of graduate learning, the goal of this book is to create a platform to discuss new ideas. Inspiring teaching practices have always been a part of higher education, just as there have always been local restaurants whose burgers blow the franchises out of the water. Folks are able to find those spots when they travel to a town simply because they hear about them. Restaurateurs are inspired to try their hand at also building their dream restaurant because they saw it work for others. We must talk about it— tell stories, share insight, and build both the desire and the capacity to approach the graduate classroom differently.[19]

Hip-hop spread because the youth involved in its community had the confidence to show up and show out. Posture is not just a philosophical idea, it is real. It is about positioning yourself. It's about placing yourself in the spotlight. It's about taking the microphone and not passing on the opportunity to get on stage. If you get nothing else from this chapter, walk away inspired to simply say yes. Claim your space. Do it, talk about it, share it, promote it, and market it. The "it" is your talent, your magic, your approach. You. Your brilliance. Be proud of the skills you bring and the difference that you make. Don't take it for granted. Often what we are able to accomplish in our work is pretty incredible. Some days we have small wins and other days it's a major victory. We accomplish what seemed impossible. Some educators also push boundaries and defy the limits given to them. When you have a boundary-pushing moment, celebrate it. And remember, sometimes we've got to show off and show out just because it's fun to be at the top of your game. It's okay to enjoy it a bit. Bling out—get your accolades, smell your flowers, and embrace your swag. Life is short and so is our time to shine.

## CHAPTER 5

# Cultural Roots
## Inherited Values, Beliefs, and Traditions

While hip-hop as a specific art form was birthed in 1973, its roots go deeper than the 1970s. As a musical genre, hip-hop is an eclectic blend of multiple musical sensibilities and styles including jazz, blues, reggae, dancehall, and disco. It also pulls from other art forms like poetry, storytelling, and even the gospel tradition of the pastor mixing and flowing between talking and singing. But all of it is fundamentally African.

Why go back to the roots? I can best explain the importance of cultural heritage by extracting inspiration and wisdom from my own family experience. As a young woman, my mother was an avid gardener. She taught us that regardless of how fruitful any planted thing becomes, it is important to conduct routine checks and inspections both above and below ground. Examining the roots help you to understand the condition of a plant long before changes start to occur to its leaves. We have a plant right now in our home that looks beautiful. But as I look inside the pot at the soil, I can see that it has been overwatered and is rotting. It won't be long before the leaves begin to die. Likewise, inspecting the roots of a fruitful tree helps you to understand much about why it is producing such incredible bounty. As the saying goes, the deeper the roots, the greater the fruits. To paint a portrait of the hip-hop mindset, we must begin with the African cultural legacies that provide the roots of all African Diasporic cultural production. A "diaspora" refers to the dispersion of a cultural people outside their land of origin. The 300-year European slave trade played a major role in establishing the modern African Diaspora, comprised of people of African descent who are spread mostly throughout the Caribbean, Latin America, North America, and Europe.

Ethnic erasure was fundamentally necessary for the success of slavery and oppression. Because of this erasure, it has been difficult to see the roots of hip-hop further back than at most a few decades before 1973. Afrika Bambaataa's trip to Africa and his renaming of both himself and his organization signify early efforts in hip-hop to connect it to a longer cultural history and experience. By simply listening to hip-hop music and observing hip-hop dance, it is easy to see how the drumbeats and body movements are forms of cultural heritage and tradition being carried forward and reimagined. But my concern here is more than music. I am examining the cultural aesthetic of hip-hop—the ethics, attitudes, beliefs, and aura of the culture that make it a valuable, beautiful cultural asset. Within the hip-hop mindset are clear linkages to the African heritage.

Several major dimensions of Black culture have been cited in the literature as important forms of cultural legacy. These dimensions of culture are demonstrated and carried forth across various African Diasporic communities. Known as "Africanisms," these shared cultural ways of being and acting can often be clearly observed and recognized, yet still remain as unconscious practices that are taken for granted as everyday life.[1] The innovation, ingenuity, entrepreneurship, and critical thought that young people have demonstrated through their development of and participation in hip-hop is part of a rich cultural legacy that the world has long been trying to govern, steal, own, and appropriate (colonize, enslave, oppress, and manufacture).

> While believing deeply in the humanity of everyone, we are haunted by decades of educational research and instructional practices which demonstrate that the humanity and needs of Black children in the Diaspora have been pervasively and persistently ignored . . . Using Black students' cultural strengths as integral parts of instruction and socialization is important for beginning the healing process which is needed because we have been (and are being) dispossessed from our past, connections to our culture, original homelands, languages, and each other.[2]

Among the characteristic legacies and dimensions of African culture, as discussed by Boykin, Hale, King, and Boutte among others, 11 are prominent: *spirituality, harmony, movement, verve, affect, communalism/ collectivity, expressive individualism, oral tradition, social time perspective, perseverance,* and *improvisation*.[3] All of these cultural dimensions are demonstrated in some form within hip-hop culture. However, eight of these Africanisms seem to me to be particularly fundamental to the roots of hip-hop.

## EIGHT AFRICANISMS FUNDAMENTAL TO HIP-HOP CULTURE

*Verve—a propensity for relatively high levels of stimulation and for action that is energetic and lively.* Yes, it's generally believed that Africans are hyped people—energetic, loud, lively. So is hip-hop. Hip-hop values hype so much that a paid position was created on stage called a *hype man* whose role is to excite the crowd during a hip-hop performance. The persona of hip-hop is never mild or modest, shy, or quiet. In hip-hop music, spirit, and culture, the goal is to (as Dr. Dre asserts) "Keep Their Heads Ringin'." Booming bass, aggressive emcees, audacious acts, over-the-top antics, showiness, boastfulness—hip-hop is loud, energetic and in your face. It is always on 10 in some way or another. An artist like Busta Rhymes is stylistically hyped—possessing a loud and fast flow with animated body movements. Nas might come off as cool and chill in his flow and movement, but his presentation puts him over the top: He might be sitting on a throne, adorned in gold, diamonds, and a floor-length fur coat. It is all loud. But the verve in hip-hop is not just about ego; it is about energy. We are attracted to hip-hop because it hypes us, it moves us, it has an infectious energy. How do you feel when you are listening to your favorite hip-hop song? Probably either on top of the world or ready to take on the world. But undoubtedly you feel energized, uninhibited, and alive. This legacy of *verve* aligns with the hip-hop practice of commanding attention. It is a function of approach.

*Affect—an emphasis on emotions and feelings, together with a specific sensitivity to emotional cues and a tendency to be emotionally expressive.* One of the most important things hip-hop gives its community is the permission to feel and to express those feelings. From anger to rage, from love to lust, from top dog confidence to underdog hunger, being centered in a hip-hop mindset is to be centered in authenticity and truth and to express that truth regardless of the consequences. Hip-hop is one of the few spaces in society where marginalized youth are not only rewarded for speaking truth to power, but their exceptionality is marked by how bold and expressive they are. The more vivid the emotion the better. Reaching back, N.W.A's 1988 classic *Fuck tha Police* (Priority/Ruthless Records) is a perfect example of hip-hop being a space where the rage and frustration felt in the community culminate in a rap song that says exactly what people who don't have a voice or platform want to express. While hip-hop music and culture make a space of strong expression of emotions, I choose here to focus on rage because rage is not only often discouraged but typically outright shut down in American society. Where is there a space where citizens are allowed to express rage? Not in school. Not in a courtroom. Not in church. Not even at a political rally, city council meeting, or school board meeting. When rage starts in any of those spaces, order is quickly restored. So you have youth who are experiencing severe forms of racism, disenfranchisement, and generational oppression, while living in a world where there is no space for them to let out or let go of that emotion. We don't offer intentional spaces for youth to deal with their legitimate anger—to express it, release it, and wrestle with it. Something as simple as blasting a song and rapping along with it at the top of your lungs (with the window rolled down) becomes all you have. It is critically important.

In *Fuck tha Police,* N.W.A opens the song by commencing a mock court with Dr. Dre serving as judge in the case of *N.W.A v. Tha Police Police.* The other members of the group are the prosecuting attorneys and the first to take the stand is Ice Cube. This creative take is so brilliant, because indeed what the group is doing in this song is testifying. They are giving very emotional testimony of their experiences with the police growing up in Los Angeles. In 1988, before we had mobile phone videos to document ill treatment by the police, it was hip-hop's testimony and video reenactments that told the truth about what was happening on the streets of major cities. In Dr. Dre's "court" there were no rules to language or limits to expression. So when Ice Cube is asked if he swears to tell the truth he responds, "You goddamn right!" For the non-rappers who identify with hip-hop, this means also accepting the permission to be truthtellers. This is about allowing yourself to acknowledge and speak about your personal experiences (show up as a person, not a title). But most importantly, educators must allow themselves to feel whether it be frustration, disappointment, happiness, joy, or anger. As folx often say now, "all the feels." Within the mindset framework, authenticity aligns with this Africanism.

*Communalism/collectivity—a commitment to social connectedness, which includes an awareness that social bonds and responsibilities transcend individual privilege.* Of course, there have always been groups in hip-hop from the Sugar Hill Gang to Grandmaster Flash and the Furious Five to Salt-N-Pepa to A Tribe Called Quest to G-Unit to Migos. The squad remains a serious thing. There are also hip-hop dance crews and graffiti crews. I see these squads as communities of practice. These are the intimate group of friends who share your passion, who give you private critiques, and who encourage you when you bomb at the big show. We all need this. Many fields require endless hours of solo work. Being a writer is one of them. At the end of the day, it's a solo effort sitting at the computer typing up this book. But, along the way, it helps to have friendly, caring, encouraging ears with whom you can share your work and bounce off ideas.

We need kinfolk that we can count on. As I deeply analyzed the kinship that I observed within the hip-hop documentaries, live dance competitions, and cyphers, what struck me the most was the mutual respect and love displayed within crews. Members valued one another. I will say that this rings true with my most trusted comrades in the struggle; we genuinely value each other's brilliance. We create spaces where our unique ways of thinking, dreaming, and creating are deeply valued for their similarities and differences. For this discussion, I want to go back to that group of boys that I talked about in Chapter 1. They had formed a cypher in the middle of the grocery store parking lot, and I walked over to listen. I'm not sure why they were in the parking lot that day. It could have been a teacher workday and school was out. Or they might have skipped or been kicked out of school. What I do know is that in that parking lot each one of them demonstrated the capacity to write, memorize, speak, and be ambitious. Those boys organically created a *community of practice.*

Etienne and Bevery Wenger-Trayner define communities of practice as "groups of people who share a concern or a passion for something they do and learn how to do it better as they interact regularly."[4] Undoubtedly, gatherings like the one I observed happen often in hip-hop and are much broader and deeper than what a culturally disrespectful eye might observe as a bunch of boys fooling around with rap. For a community of practice to form, there must first be a shared domain of interest. However, such a group isn't simply a bunch of friends who like the same things. Members are all committed to action in an area (though they may have different levels of commitment and competence). Members of a community of practice are practitioners who want to improve their practice. So, they gather willingly, look forward to group encounters, appreciate them when they are over, and practice until the next time. As Wenger-Trayner and Wenger-Trayner explain, "They value their collective competence and learn from each other, even though few people outside the group may value or even recognize their expertise."[5] The community of practice understands your ability even if others don't even recognize what you are doing as a viable craft. Someone with a gaze outside the domain of hip-hop culture might not have observed and interpreted the boys as a group of thinkers, writers, and public speakers. Depending on the perspective, a group of young Black boys gathered in a parking lot rapping during school hours might be the perfect example of academic apathy.

What drew me over to listen to the boys is the same thing that pulled them to gather in the parking lot in the first place—an appreciation of and a love for hip-hop. I observed what they were doing as acts of brilliance because I belong to the network, even though this was my first interaction with their particular community. Where society in general socialized me to look at these boys and see at worst deviant and at best trivial behavior, hip-hop has taught me to see talent, dedication, and intellectual potential. So while a group of middle schoolers might normally shut down, pack up, and move on when an adult approached them, these boys kept rocking on because I entered the space smiling, also bobbing my head, listening deeply, and genuinely reacting to their work through applause, laughter, and many, many "Ohhhs!" and "Auuughs!" That's what happens when you understand, value, and are connected to students' cultures.

*Expressive individualism—the cultivation of a distinctive personality and proclivity for spontaneous and genuine personal expression.* While community is critical within hip-hop, so is a sense of personal identity. Drake and Lil Wayne may be a part of the same crew, but they are totally different.

What they share is a passion and dedication to make a lasting mark in hip-hop. Hip-hop crews demonstrate in action (without training or formal education to guide them) the idea that diversity matters. Every person in the crew brings something different to the table—they complete the puzzle through their unique flavor. To continue with the Young Money Entertainment example, Drake and Nicki Minaj stand strong on their own. When you pull them together as part of a crew, that crew becomes the equivalent of a championship sports team. In my own work, as I think about my crew of colleagues, we each bring a different strength or talent to the table. We are committed to similar outcomes and goals, but we think and contribute differently, some through the arts, some through traditional scholarship, and some through community programming. We each shine in our own dimension, and we also join forces and build together. We need a lot more of this in the field of education. The ability to cultivate one's distinct professional personality, or in other words to just "be you," is vital. Too often, teachers are being molded and trained to be the same rather than distinctly different. A hip-hop crew wants that difference to shine, rather than be shut down. As an educator, start the process of becoming more of yourself by first thinking deeply about who you are professionally. What is your contribution? What is your talent? What magic do you bring to your work? This Africanism aligns with the hip-hop value for originality and uniqueness.

*Oral tradition—strengths in oral/aural modes of communication, in which both speaking and listening are treated as performances, and cultivation of oral virtuosity—the ability to use alliterative, metaphorically colorful, graphic forms of spoken language. This does not mean that strengths do not exist in written and other literacy traditions as well.* The African cultural legacy of oral tradition and its ties to hip-hop is a no-brainer. It aligns with hip-hop practices related to creativity, ingenuity, confidence, and claiming space. The emcee in hip-hop is not the introducer or host of the show, but the rhymer, the poet and one of the central figures within hip-hop music. The oral tradition in hip-hop concerns one's flow, style, and creative content using alliteration, metaphor, and double entendre. The microphone is one of the quintessential tools of hip-hop, and it is a visual symbol that indicates one's voice matters. Passing the mic or grabbing the mic is an important act of creating or taking space to allow new voices to speak. Dropping the mic is a swag-filled act of confidence that indicates there is nothing left to be said: I said it all. Voice—finding your voice, speaking your truth, saying it slick and creative, commanding attention, and being a dynamic speaker—is key to hip-hop culture.

How does this connect to fields like education? There are many fields that require its professionals to perform on a daily basis; teaching is one of them. Educators at any level must possess the ability to hold the attention of an audience. Those who have the ability to move the crowd (through their speaking or actions) often excel. Those who take the performativity of teaching as seriously as, let's say, Beyoncé takes performing (innovative choreography, constant practice, dress rehearsals, mic checks) capture students' attention because they pay so much attention to their craft. Understanding the power of your voice and the way that you show up as an orator in your classrooms is critical.

*Social time perspective—an orientation in which time is treated as passing through a social space rather than a material one, and in which time can be recurring, personal, and phenomenological.* Whether calling it "African Time" or "CP [colored people's] Time," the African Diasporic community is notorious for viewing time as a flexible concept. Hip-hop is no different. Lauryn Hill took it too far with her now infamous 4-hour-late concerts. But waiting for everything to be right, rather than pushing for things to be on time, is very much a concept within hip-hop culture. In her article, "Global breakdancing and the intercultural body," Halifu Osumare shares her experiences observing hip-hop culture in the club scene in Honolulu:

> When I arrived at nine o'clock, the deejay was spinning "trip hop" style disks in the "chill room" upstairs until the formal dance show was supposed to start at ten o'clock downstairs.' Critical mass is important: the event did not begin until midnight; size of crowd and group energy are the determining factors for starting time in hip hop culture.[6]

*Critical mass is important.* Regardless of what is advertised on the poster, a party doesn't start until the place is packed, or it will look like a failure. In this case, the promoters had created a *chill room*, a space for folx who showed up on time to go chill and listen to music. As the crowd thickens, they are organically pushed out of the chill room into the main party area where the show begins. In many ways, this is about cultivating a culture of care and mattering. Ensuring that the community is present is important. Within the education arena, this might mean more than checking to ensure that all bodies are in the classroom. A student being physically present and a student being mentally present are two different things. This is about not taking the stage until you have an audience. Ensuring there is transitional time to get into the mood of learning is necessary. This gives the students time to address issues or release emotions that may have occurred that morning, to grab a snack if their bellies are still empty, to greet and say "Whatsup" to friends and comrades. There is much to do within the time constraints of any school setting, whether it is a high school or college classroom. But no learning will occur (whether you are talking or not) until the crowd is ready and present. Each educator thinking through creative ways to account for this reality in their own classrooms is important. This pulls us back to the hip-hop mindset of honor and kinship—respecting the community and focusing on people rather than rules.

*Movement—an emphasis on the interweaving of movement, rhythm, percussiveness, music, and dance, all of which are taken as central to psychological health.* The first time that I critically understood dance to be a form of racial and economic therapy was at a museum exhibit about juke joints at the University of South Carolina. The exhibit never explicitly made this point, but the curator did an excellent job of transforming the space into an embodiment of Black people's exhaustion and frustration with oppression. You could feel it. The mannequins dressed in nightclub attire personified both a desire to be beautiful and the heavy weight of racial and economic exhaustion. The built environment of the juke joint forced you to confront the poverty of the neighborhood. These weren't fancy places. The real photographs of juke joints across the South were placed in frames on the walls to represent decorations. But they were documentation that what was being recreated in the exhibit really existed. This was not an exaggeration or product of the artists' imaginations. As I walked through the space, it became vividly clear how dancing, partying, and moving was an act of release. This is what made the juke joint an important space of social therapy on Friday and Saturday nights. In the interviews conducted for this book, I ask each person if they can dance. Several people mention dance as a form of healing that can only be achieved through moving and accessing the body.

Hip-hop culture has an explicit focus on movement through both the performance of breakdance and the everyday performativity of body language. The creation of breakdance positions movement as so essential that a *break* was established in the music in order to create a space to focus on dance—to show out on the dance floor. At a hip-hop party, space is created both in the music by the DJ and on the dance floor by the crowd. When dance cyphers form, it is almost a ritualistic activity with everyone who is present moving back to give respect and room to showcase the dancers. I use the term "air-walking" in the concluding chapter of this book, because the hip-hop dance performance is one that defies all rational thought. Whether by spinning on their heads or walking on air, hip-hop dancers have pushed us to new heights when it comes to the capacity of body movement.

Beyond dance, movement itself has meaning. The performativity of movement in everyday body language is essential to hip-hop. Osumare explains the concept of performativity:

> I define performativity as an often unconscious but meaningful series of bodily postures, gestures, and movements that implicitly signify and mark a sense of social identity or identities in everyday pedestrian activity . . . Performativity might be understood as the bodily methodology by which we project our sense of ourselves into the world.[7]

The way you walk, stand, and project through your body communicates strong messages. In the book *Sing a Rhythm, Dance a Blues,* Monique W. Morris shares an excerpt of a piece of writing where an educator discusses how students can see the way that teachers look at them.[8] She stresses that the issue isn't just that they are being watched; it is the *way* that teachers look at them. Without saying any words, the gaze, the eyes, the facial expressions speak volumes of the disgust that some educators have for some students. We communicate much with our bodies. And the students were basically saying, "We *see* you." A hip-hop mindset demands your awareness regarding how you are using your movements. It requires intentionality in what you are communicating through your movements. Are you communicating love, welcome, confidence, self-assuredness, and openness? Or are you communicating something totally different?

*Perseverance—ability to maintain a sense of agency and strength in the face of adversities.* So many hip-hop songs have this theme of persevering from difficult starts. The act of remembering as a source of affirmation and motivation is a cultural legacy present throughout the African Diaspora and hip-hop culture. The Notorious B.I.G. talked about it in the song "Juicy," reflecting on how he transformed his life from bad to good through hip-hop. Drake's reflection in his song "Started From the Bottom" became almost an anthem for the historically disenfranchised. When you started from the bottom, being on top feels extra good.

The list of motivational songs goes on: Childish Gambino's "I'm Alright," Rick Ross's "Hold Me Back," Meek Mill's "Dreams and Nightmares," Young Jeezy's "Put On," Kid Cudi's "Pursuit of Happiness," and Wale's "Ambition." There is a very constant theme of perseverance in rap lyrics. It makes sense that a community of people who are, in many ways, the quintessential symbol of disenfranchisement, oppression, and discrimination, would speak on how they survived this experience if given a microphone to talk to the world. Again, lyrics are a form of testimony to the tenacity of a community—to not just make it and stay alive, but thrive and come out winning.

Professionals working in different areas of hip-hop culture, particularly as nonprofit leaders or university scholars, have similar stories to tell. Academia and the nonprofit world are professional fields that are, in many cases, very exclusive. While many people are aware of higher education's history of exclusivity, the nonprofit world is often viewed as the open, democratic alternative. But ask any executive director; nonprofit work is filled with politics and social networks that decide how long your organization will live. Working in these fields often requires folx to play tough games in order to succeed. So perseverance in these realms looks like having the ability not just to keep your job, but to blaze trails, innovating and expanding these arenas to create a whole new field of study or a new nonprofit area focused exclusively on hip-hop. Folx like Martha Diaz, P. Thandi Hicks Harper, Toni Blackman, and Tricia Rose were so brilliant that they pioneered hip-hop career fields completely outside of the hip-hop industry.

All of this brings us to the critical issue of efficacy. Both self-efficacy and cultural efficacy allow members of the hip-hop community to audaciously believe that they can not only be a professor, but that they will be a professor *of hip-hop*. On the one hand is a demonstrated confidence or belief in one's ability to play academic ball in the big leagues; on the other is the demonstrated confidence or belief in one's culture as important and valuable enough to dedicate one's career to studying it. Forty years ago, there was not one college professor who believed that they could earn tenure by studying hip-hop. Today, we have academic superstars in hip-hop studies, and the largest educational research association in the country, the American Education Research Association, has a special interest group of academics dedicated to the research and study of hip-hop. Harvard University has developed a Hip-Hop Archive and Research Institute. These developments illustrate that our sense of cultural swag and our demonstration of our African cultural inheritance has allowed professionals outside the entertainment industry to claim their own space as champions of hip-hop.

Exploring the life experiences of these professionals offers younger professionals a meaningful opportunity to conceive how it's possible to build successful careers that are focused not just on creating hip-hop educational spaces, but on embracing hip-hop as an overall ethic of practice. The pressures to conform are strong in professional environments. It is powerful to read literature that illuminates who we are and that encourages us to keep becoming more of ourselves. 'Cause we are hella dope.

## CHAPTER 6

# Can I Kick It?

## The Hip-Hop Mindset in Professional Practice

How does all of this look in practice? What does it look like to show up hip-hop as a professional? In this chapter, I share snapshots of professionals who unapologetically embrace a hip-hop mindset. I came to understand and build a framework of the hip-hop mindset not only by a deep dive into the knowledge base (books, documentaries, journal articles, song lyrics), but also through a series of incredible conversations with professionals who are unmistakably bad and brilliant. I talked with academic scholars, nonprofit leaders, P–12 educators, college professors, writers, and community leaders. All of the conversations are structured the same, with the same open-ended questions. Rather than interrupting their talk with framing and analysis, I offer our conversations with minimal editing as an invitation for you to kick it with us.

"Kicking it" isn't just simply sitting around talking. It is about truth-telling, slick talking, native-tonguing. You kick it in spaces of comfort and welcome. You kick it in spaces where you are respected, where your talents are appreciated, and where your words matter. In soccer, when you "dribble" the ball it involves gentle strokes, but when you "kick it" you are going for the goal with strength, power, momentum. So when an emcee asks if they can "kick it," they aren't just asking if they can speak. Rather, they are asking if you are ready for the fire that they are about to start. It is in that spirit that I invited this group of elite professionals to "kick it"—to speak freely, fully, and boldly about the power and presence of hip-hop in their lives.

## TONI BLACKMAN

*CEO, Toni Blackman Presents*
*Visiting scholar, NYU*
*Artist, educator, cultural*
*    ambassador*
*Brooklyn, New York*

*This book is about understanding*
*the utility of hip-hop culture. So*
*talk to me about how you use hip-*
*hop in your life, not just teaching it or studying it as a subject. Do you em-*
*brace it in how you show up in the world?*
I was very active in the Zulu Nation when I was young. We would do service, but it wasn't called community service. We just did what needed to be done. We showed up for the community. If the elderly home needed help moving out crates, here comes Zulu Nation. If there was a block that needed cleaning, here comes Zulu Nation. If there was a youth event and they needed grownups to chaperone, here comes Zulu Nation. If you were really hip-hop, you served, you showed up. So, if anything, I saw myself as a humanitarian. I care about humans. That shaped me. The other way hip-hop influences my life is the idea of making something out of nothing. That is literally my life story. My whole career has been that concept: a pioneer in hip-hop education, a pioneer in hip-hop theater, a pioneer in hip-hop diplomacy. And in recent years, a pioneer in hip-hop spirituality. That's my design, to create. If it doesn't exist, and I want it, I create it. If it hasn't been built, I build it. And I'm not afraid to do so.

*As a professional who embraces hip-hop, what are the skills that you get*
*from hip-hop?*
In my upcoming book, *Wisdom of the Cypher*, I'm documenting the personal growth lessons and principles gleaned from my work facilitating cyphers. The freestyle cypher is about heightening your access to your creativity. It's about giving you greater access to new words and phrases and building your confidence. We can sometimes have a false sense of confidence as a performer. Just because you are comfortable presenting, speaking, or facilitating, doesn't mean that you are truly confident from the inside out. True confidence is when you are capable of mastering the moment regardless of what happens. So whether or not you're prepared, whether or not you rehearsed, whether or not the sound goes out, whether or not the person you dislike is in the front row, whether or not you just had a fight with your mate, whether or not one of your kids just pissed you off, you can still come and rock the crowd and make the most of the moment. That's one of the things that hip-hop gifts you. Because inevitably, at a hip-hop show,

something's going wrong. It's training. If you participate as an emcee who battles, a dancer who battles, or a DJ who battles, having the ability to rock on no matter what is essential. But that's also a critical skill for everyone, not just artists.

*What about attitudes?*
Hip-hop gives you a sense of drive and determination that comes from hip-hop not being embraced for so many years. It's embraced now in a big way. But it was a subculture for a very long time. And so hip-hop still possesses that element of, "I'm going to go get it. I'm going to make it happen." My first professional hip-hop workshops were with teachers. I facilitated workshops for the non-profit organization, Teaching for Change, in DC. In this role, I led a storytelling program with immigrant mothers, to get them to read to their children. I had translators because many of the mothers spoke very little English. But my mentor Deborah was fascinated that even though I couldn't speak their language, it didn't stop me from connecting with the mothers. There were three languages in that room, and I only spoke one. But I was determined to connect. That's hip-hop. It was because of the foundation of hip-hop, I had no fear. I was trained amongst some really, really dope emcees, masters of the craft, who taught me how to shift my flow, fluctuate my voice, how to tap into melody when I'm rapping, how to shift the rhythm. And in doing that, the person who does not understand every word, they understand music. They understand the musicality of your voice, they understand the rhythm of your flow, they understand the pacing of your breath. And guess what, you could move the crowd with just that. This culture is valuable and powerful. Working with those mothers and teaching DC school teachers about hip-hop grounded me in the power of culture, period. It positioned me to be confident, and to be clear about my love for the culture.

*What beliefs about yourself do you get from hip-hop?*
This one came from both hip-hop and from attending Howard University: I feel like I can do anything. I also believe in the power of energy. My belief in energy came from the hip-hop cypher. While living in DC, I did a lot of work with the 9:30 Club. I saw KRS-One probably a hundred times. When he did a show, I liked to go sit at the top and look down so that I could just watch KRS-One on stage. KRS-One commands the stage like nobody's business. He commands attention. He calls for energy. He starts backstage, then he walks in and says, "Okaaaay." He never has to say, "Come close." He just says "Okaaaaay," and the whole crowd just rushes to the stage. It's fascinating. Because if you compare that to other rap artists who are giving detailed instructions: "Everybody come to the front. Stand up, put your hands up," they're telling the audience to be inspired. The performer is telling the audience to respond *as if* they're inspired instead of just inspiring

the audience. I studied energy from that balcony, just watching KRS-One. And I remember feeling it. I believe that we can move, touch, and inspire people if we learn how to tap into our energy. A lot of us are afraid of our own energy. We are afraid of our own power. We're afraid of losing control. We're afraid of being seen. We're afraid of being vulnerable. We're afraid of being transparent. But that's where the power is. That's where the spirit is. That's where the healing is. And it's a beautiful thing. It's imperative that we each learn to harness it.

*What is professional success to you?*
I think I went through a severe burnout crash in 2016. I had several serious health ailments. I spent a whole month in the bed. I could barely walk five blocks. I felt like I was going to die. And I was laying there like, "What if this is it?" And I really started thinking about what does success look like and if that were my ending, had I been successful? I thought about it a lot. I realized the organization I worked for did not give a damn about my health. I had a trip booked to Senegal. I was going there to work a festival and then planned to stay a few weeks. But I pulled out of everything and just went to Senegal to eat fresh watermelon, papaya, and fish, and sit by the beach. During that quiet time, I realized I'm successful on paper. I'm successful on my resume. I'm successful in my bio. But I didn't feel successful in my gut. I was not tapping into my greatness. And although I had the applause and the prestigious fellowships, the reality was all of those things only represented about 25% of my potential. So now I'm focused on executing the things that will truly honor my destiny. That means me letting go of resentment, me letting go of disappointment. I had a whole lot of heartbreak with my hip-hop organizing. There was a lot of disappointment, betrayal, and pain based upon my being a woman. You carry those little hurts. You carry the wounds. There are certain standards to which women are held, that men are not. There are certain boys' clubs that women will never get into. There are these double standards. I'm finally at a stage where I'm letting it all go. Success will be liberation. Honoring my fire. Because too often as women, we are told that you can't be too strong, don't be too soft, don't be too loud, don't be too quiet, don't be too smart, don't be too this, don't be too that. So right now, my success is liberating myself from all of that.

*Take a moment to do some trash-talking. Tell me about your greatest accomplishments.*
Becoming the first U.S. hip-hop ambassador, I'm very proud of that. As a woman, knowing that it was my work that got me recognized. It was my sacrifice. It was my vision that got me recognized. So I'm very proud of the work that I did. It became the foundation for a comprehensive hip-hop diplomacy program with U.S. Department of State. I'm proud of Freestyle

Union, which ran in Washington, D.C., for 25 years. I'm proud of Rhyme Like a Girl, which has been running for 18 years. These projects that I created have benefited hundreds of artists. At least five women that came through Rhyme Like a Girl have become hip-hop ambassadors with the State Department and have toured internationally. I'm very proud of that work. I have artists that I've mentored who are brilliant and successful. I'm always proud when I can see that my ideas were effective, impacted and changed other people's lives in a meaningful way.

*What about challenges? Have there been any challenges in embracing a hip-hop mindset or just being authentic?*
As a young professional, I had to rewrite a future. I came from an era before entrepreneurship was trendy. I've always been creative, always been entre-preneurial. But I kept trying to fit the square peg into the round hole, forcing myself to choose a career. When I look back at how much time and energy I used trying to fit in with a standard idea of a career, it's crazy. It never fit. Never. Now, I crack up sometimes when I see myself in here with my back-drop screen and my lighting kit, the tripod, the recording equipment, and my speakers. And I'm like, "Yes, this is me." Why did I try for so many years to be this other? When you fight yourself, you will be challenged. When you deny yourself, when you reject yourself, you will be challenged. You can overwork and overachieve, and even get awards. But underneath it, you will still feel challenged because it's not your true self.

*What's one word that best describes hip-hop culture?*
Love

*What's your stage song?*
"Elevators" by Outkast or "Simon Says" by Pharoahe Monch. It depends on my mood.

*Last question. Can you dance?*
Yes. I don't understand people who say they don't even try to dance. Dance is medicinal. Dance is life. It's so important. Don't ever stop. Don't ever put the mic down. Just because you're not seeking a career in it, just because you have gray hairs, just because you have a grandkid, just because you get married, just because you turned 30 or 35 doesn't mean you have to stop rapping or dancing. You didn't start rapping to become Jay-Z, you started rapping because it felt good. We have to stop cutting the cord to the fun in our lives. Culture doesn't go away. It doesn't die. You don't throw it away like a pair of old shoes. So how are you going to say you can't dance but the 7-year-olds can? What's that? I think that is sick and twisted, and I think it is unfortunate. It's one of the reasons why there is so much unhealthiness, because we don't honor the spirit of celebration.

## MARTHA DIAZ

*Founder, Hip Hop Education Center &
    Hip Hop CU (CommUniversity)
Educator, curator, archivist, social
    entrepreneur
Los Angeles, California*

*This book is about understanding the utility of hip-hop culture. So talk to me about how you use hip-hop in your life, not just teaching it or studying it as a subject. Do you embrace it in how you show up in the world?*
I discovered hip-hop when I was about 10 years old in Paterson, New Jersey. I'm first generation Colombian American. We didn't have any family here in the United States. So when I discovered hip-hop, it became my surrogate family. I was filled with this community that helped me understand the world and my purpose in it. I was largely someone who felt like I didn't belong in this world. I was very shy and I came from a very strict household. I was a quiet person because of that and hip-hop gave me the freedom to express myself. It helped me to feel like I mattered, like my voice mattered. Hip-hop gave me the ability to speak up. Hip-hop also gave me the idea that I could do whatever I wanted. I could dance. And if I couldn't dance, I could DJ. And if I couldn't DJ, I could emcee. And if I couldn't emcee, I could become a hip-hop scholar, a hip-hop historian, a hip-hop archivist, a hip-hop media producer. Those are all of the roles that I have played within hip-hop. I was able to create a pathway that led to many opportunities. If I had not discovered hip-hop, I would be a boring, "just follow the herd" kind of girl.

*As a professional who embraces hip-hop, what are the skills that you get from hip-hop?*
Resourcefulness, that's for sure. Hip-hop taught me about community organizing and how to tap into my social capital. I have miraculously created institutions and produced major events with barely any money. What I've been able to do with my reputation and network is really impressive. People give so much to me because they know that I am committed to the community. They know the quality of my work. I learned that I'm really wealthy when it comes to social capital. I'm the plug. I'm always like, "Oh, you know who you should meet? You need to meet this person." Or "Do you know about this person? They are doing similar work. I don't see competition like everyone else sees competition. I see competition as being very healthy for the culture. We should be able to work with each other. The only real battle is how you are going to evolve into a better iteration of

yourself. I'm going to work with my competitor. I'm going to work with the people that challenge me the most because I want to be better. Hip-hop also gave me a futurist mindset of reimagining or dreaming new realities. In the words of Grandmaster Caz, "Hip Hop didn't invent anything, it reinvented everything." I'm constantly asking, "What would make this world a better place?" "How can I disrupt old systems and design new ones?"

*What about attitudes? Did you get any attitudes from hip-hop culture?*
My immigrant friends and I had a rebel type of attitude because the White establishment looked down on us. We were badasses. My friends gave themselves nicknames like Zorro. We weren't afraid of anything. The attitude was, "I don't care what you think, I rule the world!" I still have this attitude in my pocket. In academia, we often can't show up as our authentic self because others are easily threatened by that bravado. The response to our culture is, "You're too much right now. We have a set of rules that we abide by. This is a quiet space. It's proper." We can show up and be quiet if we need to be. But trust me, if it's on, it's on. We're not afraid to take it over the top because that is liberation. Hip-hop gives you permission to take a stand and to show up as your authentic self, even when those spaces are not meant for us. We will go in there and shine. When you look at the way Chris [Emdin] or Bettina Love show up in academia, it's bold. They're like, "No, this is how we do it. This is what we want." Jeff Duncan-Andrade at San Francisco State does it too. He's like, "No, students don't have to change; you have to change the way you teach." They are all able to articulate and challenge in a way that doesn't threaten anyone. That ability makes us so fierce as educators and professionals. We can be the Jay-Zs in the boardroom, or we can go to the hood and run a street cypher on the corner. Hip-hop allows you to just let loose, let go; to stop being rigid and be open to new ways of thinking and being. Dreaming yourself into a new existence with a fresh attitude—that's hip-hop.

*What beliefs about yourself do you get from hip-hop?*
As I grew and matured, I became more introspective. Although I was really happy in my role within the community and hip-hop culture, I still felt like I didn't deserve the opportunities or the shine. I had imposter syndrome and I would just give my power away. So I was always offering other people the opportunities that were initially offered to me. If I had an invitation to participate in something, I would pass it on to someone else. "You go. You represent for me." I would give everything away and allow others to stand in my spotlight. Until recently. I'm 51 years old and I finally started to accept my role. I began to love myself and take back my power. The new cultures in hip-hop really helped me to see myself. Right now, so many artists are being vulnerable in hip-hop and it has made me think about myself just a little

bit more. In the beginning, when I was hearing Public Enemy's "Fight the Power" and KRS-One's music, it was more about what was happening out in the world. But this new group of artists are much more vulnerable. They are expressing sadness. They are really making us think about our emotions in a different way. And I think that helped me understand myself a little bit more and gave me the courage to heal and change.

*What is professional success to you?*
I'm the first one to be born in the United States from my family in Colombia. I'm the first hip-hop activist, first artist, and first educator in my family. In the beginning of my career, my family didn't think I was successful. They were like, "What is she doing with this hip-hop music?" They thought I was rapping or in a gang, they didn't know. All they see is what is in the media. But I when I got the Nasir Jones fellowship at Harvard, they were like, "Martha is at Harvard! Oh, my God!" To them, that was major props and success. And for me, that was the least part of my trajectory of success. But the people that I know from hip-hop culture—their respect for my work is what I see as success. For example, I have known Steve Stoute for 30 years. I knew him when he was managing Kid 'n Play. Although he's hugely successful, a multimillionaire, he still sees the value in me. When I saw him recently, he said, "I'm so proud of you. I'm so happy that you were able to reinvent yourself to do everything that you do within hip-hop and education." I don't have the millions. But the fact that he respects me that much, that is success. I can ask people like Steve, or Beverly Bond, or Fab Five Freddy, "Can you come and do this for me?" and they'll do it, no money exchanged. Just because they know and trust what I do to lift our community. They just simply want to support me. That is success.

*Take a moment to do some trash-talking. Tell me about your greatest accomplishments.*
I've created movements. I started the first hip-hop film festival. I created it because I was frustrated as a filmmaker. I felt that these other film festivals didn't have the sensibility to truly care for the hip-hop filmmaker. They weren't even taking our films, our documentation, seriously. I wanted to create a space just for us. I was also teaching in schools and bringing hip-hop in the classroom. So when one of the filmmakers had a curriculum attached to his film, I thought, "Wow, that is so cool." In 2003, I decided to organize a Hip-Hop Education Summit. No one had ever done a Hip-Hop Education Summit. This was the beginning of the Hip-Hop Education movement. In 2007, I self-published a book, the first *Hip-Hop Education Guidebook*. I was really pushing a new field into existence. People were already building hip-hop education across the country. They had their bricks. They were laying the foundation. They just needed someone like me to create that

platform and connect them. I just started creating and I haven't stopped. I have come to know my worth and my value. I know that I'm a trailblazer. I'm the architect connecting the dots and building the framework. If you know someone, I probably introduced you to them. When people want to be innovative, they just look at what I'm doing. As a matter of fact, people call to get inspiration from me—some Martha magic.

*What about challenges? Have there been any challenges in embracing a hip-hop mindset or just being authentic?*
Latinos are often an afterthought in hip-hop. We aren't intentionally left out, but we are overlooked when it comes to our contributions in developing the culture. So I have often felt, "Do I belong here?" Even going into academia was a challenge. I'm a girl from the hood who wasn't supposed to make it out. I started a Hip-Hop Education Center at NYU because Dr. Pedro Noguera believed in me and was like, "You can do it, Martha, you can do it." I wasn't sure. I was still thinking, "Do I belong?" My strengths aren't public speaking or writing and that's really what the work is in academia. But I have an incredible mind for community organizing. I have a mind for problem solving and developing solutions through enterprising and innovation. I had to push against those outside beliefs that academia is only for one type of mind or one type of intelligence.

There is also a culture that fails to recognize women in our society. Whether it's hip-hop education, filmmaking, or archiving, men just glaze over me. They leave me out. This is not just a personal issue for me. Men don't cite women in general. To give an example, you have men in the entertainment industry saying that they came up with hip-hop education. I remember in 1992 when I first entered the entertainment industry working at Yo! MTV Raps, Wendy Day wanted to help artists become more knowledgeable about contracts. There was no one teaching how to negotiate, and she was sick of them getting exploited. I still have a letter of invitation from 1992 asking me to be a part of her rap coalition conference. I've been participating in hip-hop educative spaces since the beginning of the 1990s.

*What's one word that best describes hip-hop culture?*
Spirit. It is energy source straight from the creator.

*What's your stage song?*
"I'm Bossy" by Kelis.

*Last question. Can you dance?*
Can I dance? Yeah, I can dance. Of course, doesn't everyone? I guess not. I have to express myself in different ways. Sometimes I dance. Sometimes I am the DJ girl. And sometimes I am the activist with my beret on ready to change the world.

## TIMOTHY DAVID JONES

*Principal, Techniques 4 Learning, LLC*
*Writer, educator, pundit of hip-hop*
*    culture*
*Washington, D.C.*

*This book is about understanding the utility of hip-hop culture. So talk to me about how you use hip-hop in your life, not just teaching it or studying it as a subject. Do you embrace it in how you show up in the world?*
Every day. I show up hip-hop by holding on to the narrative that hip-hop is the ultimate form of synthesis. Hip-hop is that ability to take things and create something that otherwise wouldn't exist or to develop uses of things that are outside the scope of what the entity that created the item was even thinking. It's about seeing the improbable as possible. Because when you look at where we are now with hip-hop, it's like, yo, hold up—we're now getting paid to do backspins and uprocks? And you're getting paid to do the thing that used to be against the law? You went from spray painting on trains and having to run to now there are museum openings and community murals where folks are paying and commissioning you to do graffiti? Now you get to teach master classes and bring a backpack full of Krylon and not think it could land you in jail. That's beautiful. We've come a long way.

*As a professional who embraces hip-hop, what are the skills that you get from hip-hop?*
The ability to critically and creatively think. I think at times there's too much emphasis on those existing apart from one another. For me, the ability to critically and creatively think is trying to see the opportunity while other people are seeing obstacles. It's the ability to shorten that distance between what you're thinking and what you're saying—whether you're equating that to the ability to freestyle or whether you're equating that to being able to spit a rhyme that stays on a subject. Creating your own standard is important. The mindfulness of not looking for commercial approval and validation means that I'm not looking for the validation or approval from entities that I don't control.

*What about attitudes?*
Some may view it as over-confidence, some may view it as arrogance, but one of the attitudes I get from hip-hop is knowing that I'm fearfully and wonderfully made. Knowing that there is something that makes me uniquely me. So even if someone is doing the same thing that I'm doing, there's a

way that I do it that's uniquely mine. And I pull that from hip-hop. I apply that to how I may design a workshop. I apply that to how I even develop my business model. I use that to encourage myself at times when every day I don't necessarily wake up feeling like I'm on top of my game or that I should still even be in the game.

*What beliefs about yourself do you get from hip-hop?*
One piece of knowledge that I got from hip-hop is understanding that mastery is really rooted in figuring it out yourself, not being afraid of trial and error. At the end of the day, your biggest competition is really who you see in the mirror. The clearer your vision of who you are, then the better you can become. One thing that I learned from hip-hop that I never learned in school is the fact that you can gain knowledge and motivation from losing. In hip-hop, if you lose a battle or your record doesn't perform, you're able to look deeply at that loss and say, "Okay, this person did this and it was dope. How can I do something like that and make it mine?" It's sort of like, "How can I be inspired and influenced by another person without trying to copy them?" I came up where hip-hop wasn't about replication or assimilation, it was more so about observation and transformation. How can my connection to others who are winning make me better? And how can I create something and do it in a way where I don't feel diminished by your shine? Hip-hop teaches me a new definition of community.

*What is professional success to you?*
A couple of things. Being sought after for my insights is something that doesn't get old. It's very humbling, but it speaks to my success. This past week we just celebrated 10 years of having our weekly Hip-Hop Ed Twitter Chat. So, for me, that is success. It is the consistency to be able to curate practice, the consistency to be able to create conversations. Another part of my success has just been in my lyrical ability. I love to freestyle. Becoming known for being able to freestyle not just in the expected places—a cypher or on stage with a beat—but I consider this conversation a level of freestyle. When I am giving a lecture or doing a workshop, I believe that there is an element of freestyle involved. It's being able to confidently have this conversation. There is also a level of success in having the work you are doing affirmed by the fact that others are doing similar things. The fact that you are writing a whole book on the hip-hop mindset affirms the relevance of the work I've been doing. We get to connect with people who can build and grow our work. We can come together like scientists. Very rarely do scientists do something by themselves. But yet we have this narrative in education that we've got to hold everything in, our name has to be on it, we've got to produce it and master it. But the greatest breakthroughs that have changed and elevated how we live have all been the result of collaboration, folks who share a passion working hard to create, innovate or imagine.

*Take a moment to do some trash-talking. Tell me about your greatest accomplishments.*

In 1996 I was working with a group of teens at an after-school program. We decided we were going to produce a hip-hop CD. So I created this clique called Crushed ICE. ICE was an acronym for individualized creative expression. I'd been around hip-hop but I had never used my voice as an emcee. So I am teaching them how to rhyme and put different things together, but I was in the background because I was the adult. It was about the teens. We were donated studio time and production services to record one of our songs. One of my students forgot the paper that his second verse was written on, and so we're in the studio and we have this 16-bar gap. So I just said, "Yo, I'm going to go into the booth." I told the engineer let the song play and I'm just going to fill in this 16. I didn't have a verse. I wasn't supposed to be on the song. I literally freestyled 16. That moment is a moment I will never forget. That's when I felt like I became an emcee. One of my dear friends was the producer who donated the track and he's looking at me like, "Yo, son, I didn't know that you had that in you." Looking back, I now can say, "Wow, God. You had a plan." Because if he wouldn't have forgotten his paper, I would have never stepped up. And after that moment, there hasn't been an opportunity that if it's presented to me, I'll shy away from. I always fall back on that moment. I always step up. That was definitely a personal victory that influenced and set a course in life for me. Also, being a part of the first hip-hop conference to take place on a national level at a college and university. We founded "The Cultural Initiative" at Howard University from '91 to '96.

*What about challenges?*

One of the bigger challenges has been navigating this space without the academic credentials. That's being fully transparent. Honestly, I have internal battles, at times, with not being in the academy, or not having a credential, or letters behind my name. The thought will creep up, "How do you think that you can compete?" I often parallel it to that artist who went independent. A million people may not know your name, but the thousand people who do, not only do they know your name, they know your spirit. They know who you are and so they're rocking with you. There are some individuals who will never get the opportunity to be in the walls of the academy, and maybe my path is supposed to be a light for them. I can serve as an example of how you can independently connect, collaborate, and move both within and outside of higher. My niece just received her PhD from George Washington University. There was a part of me that honestly wanted to cry. I was proud of her. I really thought about how education is presented to the masses of children and youth. The fact that she was able to take her passion, turn her passion into knowledge, study her passion as knowledge, write a dissertation about her passion and then persuasively convince others that this knowledge is important and beneficial to society—being able to do that is a beautiful thing. Who wouldn't want to do that? If education were presented like that, I think folks would be more interested. It wasn't presented like this to me, and I went to college. There are a lot of undergrads who aren't being introduced to the idea of graduate school or a doctorate in a way that will make them say, "Yo, I want this because I want to wonder. I want to have the chance to just ideate. I want to be able to just think and then find a collective of other thinkers that I can build with." As a society and especially as Black folks, we get robbed of the ability to think. In our minds, if we are not physically doing, you're lazy.

Another challenge is getting people to see hip-hop beyond the way it's commercially presented, especially in dealing with K–12 schools. People will be quick to say, "Well, how are you going to talk about using the culture, but you've got this song with explicit lyrics and then in the song they're talking about how this person shot that person." Navigating that isn't easy. That's why this project is important. It helps people to understand that we aren't talking about only the music that's being made. We're talking about the mindset. It requires such a critical consciousness to deal with hip-hop. When we're talking about the stereotypes in hip-hop, the lyrical content in hip-hop, we can't judge it in a vacuum absent of the ecosystems that created it. Let's start explaining what created the environment that gives you trap music or hypersexuality. For those of us who work with young people, we need to see ourselves as mandatory reporters. If a young person came to tell you that they are in danger, but the way that they told you involved a whole lot of cursing, would you focus on the fact that they were cursing or would you focus on what it is that they're actually trying to tell you? Are you editing their language or are you focusing on the danger they are describing? If we listen to the messages that are in the music, if we listen to them as mandatory reporters, then there would be a level of action that we would take or that I hope we would take. Those lyrics should motivate us to move—not dance, but move and act in the lives of young people and on behalf of communities.

*What's one word that best describes hip-hop culture?*
Rhythm.

*What's your stage song?*
"You Don't Know" by Jay-Z. I love the energy when he performs it—when he's telling us to turn the music up higher and higher. Throughout the song he's talking in these hyperboles but because it's Jay, the hyperbole almost sounds believable. He's talking about selling water to a whale. For me, it's striving to make the hyperbole manifest as something real in my life, like I am trying to blow your mind or do the impossible.

*Last question. Can you dance?*
No. Not at all. But I do appreciate it and in my head, I'm getting it in!

## EMERY PETCHAUER

*Associate Professor and Coordinator
    of English Education Program,
    Michigan State University
Scholar, educator, DJ/turntablist,
    cultural organizer
East Lansing, MI*

*This book is about understanding
the utility of hip-hop culture. So talk to me about how you use hip-hop in
your life, not just teaching it or studying it as a subject: Do you embrace it
in how you show up in the world?*

Yes. My points of entry into hip-hop were two specific elements: breaking
and DJing. I listened to hip-hop music, heard it growing up among other
musical genres, but specifically a key point for me is when I started breaking in 1998. The beginning was 55th and Lake Shore Drive—the Point Park
District in Chicago, where community folk were engaging in creating hip-
hop arts. I started hanging out in B-boys' spaces and B-girls' spaces throughout the city. I met DJs and that led me to start carrying their records to
parties. If you know anything about deejaying, carrying records is actually
the first step to becoming a DJ. You don't even realize you're going on that
journey when they say, "Hey, come with me to this spot and carry these records." But that's the invitation into the culture, into the world. My claim to
hip-hop is rooted in literally the tens of thousands of hours that I've spent
pursuing the craft, knowledge of the craft, and performing in communal set-
tings, cyphers, events, clubs, etc. I think that's a particular claim that is also
rooted in my existence as a White person. The claim is civic. It's based upon
a participatory set of actions rather than a discernable African ancestry.

Hip-hop affects me professionally in two ways. I always try to bring my
students into community with artists who are not explicitly affiliated with the
class or institution. I always connect my students to community artists. Most
often my students are aspiring teachers. I craft assignments for them to engage
with the human assets and artistic assets that are already existing around
them, so that as educators they leverage those assets in ethical and reciprocal
ways. I try to create educational spaces where students can see themselves as
participants in the community rather than approaching community members
as a kind of transaction. So what does this have to do with hip-hop? I know
from my experiences in hip-hop that when resources and assets are better
connected, that changes the conditions and allows for really dope stuff to
happen that you couldn't have imagined. Beyond this, I think another way
hip-hop shows up in my professional life is the responsibility I feel to organize
and create space for young folks to have access to knowledge, technologies,
and creative practices in public spaces—community centers, libraries, schools.

The community organizing that I do through arts is not an outgrowth of academic work. It is an outgrowth of who I am as a person and the ways my personhood has been shaped generously by hip-hop communities.

*As a professional who embraces hip-hop, what are the skills that you get from hip-hop?*
Let me add first that some of what I'm about to name might not be unique to hip-hop. You might see these things through other types of cultural pursuits or other types of avenues. But for me, some of them are concentrated in hip-hop. The most explicit embrace of hip-hop for me is the idea of search and discovery. What I mean is searching for that undiscovered gem that everyone else has overlooked—having a sensibility that allows you to see, hear, feel, or find things others have overlooked. That's something I get from hip-hop. For me, that comes from being a hip-hop DJ and digging for records and samples. There's just a certain set of skills and sensibilities that are tied to physically searching through records and listening for certain sounds. That skill translates over into how I approach professional work or just my life in general.

Another skill that I've developed from my involvement in hip-hop is being a connector. I am able to connect people to different resources and assets. I think of myself as someone who is always searching for assets and strengths, and then organizing them in certain ways, so that communities can be stronger. I see that skill as a hip-hop sensibility because you're not looking at what you don't have and thinking about what you need to get, but instead, you're looking at what you do have and how you can organize it in certain ways to make it strong. I'm the person to bring us all together. And I would argue that is a quintessential DJ sensibility—to take these five records that probably don't have much to do with each other, but you can hear this element in record one that leads to this element in record two until you have created this broader constellation that makes all of these songs flow together. So that ability to connect and orchestrate connections across resources, I get that from hip-hop.

*What about attitudes?*
One specific attitude that I've gotten from hip-hop is hypercompetitiveness. This comes from that competitive battle aspect of hip-hop. It's a part of all hip-hop elements. There is also this attitude of generosity in hip-hop. People have been very generous with me in sharing knowledge and welcoming me into scenes when I've showed up as a new person. Generosity is something I've learned from hip-hop, and it probably pushes me to value that spirit of connecting people and putting them on.

*What beliefs about yourself do you get from hip-hop?*
Just by seeing what people have done with hip-hop, I've come to believe that there's so many incredible accomplishments that people can make when

they focus themselves. Even just in the physical part of it, people spin on their heads. Before I ever saw somebody spinning on their head, I would've never thought that was actually physically possible. So the belief that incredible accomplishments are possible has been demonstrated and illustrated through my involvement in hip-hop.

*What is professional success to you?*
Expanding opportunities for other people to get put on—grad students, artists, homies, friends, junior scholars. Professional success is sharing knowledge. And I don't just mean journal articles or books. You could share knowledge in a podcast, you can share knowledge in a newsletter, you share knowledge by teaching. I've really been focused on creating spaces for people to share knowledge with each other. Not just me sharing knowledge with others, but rather me creating space for these dope forms of community knowledge sharing. I'll give you a specific example. This last summer, I was supposed to run a virtual songwriting camp with some artist friends. I got a grant so I was able to pay them for the whole week. I was super excited. And then nobody signed up because we're in a pandemic. We were like, damn. So we flipped it. We just did a weeklong skill share among the five artists on the team. Monday, one person shared a skill for 20 minutes with reactions and feedback. Tuesday, the next person shared a skill, with feedback and reactions. We did that the whole week and recorded each of them. At the end of the week, we have this wealth of knowledge. All the instructors were emcees, producers, or DJs. Everyone's knowledge is that much greater because we did the skill share amongst each other, so we all learned and grew. And then we created this lasting video educational resource available for the community to access virtually. Creating those conditions for knowledge and skill sharing is professional success to me.

*Take a moment to do some trash-talking. Tell me about your greatest accomplishments.*
I consider it a great accomplishment when one of my students goes on to do something important. So many students have gone on to do amazing things. Kyesha Jennings was one of my undergrads at Lincoln and she's a grad student, critic, and curator now in North Carolina. I feel most successful when people like her are successful. When I see the amazing things that my former students are doing in their classrooms now as teachers, I feel accomplished.

As far as programs or initiatives that I have created, I consider the community hip-hop events I've thrown as great accomplishments because they've been spaces for people to connect, create culture, and love life. I'll give you an example. There's a hip-hop jam that I used to throw with DJ @Large called Lovers' Rock. It was every Valentine's weekend. It was a Bonnie and Clyde B-boy/B-girl battle (two-versus-two coed battle), a contest for the flyest dressed couple, a picture booth, and all of that. People would make custom outfits just for the event. People would even slow dance and kiss on the dancefloor. I'm not kidding. One year in Philly, I was outside the venue for a minute and I overhead a b-boy calling his girlfriend and saying something like, "Yeah, babe, you know, I'm at this battle they're playing all these love songs in between and everybody's dancing. So, I had to call and say I was thinking about you." This dude left the venue to call his sweet thing. Creating THAT kind of space is one of my greatest accomplishments.

*What's one word that best describes hip-hop culture?*
Embodiment.

*What's your stage song?*
"It's Just Begun" by The Jimmy Castor Bunch. I hit the stage when the horns come in.

*Last question. Can you dance?*
Absolutely.

## BETTINA L. LOVE

*William F. Russell Professor at Teachers College,*
*     Columbia University*
*New York, New York*
*Researcher, author, educator*

*This book is about understanding the utility of hip-hop culture. So talk to me about how you use hip-hop in your life, not just teaching it or studying it as a subject. Do you embrace it in how you show up in the world?*
I actually think about this often. I ask myself why I'm doing what I'm doing. Why am I act-ing the way I'm acting? Is it because of hip-hop culture? Is it because of the way I grew up? Is it both? But my thought pattern, my walk, my talk, everything about how I show up comes out of that hip-hop structure that I know. And I lean on it as a way to be in life. So the hustle, the drive, the persistence, the confidence, a lot of it comes out of hip-hop culture and how I've been indoctrinated to think.

*As a professional who embraces hip-hop, what are the skills that you get from hip-hop?*
Probably the most important skill that I get from hip-hop is to write in a very clear and concrete way—to say what I have to say. In hip-hop music, there are just lines that are so vividly clear—when Jay-Z says, if you lived the life I've lived and seen the things I've seen, you'd be in Paris wilding out too. I'm like, "Yes!" I live by that. When you've come through a lot, you have a right to get crazy in your joy. I want to write in that way, where people know exactly what I mean. They feel my words. I think that hip-hop gave me a way to communicate that's clear and concise, that's to the point and doesn't blur my message. Hip-hop made me a better writer. I'm always pushing myself asking, "How is this clear?" Now, I can't rap at all, but I do see rap in what I do. I think hip-hop is poetry. I think hip-hop is spoken word. I think hip-hop is written language to the fullest. So I think it gave me that skill of crafting language that's accessible to people.

*What about attitudes?*
I definitely have the hip-hop persona of confidence and self-assurance. I'm a little braggadocious. I am aware of my competence, and I think that comes from hip-hop culture. It's also important to say that I was a high school and college basketball player. Those two cultures of athletics and hip-hop coming together just builds a type of person who is deeply thinking about being the best. They create the type of person who is always exposed to criticism and

can take that criticism, apply it, and transform it into skill. So there is an attitude of persistence and perseverance that comes from sports and hip-hop. Some people who have an attitude like, "I don't care"—those aren't deeply competitive people. I think that hip-hop is a culture where even if you have all this confidence, this braggadocious attitude, you still want to impact your community. You still want to say something to your community. And you still care how that community responds. So that attitude transcends into being more than just arrogance, you want your community to ride with you and you want your community to validate you. You want your community to be like, "Yo, that's hot." So even with all that self-confidence, there's still this vulnerability of needing community acceptance. I think hip-hop always toes the line of "I'm good. Nope, don't need nobody. But y'all like that new song, right?" That still shows up in my world. I know my book is fire, but I'm still checking for the community response. It matters because it's for them.

*What is professional success to you?*
I'm a New Yorker. I grew up in upstate New York. I love New York. I really do. But when I wrote my first book, *Hip Hop's Li'l Sistas Speak*, it was centered in Atlanta and focused on Black girls in the South and how they consume hip-hop. I love Southern hip-hop, probably as much as I love New York hip-hop. So it mattered to me when people were like, "Yo, you wrote your ass off in that chapter on Southern hip-hop." As a writer, that is success. As a thinker, as a scholar—when you can write and people can see themselves, that's success. The fact that in my second book, *We Want to Do More than Survive*, people actually feel seen is incredible. I love it when people read it and are like, "I've been saying that in my head for years." That means I'm listening to people. That means I'm listening to the struggles and the triumphs and the beauty and the joy. People want to see their history. People want to hear their own stories. People want to feel connected. That's success, when everyday folk can pick up your work and say to themselves, "Yo, I was saying this to my friends."

As scholars and as educators, we want to provide new language. We want to provide new ideas. If what we are doing is writing as academics for other academics, I get that. That's cool. And I'm not mad at anybody who does that. But for me, success is when we are writing for everyday people and everyday people actually engage with the work. When people feel seen and heard and they are provided a new language or a new lens to apply to themselves, that's impact. When the community is provided new tools to fight for freedom, justice, and liberty or new ways to advocate for the engagement of joy and pleasure in their own lives, that's success for me.

*Take a moment to do some trash-talking. Tell me about your greatest accomplishments.*
I really enjoyed creating the Hip-Hop Civics Curriculum. That allowed me to go around the country talking to activists and working with teachers to

use my framework in the classroom. We've had over 150,000 hits on the website and people are using it in different ways. I was just having a conversation with some teachers from Boston yesterday and they were showing me all of the lessons they developed from it. The impact and reach of that work has been amazing. I'm also proud of the conversation that I had with bell hooks and that I followed my gut to push back a little bit on her thoughts about Jay-Z and Beyoncé. Those aren't easy moments, but they are the moments that define when you have grown into your greatness. I'm confident enough to have a challenging conversation with academic giants that I respect. One of the biggest accomplishments was definitely being named the Nasir Jones Hiphop Fellow at Harvard. It was a wonderful experience that exposed me to what is possible when a university puts money behind theory and the practice.

*What about challenges? Have there been any challenges in embracing a hip-hop mindset or just being authentic?*
Yeah. There are a lot of challenges. White folks are always a challenge when you do work on race. Academic journals are always a challenge. Reviewers are always a challenge. It's just always a challenge when you have to explain and explain and explain. In 2020 and moving on, I don't think that hip-hop scholarship has to explain itself as much as it did 10 or 15 years ago. Hip-hop is such a crazy culture that's always moving and evolving so you can become old-school real fast. I remember walking into a Hip-Hop Special Interest Group meeting at AERA [American Educational Research Association] and the person at the podium was like, "Our elder just walked in the room, y'all." Meanwhile, I'm looking around and I realize they are talking about me. So I'm excited that the field of hip-hop studies has a long enough history to have "elders" now. I'm excited to see where the field goes. I'm excited that it's legitimized now so they don't have to jump through the same hoops we did to have the work accepted. But I would say the biggest challenge early on was just the everyday public school and getting them to understand why this was important.

*What's one word that best describes hip-hop culture?*
Indomitable. You can try to knock us out, baby, but we have an indomitable spirit. You can come with all you've got to trip us up. We're still going to figure it out. Ingenuity to the core.

*What's your stage song?*
"Black Parade" by Beyoncé or "Bubbly" by Young Thug

*Last question. Can you dance?*
Yeah, at a party. I mean, choreography, no. But I will be the last one at the club, just having a good time. My body was made to feel loose.

## TONY KEITH JR.

*Executive Director, Educational*
*    Emcee, LLC*
*Scholar, author, artist*
*Washington, D.C.*

*This book is about understand-*
*ing the utility of hip-hop culture.*
*So talk to me about how you use*
*hip-hop in your life, not just teaching it or studying it as a subject. Do you*
*embrace it in how you show up in the world?*

I have served a lot of roles in education. I've been a teacher. I've been a
university administrator. I've been faculty. I've worked at a nonprofit. I've
worked in several different educational spaces. But in all those spaces hip-
hop culture becomes a part of the content (lesson plans, research, educational intervention) because I believe that it is a concept that will relate to
most people. Another way that I embrace hip-hop is more of embodiment.
I've always walked into my professional spaces with my jeans on and my
Chuck Taylors and my T-shirt. Even if it's an occasion where I need to level
it up, I'm always extra, extra cool. Now some of that is probably because
I'm Black, and Black people are just naturally cool. We can't help it. But
bringing some of that flavor, bringing that language, bringing that swag is
all about an embrace of hip-hop. I don't just value it, I embody it. Even in
my graduate school moments, when I consider how I brought spoken word
poetry into that world, I was embodying hip-hop because I was essentially
trying to physically do something different, be original, change the look and
feel of a dissertation. I think that type of swag is embedded in the bones and
the heartbeats of educators like us.

There's a very necessary liberatory aspect of hip-hop culture, especially
in this moment of the Black Lives Matter movement. When I think about
racism and injustice, we have to find ways that we can address these huge issues in a palatable form that can reach the masses. So my approach is using
hip-hop as a medium. Whether it's through the artistic, the performative,
the sonic, the linguistic, the kinesthetic—this is the moment we can do that.
In 2023, hip-hop will be 50 years old. Now is the time. You've got 17,000-
plus people that have written dissertations with hip-hop in it. You've got
people like you writing books on it. You've got hip-hop studies as major
and minor programs of study in college; you've got an endowed fellowship
at Harvard. You've got K-hop. If we—the people who have the capacity to
record this history in written form—don't take this time to do this work,
then the knowledge about hip-hop will be lost. I feel compelled. What I'm
trying to bring to the world is that historical piece. In a lot of the early hip-
hop music, the work was connected to their ancestral past. They knew they

came from African people. There was this level of understanding about their Blackness that I didn't necessarily understand until I got older. But now I know from firsthand experience the power of hip-hop to change the narrative of Black people. Because it did it for me. I know the power of hip-hop in education. I've experienced it as a student and a teacher.

*As a professional who embraces hip-hop, what are the skills that you get from hip-hop?*
The first thing that comes to my mind is storytelling. I know for sure that whether it's an academic presentation or defending my dissertation or teaching, there is an element of storytelling that is super important because what I say can impact the people who are listening in the audience. So much of that is hip-hop—that idea of being connected to your audience through story. Hip-hop is about asking yourself, How can I make this accessible, make it plain? Let's make sure that the knowledge matters to the community. The other skill is the ability to remix. When I think about my professional experience as an educator, whether you're working at a university cultural center or a nonprofit organization or a public school, you have limited resources. Particularly when you are serving mostly Black students, you typically know that you don't have the resources that you probably should have. So your approach becomes, "Let me see how I can sample this curriculum. Let me see how I can pull together this video. Let me see how I can remix every space we have—even if it's a hallway." You are in these spaces where you've got to make this work given what you have. Hip-hop comes from that evolution of creating out of scarcity. It is about identifying resources in the community to help you do the thing. So, honestly, I think another skill that I have gained from hip-hop is without a doubt leadership. Being able to inspire people towards a common goal. When I think about the nonprofits where I've worked, I didn't realize how much race intersected with how the organizations were run. But when you are working in organizations that are run by White people with a staff of mostly White women educators, but you're serving predominately Black and Brown kids, it's like, no, we've got to shift this to match who we're serving. But doing that, engaging that process of systemic change, takes guts. Addressing those type of issues isn't easy. But it's so necessary.

*What about attitudes?*
Being an unapologetic bad ass. My focus is to straight up disrupt the system—that very artsy revolutionary vibe. Some of that comes from the origin of hip-hop and the ways that racism and poverty intersect in that experience. People had to plug through hard times and because of that, they developed a layer of skin that's extra thick and tough. There is also this extra boost of confidence that you get from being resilient. You feel like you can take on anything. And the last attitude I get from hip-hop: When it

comes down to it, hip-hop is also a lot of fun. From the beginning, Afrika Bambaataa was always like, it's about "peace, love, unity, and having fun." That's truth. I can't even explain the fun that I have embodying hip-hop, wherever I go. I know that the moment I walk into a space with young people it's about to be good times. My attitude is automatically bright just anticipating the experience. When I go do work in prisons or jails, I know exactly how I can relate to the audience. There's no need for anxiety or stress. I know we are going to get busy with hip-hop and so I just relax and have fun. Schools and prisons can be really restrictive spaces. So being free, being yourself, being hip-hop is like screaming relief. A lot of people will say, "Tony has such a bubbly personality." And what I'm learning is there is truth to that. I've been bopping, laughing, and being loud since I was a kid growing up in hip-hop. I grew up with fun as my culture. I lead with fun. I bring fun with me into these spaces.

*What beliefs about yourself do you get from hip-hop?*
I have this belief that my work speaks for itself, all the time. For me, how I look when I walk into a space has nothing to do with the work that I create in that space. Whatever it is that I'm presenting, teaching, or offering up, the quality of my work is not based on my outfit. I come as I am. Like I said, I come dressed in a hip-hop vibe. I'm not trying to dress to please others. That's hip-hop. Being self-confident. Maybe that is also the sense of competence that's a part of hip-hop. I believe that my work is untouchable; I put in extra work to make sure my work is untouchable. I've been fortunate to be surrounded by so many Black people, especially Black women who seem to get that, who pushed me to understand that. They all taught me how to show up—to go into spaces on point and as myself. Because, originally, I was definitely like, "Let me put on my suit and my tie." But I think that there's something about needing to learn that you are enough and being exposed to educators who teach that to you. You learn to carry yourself in a way that says, "Look, I am bringing my best. If you want to talk about my slacks that's a conversation. Or we can focus on talking about this policy." I have been fortunate to travel to parts of Africa and I've seen African people walk into professional spaces dressed in their cultural clothes. And I was like, why can't I do that?

Another belief I get from hip-hop is the mindset that if you're going to do something, then *do* it—don't half do it. I did a presentation a couple months ago on social justice. But I focused on understanding how urgent the moment is—how much students need us to be excellent right now. COVID-19 is virtual learning. Just because we are home, now is not the time for you to get lazy. Your pedagogy can't be lazy. It's unacceptable. So I come into those spaces with a high expectation of not just myself, but my colleagues too. They aren't exempt. I'm like, no, you better bring it. Bring all you've got. Because when you walk into a space, whether it's to teach or to lead, your whole self needs to be right. You're bringing that energy in there. When I come with an energy knowing I'm about to get busy, you know what happens? I get busy.

*What is professional success to you?*
Professional success for me is when whatever work I'm involved in has created some sort of change. Whether it's a change in a person's mindset, whether it's a change in a policy, whether it's a change in the way we do a program, my work has to have some form of impact. It's not about money. Regardless of how much I'm earning, I care more about the impact. Now, of course, I haven't always been there. At one point, when I was younger, I used to believe that success was titles and salary—the traditional beliefs about professionalism. Now, I just want to change and uplift and help and love my community. And to be known for it. Because, I'm clear—I don't want to be someone who's done some amazing things. I want people to know that I contributed those things.

*Take a moment to do some trash-talking. Tell me about your greatest accomplishments.*
The major accomplishment right now would be my dissertation. Of course it was a big deal to be the first in my family to ever get a doctorate. But the way that I approached it—focusing on hip-hop—was also an accomplishment for me. Particularly because in academia hip-hop is not considered as high-level intellectual scholarship. And so for me to be able to thrive and defend the joy of using hip-hop feels good. When I wrote that thing, I was serious. I came in thinking I'm going to give it all I've got. And that's why there weren't many revisions. That's why I was able to propose and defend in six months. That was my biggest achievement because I did something that mattered to me. I knew it also mattered to the people that I cared about because I shared it with them. Before I submitted my dissertation to the committee, I sent it to poets and DC hip-hop artists asking them for their thoughts and feedback. The community got it first. The same thing happened when it came down to the defense of the dissertation, I did a community-based defense first [at Busboys and Poets Restaurant in Washington, D.C.]. And that pulled the community completely into the experience. They were more aware of what it all meant. They were able to know what a dissertation was. They understood more clearly what I was doing. It wasn't scary for them. So many people who came to that public defense at the restaurant are now like, "I can't wait to go get my PhD." That's also success to me. I came into it, setting out to do something with it that mattered to me and mattered to the community. And I did. I did it the way I wanted and it won the Dissertation of the Year Award in my college.

*What about challenges? Have there been any challenges in embracing a hip-hop mindset or just being authentic?*
The biggest challenge that I have had was trying to determine where my niche was in the scholarly community because I have navigated this work most recently as an independent scholar. I had to let go of those traditional ideas of what it means to be connected in academia. So, not needing to be attached to an institution, or not necessarily having deep personal relationships with all of the big names in your field. That was a narrative I was telling myself, that I needed those things. I don't feel that way anymore. I mean that's actually hip-hop—creating your own success, rising to superstar from the margin. I know that what I have now I've built and I'm still building. But there aren't a lot of examples in academia of folks who do it differently.

*What's one word that best describes hip-hop culture?*
Love.

*What's your stage song?*
My stage song is definitely KRS-One's "The MC" (1997). I feel like he's rapping an entire theme song about me, who for a living, is an actual Ed Emcee. It's the philosophy of it all for me. KRS-One, to me, is like an "OG Ed Emcee"!

*Last question. Can you dance?*
Absolutely. I'm clear. I get busy.

## IAN LEVY

*Associate Professor, Counseling
    and Therapy, Manhattan
    College*
*Counselor, scholar, emcee*
*New York, NY*

*This book is about understanding the utility of hip-hop culture. So talk to me about how you use hip-hop in your life, not just teaching it or studying it as a subject. Do you embrace it in how you show up in the world?*

I had a bunch of self-doubt from things that I went through in high school. I couldn't talk about them when they happened. When I got into college cyphers in dorm rooms and around campus, I just started emoting through my rhymes. And I was met with validation and support in these hip-hop spaces. That's important to stress. It wasn't just one group of folks who were really mature and thoughtful who made me feel welcomed. *All* the spaces welcomed my experience and my approach. That was just a hip-hop way to be—being okay with whoever the person was.

So after feeling so affirmed, I began to dig in to being an emcee. In the same way that Nas wrote one of his songs backwards and that was a dope concept, I became obsessed with this idea of finding concepts and flipping them into something interesting and dope. But my "concepts" weren't stories from the streets, they were areas of personal growth. I would take my weaknesses and flip them into content for a song. Instead of saying, This is a vulnerability and I'm the worst, I would think, This is such a real experience and it's going to be a crazy dope track, I cannot wait to write this song. That was my experience with using hip-hop to reflect, process, and critique myself. The more personal I got, the more relatable it was to more people. This encouraged me to be more personal as a professor. In my classes, I'll share personal narratives about my experiences or whatever issues I've faced. I'll share my thoughts and feelings and frustrations. I'll share that I've made mistakes. I'll be very honest and reflective. Hip-hop has certainly been a place that's helped me learn that. There's a freshness and an authenticity to it. Come here as yourself. When I started going to the hip-hop spaces in college, I was rhyming about high school in the suburbs and feeling like I wasn't smart enough to be in the upper-level math classes. I was rapping about the nerdiest content ever. But it didn't matter because I wasn't trying to be anything I wasn't. And for that reason, I was accepted by the communities that I stepped into, simply because I was able to step in and be authentic.

*As a professional who embraces hip-hop, what are the skills that you get from hip-hop?*
What sticks out the most is writing. My writing has significantly improved from engaging in hip-hop spaces. I know more words than I knew before I fell in love with hip-hop. If I hear a word that sounds sick in a rhyme and I don't know what that word means, I'll look it up. My vocabulary has increased. I've also learned how to write in a more descriptive way because of hip-hop. The second thing is public speaking. Being able to grab the mic and speak in the moment, not having to memorize things or use notes, is a skill that I have gotten from hip-hop. I'm able to trust that I can form and connect thoughts that flow together. I'm comfortable. My mentor, Chris Emdin, refers to it as being a "spitter." What he is talking about is the way that you can get on the mic and speak in a really engaging way—to command attention. I think that's necessary. I see presentations that are boring PowerPoint presentations or people just reciting other people's stuff. And I can tell that they don't have an emotional connection to it. I feel people sharing a story that I know they've shared 200 times, because I can hear it in the way that they're delivering it, that their heart's not in it. I pick up on authenticity. That's something hip-hop taught me. Real recognizes real. Academia is good at making you believe that you don't need to be emotional and that you should be very scientific and objective. Hip-hop preaches the opposite. Hip-hop preaches we want to hear what you have to say, what you've been through, your pain and your happiness, everything. The range of your emotional experiences is demanded in hip-hop. And I've learned how to bring those emotional experiences to the stage. I say stage but it might really be teaching class or giving a conference presentation. But I treat it like a performance, I really do.

*What about attitudes?*
There's a certain confidence that I draw from hip-hop or that I'm at least trying to develop more deeply in myself because of hip-hop. When you think about famous emcee battles, if someone threw a stab at an emcee on their track, the other emcee was undoubtedly going to say something back on theirs. I've learned that confidence to defend myself. I'm not going to let a comment just sit there. I'm going to figure out how to address it. Learning how to navigate slick things that are said in a department meeting or comments about your work isn't easy. I do have colleagues who won't let disrespect stand. I'm not saying that they will confront in some disrespectful way. But they will confidently approach that conflict. That's a hip-hop mentality that I'm continuing to build up in myself. I'm also trying to adopt something else that hip-hop preaches—the attitude that I don't care what

other people think. The belief that I'm just out here being myself and the world can live with it is a hip-hop mindset. I love when I hear that kind of message in a song. I haven't been able to fully embody that attitude yet. I have moments of it, but I can't sustain it as a way of being in life yet. I'm an emotional dude. Things do bother me. But that's been an attitude that I've tried to adopt in my life—strong confidence.

*What beliefs about yourself do you get from hip-hop?*
I believe in a team approach or a squad approach to scholarship and to social change. I rock with #hiphoped, that is my team. That's my place that I can go to share ideas, to collaborate, to form partnerships, to build. Dr. [Chris] Emdin, that's my big brother. I'll hit him up and ask for guidance and he'll put me on to new scholarship or people. Getting feedback or ideas and not running from the difficulty of a problem—that's hip-hop. Something that I learned from the hip-hop community is that if you want to go far in this world and in this work, do it with a team. If you want to have a temporary moment where you're popping, then go solo. But, if you really want to have lasting impacts, you need to go with the team. I have my individual work, but my individual work fits within a team of people that are doing their own individual work and collectively we're all doing work together.

Another belief is integrity. I spoke about authenticity before, but integrity is a bit different. That's something that has been solidified for me over time, the ability to walk away from things that don't feel right. I trust that if I keep doing meaningful work my time is going to come in terms of the money and shine. But integrity is most important. If you sell out in education, the same way as when you sell out in hip-hop, people are not going to rock with you anymore. And it's more important for people to rock with me than it is for me to have acclaim and or some temporary extra bread. I'd rather have lasting impact within the world.

*What is professional success to you?*
I know very clearly what I want. I want to have a center for hip-hop and school counseling research and practice. I want to run that center and I want it to be on a college campus. I want to have graduate students, whether it's master's or doctoral, coming to that center to learn about how to use hip-hop in school counseling practice. I became a scholar through the practical work I did. I worked in a high school as a school counselor, and I built a studio at the school where we created mixtapes around different emotional themes. One of my goals was to go into higher education so I could train more school counselors to do that type of work. That's the mission. That's what success means to me—to be able to go into work every day, to teach classes on hip-hop, to write about hip-hop, to research hip-hop in counseling practice, and then to help support the next wave of scholars.

*Take a moment to do some trash-talking. Tell me about your greatest accomplishments.*

Probably the most hip-hop thing that ever happened to me was after the *New York Times* wrote a piece on my high school program, my students and I were invited to visit the *Sway in the Morning* show. We had around 18 students with us and Lil Bibby was also on the show that day because they were celebrating that he had just gotten his GED. Just from a pure hip-hop sense, not even as an educator, just as a lover of hip-hop, anyone that has had the very healthy teenage and young adult dream of being a rapper, also dreams of being on *Sway*. That's the equivalent of the Ed Sullivan show my parents grew up watching. If you get on there and you crush it, that's the ultimate success. I did not expect at 21 years old that I would be on *Sway in the Morning* with 18 of my students showcasing work we were doing at a high school, but that's how it happens. That moment was actually a bridge for me, the pinnacle of one old dream and the beginning of a whole new professional journey. My original emcee dream was realized. I spit a rhyme on *Sway in the Morning*—not many other emcees can say that. I'll take that one to that grave with me. But the experience also opened my mind to better understand my professional gifts. Sway and I were walking down the hallway together and I thanked him for having my students on the show. He looked at me and said, "I just want to see y'all win." That was a huge encouragement. I'm still pushing to win. That was the moment where I understood I had an expertise. So I was like, okay, it's time to really start working towards this. I need to write more about it. I need to figure out how to train people to do it. It was a turning point for me.

*What about challenges? Have there been any challenges in embracing a hip-hop mindset or just being authentic?*

There's all the classic challenges of doing hip-hop within school administration or other staff who hold on to very stereotypical perceptions of hip-hop. School leaders assuming that we're just making loud noises and promoting misogyny, which is not what's happening when we're doing hip-hop work. That's not to say, of course, that misogynistic or violent things don't come up in what students write, but then they become things that we talk about and process and work through. And it's beautiful. But there's a lot of erroneous fear around what we're going to do to youth if we expose them to hip-hop in schools. There's certainly also a pushback that I have received in academia. I did this cool research study focused on using hip-hop in counseling practice and there were some really transformative findings. I submitted it to a journal in my field, which I'll name. I'm not afraid to name it. It was the *Counselor Education and Supervision* journal, which is a big counselor education journal. The title was something like, "Hip-Hop and Spoken Word Therapy." It was desk-rejected. That means the editor saw it and didn't even send it out for peer review. Their critique back to me was that my methods were overly complex. What was crazy is that I submitted it under the category of "Innovative Methods." They had that as a category for the types of manuscripts that they were seeking. I interpreted innovative as meaning that your work was supposed to be complex, supposed to be new, supposed to be dope. But it's rejected. Coincidentally, there was an awesome smaller journal called the *Journal of Preparation and Supervision in Counseling*. They accepted it with no revisions and one of the editors sent a personal note, saying this is a perfect fit for a counselor education journal. Many of these fields are not ready for hip-hop and they hold on to negative perceptions of hip-hop, and honestly of Black and Brown people. Breaking through the gatekeepers of these so-called high impact journals is such a challenge.

*What's one word that best describes hip-hop culture?*
Complex.

*What's your stage song?*
"Hussle and Motivate" by Nipsey Hussle. That beat is just too crazy, the way they slowed down and chopped up that "Hard Knock Life (Ghetto Anthem)" (by Jay-Z) sample gets me hype every time.

*Last question. Can you dance?*
I can't. I'm willing to, though. I'm willing to make a fool of myself dancing in a party having a good time.

## ANDRE PERRY

*Senior Fellow, Brookings Institution*
*Researcher, author, news*
*    correspondent*
*Washington, DC*

*This book is about understanding the utility of hip-hop culture. So talk to me about how you use hip-hop in your life, not just teaching it or studying it as a subject. Do you embrace it in how you show up in the world?*

Oh, no doubt. I approach an academic presentation or a television appearance as a correspondent as if I'm rocking the mic. I might use academic terms, but the goal is still very similar to the goal of an emcee: to communicate in a way that will make people feel it, that will move them. In my writing, I certainly use data and I often present pretty lofty concepts, but I deliver it in a way that people understand. I put it in the context of our lives and make it real. That's hip-hop. That's a way of being and a mindset that people who know hip-hop understand. Your words don't matter if the crowd doesn't react to them.

There's also a level of hunger that I think is quintessentially hip-hop. I want it like a hungry rapper. I think that's a universal hip-hop feeling of "wanting to get on." All kinds of people know what it is to seek opportunity. But that idea was introduced to me largely through hip-hop. There is this intense desire to get an opportunity, to get on the stage, to get a record deal, to get in a magazine, to be known and to be recognized. Not just for the fame, but to literally be seen and heard. It's about having a level of importance and impact. When I saw Run-D.M.C. perform during the Fresh Fest Tour in the '80s, in his intro he goes, "There's been a whole lot of people on this stage here tonight, but I want you to know one thing: This is MY house!" When you think about that it's like, wow, he was claiming space in front of thousands of people. And honestly, I also try to claim space in my professional realm. I approach my work with the mindset that there's been a whole lot of people before me and there might be people after me, but today this is MY house. I'm going to set the stage. I'm going to jump it off. People recognize that. Even for folks who aren't really a part of the culture, they still understand that they can't approach me any kind of way. They can see that I come from a tree, a hip hop tradition. When you have roots, people know it's hard to pull on you. Even if they don't understand it, they respect it.

*As a professional who embraces hip-hop, what are the skills that you get from hip-hop?*
Number one is communication skills. I have definitely learned verbal skills from hip-hop—proper word use and the right combination of words. No question, wordplay is one of my strong skills. I also like my writing to describe the world around me. I want people to see the world through my words and that comes from the style of hip-hop that I really love. I love storytelling. I love the folks who can lay out the description of a situation or bring you into a room just by describing it. And I do the same thing. I want people to smell the communities, see the communities, feel the communities that I'm writing about. And my introduction to doing that was not some great English course or something. It was hip-hop. It was Biggie. It was Mos Def. That's where I learned it. The other skill is how to move in the world. I'm talking about my physical movements here. When I'm giving a presentation, I know how to get the crowd going and get the crowd hyped. I get that from hip-hop. I observed in hip-hop how emcees control the mic and the stage, how they keep a crowd's attention. I even think we learn from the producer or DJ. Mixing and flow are important skillsets. In my latest book, I talk about education, I talk about housing, I talk about business development; you must be able to mix that properly. In hip-hop flow is everything. You can't have great content (important data) with a flow that is wack. No one will listen. You will lose people.

*What about attitudes?*
Oh man, I go into battle mode real quick. Sometimes it's the friendly banter that a lot of Black people are very comfortable with—we get it from "the dozens" and from hip-hop battling. I have no problem mixing it up with somebody. I'm talking about getting into debates where other people might get emotionally charged by an engagement. I love engagement. I love the intellectual battle. Sometimes you take a loss. But it's in that engagement, when it's back and forth like a cypher, that's where new knowledge comes out. That's where you sharpen your ideas and thoughts. There's no question, hip-hop culture taught me to embrace the battle and not run from it. That attitude of let's go, let's do this; let's put up your skills versus my skills and see who comes out on top. I definitely have that attitude.

*What beliefs about yourself do you get from hip-hop?*
There are some belief systems that I will take with me to the grave. I don't believe in biting [copying]. I want to have my own style. My form is this mixed methods approach: I talk about numbers, I talk about life. That's my style. I got that from this incessant need to be original in hip-hop. That's what separates the great emcees from the mediocre ones. The ones that have their own style, brand, or thought process, those are the greats. I've also

learned or believe in building with other men. What's interesting is that hip-hop and sports are the only places where men actually do things together and we are allowed to have some kind of emotional reaction to the stuff that we're doing. In both cultures men are dapping, laughing, hugging, cheering. Hip-hop is one of the few spaces where men can actually work together. But in that masculine space, hip-hop is a blessing and a curse. I think that I've learned or been influenced by a lot of the misogynistic things that have been in hip-hop. As I have grown into my manhood, I've questioned a lot of the things I've believed in or the ways that I've treated women. Growing up in hip-hop, you do have to question yourself. What am I doing? What is this behavior about? Some of the attitudes and belief systems that are in hip-hop are not devoid of the sociological problems that we all face. So it's complicated, as are most cultures.

*What is professional success to you?*
When I go back home, and my home community accepts me. That's success. Part of being in my position, I get lots of praise and criticism. You learn to just take both in stride. Never get too high, never get too low. But when I get praise from home it's like, wow, I'm a credit. That's how older folks used to say it, "You're a credit" or "You didn't forget home." That's another theme in hip-hop: don't forget where you came from. You hear that a lot because for some people, success has meant leaving home. Success for me means going back home with something that I did for them. Whenever I go back and I'm giving these talks, I can look at the audience and see there are some people who aren't really listening to me, they're just proud of me. They're just there. And afterwards they're in the crowd telling people, "Yeah, we went to the same high school." They are just proud. My presence validates their existence and that is success for me. When I go home, I feel like a million bucks. I feel unstoppable. When I can go home and people recognize that I've added value to their lives, that is success.

*Take a moment to do some trash-talking. Tell me about your greatest accomplishments.*
There have been so many high points. I've had dinners with presidents. I had a dinner with Bill Clinton that lasted like four hours. Incredible dinner. Then there's the fact that I'm on television all the time. I have articles in *The New York Times*, *The Root*, and *The Washington Post*. I've presented in front of thousands of people. I have a popular book out right now. Those are all big deals. But honestly, the best moment was when I recently went home and this older Black woman—she reminded me so much of my grandparents— came up to me after my lecture. She got really close and says, "Now you're talking truth. You were up there saying the same thing that we've been saying all these years. And you got the numbers to back it up." When I get that, man, those are the moments where I go, okay, I did something real.

Because the truth is it all comes from them. I did this one report where we scraped Yelp data. We examined businesses in Black neighborhoods and White neighborhoods. And we showed that businesses owned by people of color—Black, Brown, and Asian folks in particular—often score higher Yelp reviews than their White counterparts. This defies the myth that our services aren't as good, that we don't run quality businesses. But I did that study in the first place because of something our Black elders used to say: "Our ice is just as cold." I do that a lot. I'll hear something that someone says and my response is, "Well, that's actually an experiment." I really need to thank folks on the street because I'll hear something and rather than keep walking, I consider it and turn it over in my head. I blow it up. Before you know, it, I have an essay, I have a chapter, I have a report, and it all comes from centering Black people and centering their words. Hip-hop has always done that; we have always been in the center of the lyrics, not talked about in relation to Whiteness.

*What about challenges? Have there been any challenges in embracing a hip-hop mindset or just being authentic?*
Oh yeah. White people can always be a challenge when you focus on racism in your work. There are many White people who don't want to hear about ending structural racism. There are also the people of all races who aren't familiar with hip-hop. They're threatened by hip-hop. So when I present concepts like ending structural racism through a lens that is saturated with a hip-hop attitude, that's threatening to a lot of people. I've been attacked politically. My family's been attacked because we are fighting for justice. The blowback from governors, mayors, funders, or administrators can be severe. I mean severe. I've left jobs. I've left tenure track positions. I've had to endure meanspirited criticism. But like I said, you're not going to shame a hip-hop head. We've been through it all. I also know that racism is real and the response that I often receive isn't because of me, it's because of what I represent—what I'm trying to do. So I can compartmentalize that in a way that saves my self-esteem. For example, my tagline—"There's nothing wrong with Black people that ending racism can't solve"—people get offended by that. Because, for so many White people, it's been a national narrative that the conditions of Black cities and Black neighborhoods are a direct result of the people in them, not the policy violence inflicted upon Black people. I reject that.

*What's one word that best describes hip-hop culture?*
Audacious. It is bold enough to defy what everyone says. To move through life with a hip-hop mindset is to boldly go where everyone else says you can't and you shouldn't. I remember listening to LL Cool J's "I'm Bad," and I remember going "Damn, is he that damn confident? How can I get some of that?" Because we're supposed to be humble, and we're supposed to be

subservient, and we're supposed to keep our head down. We're not supposed to have our own thoughts and ideas. He personified confidence and for young Black and Brown people to scream confidence in a society that's trying to suffocate them is audacious.

*What's your stage song?*
"Fear Not of Man" by Mos Def.

*Last question. Can you dance?*
Of course. I still got a little bit. I try to keep up with the young people—not to the point where it's embarrassing. But I can do it. Dance is a communal activity. It's our way to express our love for each other and it's quintessentially African. It's one of the things we use to feel free.

## EDMUND ADJAPONG

*Assistant Professor of Education,*
   *Seton Hall University*
*Researcher, author, educator*
*Bronx, NY*

*This book is about understanding the utility of hip-hop culture. So talk to me about how you use hip-hop in your life, not just teaching it or studying it as a subject. Do you embrace it in how you show up in the world?*

My work is driven by hip-hop. Hip-hop is very community-based. Hip-hop drives my work because I recognize the connection between culture, community, and the deep, deep roots around social justice. What really encouraged me to become an educator was asking myself, How can I give back to my community? Because we get the narratives of successful people leaving; but with hip-hop artists, even when they become wealthy and physically leave the neighborhood, hip-hop as a culture is embedded so deeply within the community, it's like the artist is still culturally there too. The community is all in their work. The artist is still there to support. I want to be a supporter of the culture in that sense. Inherently, my goals with hip-hop are to teach hip-hop in schools, K–12 schools, so that young people can understand their culture. A lot of college students of color start college understanding that they have values and while they are in college they become very socially active as leaders. That's when they begin to connect the culture, the values, the beliefs, to the activism and social action. But it shouldn't take that long for young people to have that experience. That's what allows me to embody hip-hop without being an artist. I'm not an emcee. But I can still embody hip-hop culture within my practice as an educator.

*As a professional who embraces hip-hop, what are the skills that you get from hip-hop?*

I think resilience is probably one of the main things that I've taken from hip-hop. When I think about my childhood and my upbringing, hip-hop was always a big part of my life. But when I think about the really difficult times in life, especially in education, hip-hop and my education journey are so intertwined. I could never have become a professor without hip-hop. I wouldn't have even become a teacher. I wouldn't have continued to college without hip-hop. It was a driving force in my life. When I realized that I wanted to attain some level of success, hip-hop was that motivator. Jay-Z is my favorite artist. He motivated my sense of hustle, that sense of ambition. Resilience is about making sure that you meet whatever goal that you set for yourself. That's hip-hop. Even the consumers of hip-hop or those who embody and identify as fans of hip-hop culture, there's this shared sense of the struggles and the challenges that you face on your life journey. Everyone is tapping their resiliency. As hip-hop continues to become increasingly popular globally, we can truly say hip-hop is for everybody. Especially now that we have older folks who are hip-hop. It's getting to a point where there will not be a generation alive who didn't grow up with hip-hop. That's crazy. And there's so much diversity in it. I know hip-hop allowed me to be more empathetic and understanding about others' experiences. But most importantly, hip-hop has encouraged me to be critical of the world and it made me recognize that there were other people who shared similar experiences to me.

*What about attitudes?*
I think hip-hop gives me kind of a bravado attitude. I don't know how to describe it—owning your space, owning your place. To be successful as an academic and in order to be successful in hip-hop, you have to be confident. And I think you also have to be authentic. So in many ways you really must have high self-awareness. You must be aware of your talents and what makes you special—that's the confidence. You must be aware of who you really are—that's the authenticity. If you don't know who you are, then the world can depict or perceive you as other. They can make even you believe you don't belong. Knowing who you are allows you to also know that you deserve to be here. I think that has helped me a lot in academia. It's been really useful when I'm navigating spaces where I'm the only Black person or I'm the youngest person.

*What beliefs about yourself do you get from hip-hop?*
This is going to sound clichéd, but hip-hop really allows me to believe that anything's possible. When you think about the history of hip-hop and how hip-hop started, nobody would ever imagine that hip-hop would have gotten this far. It's really mindblowing when you think about how hip-hop permeates other cultures, other countries. That's a testament to the power and beauty of Blackness. That's a testament to our resilience because we were the ones who created the art form—the culture. I can only imagine the young people who created it, maybe with no intention for it to go anywhere, how do they feel? Look at where it's reached. Anything is possible.

*What is professional success to you?*
Listen, I would not be who I am if it weren't for Jay-Z as an artist. I admittedly try to emulate him. Jay-Z is super confident, hyper self-aware, and

reflective. But I also love his growth as an artist. He's an artist who shares his personal growth with his audience. I appreciate that so much. His professional growth aligns with my professional growth because I know what I want and I know that if I want to achieve Jay-Z type of success in my realm, I just need to keep going. I know that there are things that I've got to do. I also know that there are challenges, there will be downfalls, there will be pitfalls. Success is never a linear line. I appreciate him showing us that he is human because it allows me to be human too. Even if we have different professions, we still face similar challenges in our pursuit of success. This has always been a thing for me—really absorbing hip-hop. When I was a teenager, I would go home and read hip-hop blogs for hours. I was really interested in hip-hop culture, not just about the music. I love the music, but I have always been super curious about what was going on in the careers of hip-hop artists. I have really been following how people live and navigate in the hip-hop industry. Seeing hip-hop artists get to a point where they have real power and privilege to do big things for themselves and for their communities, to have such a global influence, shows me that I can do whatever I want within my arena as well.

*Take a moment to do some trash-talking. Tell me about your greatest accomplishments.*
I think something I'm real proud of is my research. When I was a doctoral student at Columbia [University Teachers College], I experienced what I call "the Ivy League blues." Do I belong here? Should I be studying this? I was in a science ed program. Everyone else was always studying things like how students perceived planets or the latest innovations in science education. Everyone there was deep in science and I'm there for hip-hop. You know what I mean? But now it's cool. I'm super proud of my research—what it's done and how it continues to grow. I'm probably most proud of how it's impacted others. That's really all I want; I just want to contribute to the hip-hop education field and contribute to the culture in my own personal way. I'm also proud of myself. Just me as a Black male academic who preaches hip-hop and talks about hip-hop in all of my classes, all my spaces at a predominantly White institution—I'm proud of that. Standing my ground. Staying the course. I'm proud that I have the privilege and the opportunity to do this. Because not everybody does on this level. I really want to be grateful for that and do it well. I just want to serve the culture well because I feel like the culture has done so much for me.

*What about challenges? Have there been any challenges in embracing a hip-hop mindset or just being authentic?*
I think the biggest challenge with embracing hip-hop is the negative perceptions that hip-hop gets. I always talk about how hip-hop literally gets a "negative rap." But hip-hop is not *only* those things. Hip-hop is not only

misogynistic. It's not only homophobic and transphobic. If they are embedded in hip-hop, it's important for us to recognize that we need to be critical of those things as a community, as a culture. I can appreciate that when I use hip-hop in my classes, it allows us the space to have those critical conversations. But generally, I do feel like the challenge is I'm always explaining. "I'm the hip-hop guy and I just want to start by saying hip-hop is not only this . . ." I wish I could go into a space and just talk—just talk the way we are talking right now. So one challenge for me is always having to defend the culture. But, honestly, the challenge is really society's perceptions of what our culture is broadly. Society has a negative perception of hip-hop because society has a negative perception of Black and Brown people. But when hip-hop benefits society, when hip-hop is bringing in billions of dollars, when hip-hop is helping companies and industries sell their products, nobody is questioning hip-hop, they're just trying to use it in any way they can. And we're over here also trying to use the culture for ourselves—to uplift ourselves, to educate ourselves—and we get pushback for using it in a positive way. I talk a lot about how the academy robs Black and Brown people of their joy. When will the academy become a space where we can allow joy in our work and scholarship without having to defend ourselves for wanting it? I find there's room for cultural joy when I'm working with young kids because I don't have to have those preface conversations with them. We just dive right in to hip-hop. When working with adults and in higher education I wish that we were able to have more unrestricted joy, more freedom.

*What's one word that best describes hip-hop culture?*
Innovative.

*What's your stage song?*
"What More Can I Say" by Jay-Z

*Last question. Can you dance?*
I'm not a dancer. But I got some rhythm.

## MAZI MUTAFA

*Executive Director, Words, Beats &*
*Life, Inc.*
*Administrator, organizer, educator*
*Washington, DC*

*This book is about understanding the utility of hip-hop culture. So talk to me about how you use hip-hop in your life, not just teaching it or studying it as a subject. Do you embrace it in how you show up in the world?*
Yes, in part, because of the way that I think about hip-hop as a practice. Some folks bring a pure artist sensibility to their work approach. I am bringing a hip-hop approach, but there are more people involved and deeply invested in the hip-hop industry than just artists. Even the artists who become label execs, there is a mind shift that has to occur once you are running the company. You begin to understand that if I don't have money, I can't actually pay your royalties. I can't distribute your music. An academic named Marshall McLuhan said something like, "I don't know who discovered the ocean, but it probably wasn't the fish." So sometimes not being an artist helps me see the art differently. It helps me see its application differently and understand its value differently. You might be a DJ who can rock a party, and you're like, "Yo, I got people to sweat out there." But I see it as a community-building activity. My view doesn't negate yours; I look at it differently as someone who is putting on the event versus performing at the event. Sometimes cultural creators negate the art of curation—being able to bring people together. It still has to be beautiful. It still has to be magical in the sense that it's transformational.

*As a professional who embraces hip-hop, what are the skills that you get from hip-hop?*
Hip-hop is rooted in this idea of remix. When approaching a challenge, my first question is, how is it that people have approached this challenge before? Then I'm asking, what was their outcome, what was the scale of their success or failure? And finally, what could help it have broader appeal? So this idea of always looking to see what people haven't seen is very much a hip-hop sensibility. The desire to be inventive and mixing things up is tied to that idea of crate digging and looking for samples or parts of music that have and haven't been used before to add them to an existing composition to create something new. In my work, whether that's a new kind of program, a new event or new policy, I'm always asking, how have people done it before and then how can we not simply replicate that, but really reimagine

it, still using that original thing as a foundation. The idea of sampling is very much a part of my own practice. The real push is how to tell a different story to achieve greater impact.

*What about attitudes?*
One of the things that's most interesting is that for most of my adult life, I've been an opposition type person. I would say things that I felt and believed, but other people usually didn't agree. And I felt comfortable in that outsider role, always being in opposition. Then over time, the shift occurred where I would say things and people would agree. Similarly, at one point in time, hip-hop wasn't on the radio because it was too different. And then there came a point where it was everywhere. One of the challenges with that new level of acceptance is transitioning from being oppositional. I saw this great video recently on the evolution of women and sexuality in hip-hop. It ended with "WAP" (by Cardi B, featuring Megan Thee Stallion). It was interesting to look at how, over time, the narratives didn't necessarily change that much, but the venues where the music was played changed. So if you go from "BWP" (Bitches with Problems), which most people haven't necessarily heard, to "WAP" now being a song on the radio and on YouTube, the messages have really stayed the same but are now just received by a larger audience. As a college student, I was that young rebel in a space where it felt like everybody was conforming—everybody wanted to be R&B and I just wanted to be N.W.A, you know? I think what's happened over time is that more folks have come to embrace and uplift N.W.A. I recently started this hashtag "#NWAwasright." What's happened over time is not that I've stopped being what I used to be called, which was "Militant Mazi," it's just that my audience isn't necessarily oppositional to ideas they used to label as militant. And my approach is different too. I realize now that if there is something that I've been thinking about, other people might not have a frame of reference—they may not have ever thought about the things I've been thinking about. And so, rather than assuming that they just don't want to be down or that they disagree, maybe I should begin from a place of listening as opposed to talking so that we can imagine ways to build together. So it's really about getting back to this idea of creating a remix that will grow an audience as opposed to repelling one.

*What beliefs about yourself do you get from hip-hop?*
Here is a really clear example: Because of who's on television or on the radio in rap music, most people assume that because I run a hip-hop organization, the primary audience for the work that I do is African American. It is the majority of the audience, but it is not the primary audience in the sense that I really look at our work as medicine for the human family. Hip-hop has widened my audience and my community as far as service. My beliefs about WBL (Words, Beats & Life, Inc.) and the global

reach of hip-hop have literally impacted my beliefs about how I work and even where I work. It might have started local but it's now global, just like hip-hop itself.

*What is professional success to you?*
It's interesting. I'm almost violently opposed to braggadocio in my professional life for really one reason: because in my experience and even looking at hip-hop, braggadocio also brings animosity. So when you're successful and you celebrate it in a way that is like, "Yo, I'm the shit," there will always be some people who will have an almost reflex response, "No, you ain't shit." That response is always going to be there by somebody. So I almost always discouraged my staff from publicly celebrating. We do internally celebrate. It's more valuable to our organization if our partners, alums, and supporters brag about us than if we brag about ourselves. I think that the song is "Heart of the City" by Jay-Z, where he talks about how long he has been repping the community through hip-hop and asks, "Where's the love?" It's this idea that he's done the work and the question is, Are you celebrating it? Having the community celebrate it matters. For me, professional success is building things that the artists in our community can't build alone. If an amazing poet in the neighborhood can put on an event, my organization should not be doing that event. We should be doing something that an individual couldn't do. It's always about creating something that's bigger than what is and that requires us to engage with more than what we have and more than who we have. I feel like a big part of professional success is collaboration and community building. Big goals.

*Take a moment to do some trash-talking. Tell me about your greatest accomplishments.*
I would say that our greatest success has been inspiring the community or the young people who've been involved with our programs, to chase their own dreams. That's happened through things like the WBL Academy, but it's also happened through things like social media. We've had people from all over the world contact us. People across the globe have been following what we've been doing here in Washington, D.C., and working to replicate it in their own cities or countries. I just met the new curator for this museum in DC called Planet Word. She shared that she'd been following Words, Beats & Life since she ran an afterschool program in Seattle. She's like, "I was literally just studying your website, taking your ideas to implement them in my city." I also met a graduate student from Germany who was writing about the transformational power of hip-hop and was literally asking me the most granular details of our programs, things that we never really talked about or really promoted. Doing work that people think is valuable enough to imitate, to innovate, or to write about, has been a tremendous part of our success. But it's also looking at the lives that the young

people who've come through our programs now lead—from the education they've achieved to the artistic endeavors that they've pursued.

*What about challenges?*
In some ways it would be so much easier to follow the path to success I witness others take. I have chosen a different path that can have real obstacles and roadblocks. But I realize that the work I do isn't really a job. It's my purpose, it's the reason I wake up every day and put my all into creating space for growth and transformation. It is not easy, but it is definitely worth it. I have heard the testimonies about our impact. I have seen our former students graduate from college and become professional artists and parents. It is amazing to see how a life can be transformed by creativity, how a community can be made better and how hip-hop itself can grow. My effort is to make quality arts education accessible to every young person in Washington, D.C. It's also to build a pipeline to creative employment that allows more people to make a living of creativity. My work is to center the voices, experiences, and aspirations of the most marginalized in our communities. I truly believe in the power of person-to-person diplomacy at home and abroad and the need to tie that diplomacy to economic collaboration and investments. I do all this for the community, and the future of the culture of hip-hop.

*What's one word that best describes hip-hop culture?*
Transformational.

*What's your stage song?*
"The World is Yours" by Nas.

*Last question. Can you dance?*
Nope, not at all.

## AYSHA UPCHURCH

*Lecturer and Director, HipHopEX*
*Harvard Graduate School of Education*
*Artist, educator, consultant*
*Cambridge, MA*

*This book is about understanding the utility of hip-hop culture. So talk to me about how you use hip-hop in your life, not just teaching it or studying it as a subject. Do you embrace it in how you show up in the world?*

I came into education the hard way: "Hey, come be a community teaching artist. You don't know anything about the kids, you don't know anything about the space, you don't anything about the rules, and can you do this and be brilliant in the hallway because we don't have any available rooms?" In those circumstances, you have to be able to freestyle and not bullshit. Because understand, freestyling and bullshitting are two different things. To freestyle and flow, you have to be creative and innovative. I've seen some colleagues who are well-known professors, when their PowerPoint breaks down they can't do anything. I really consider myself a facilitator and a DJ. In lecture spaces, I facilitate workshops on topics like conflict resolution, equity, and diversity. But as I approach this work, I am thinking about the DJ. At all of the most hype parties, who was the most essential person? The DJ. Because the DJ had the ability to read the space. They come prepared with the right crates. They also know where to pull from—they can tell if people want more or less of something. The sensibility of knowing and feeling the crowd is so important. So if the feedback is silence, you've got to amp it up. If the energy is really high, you've got to keep it going.

*As a professional who embraces hip-hop, what are the skills that you get from hip-hop?*

It enhances your linguistic skills. I'm not just talking about from emceeing. There's so much kinesthetic reading, responding and nonverbal communication in hip-hop. My communication skills—my ability to listen—are better. I'm a dancer, so I have to know where the downbeat is. The way my ear listens as a dancer also transfers to being able to listen in conversations. If I have students who are going at it or students who are zoning out, I need to be able to go, okay, where's the downbeat? In other words, how are we going to get on that same two-step, or how do we get our different ideas to complement each other? Listening is such a critical skill within so many realms of life.

Another skillset is always being ready to be pushed. Emcees are never happy with just one track that went well. No one wants to be the dancer who hit the circle one time. I want to be pushed. And that means that you must be able to embrace feedback whether you wanted it or not, whether it's good or bad, and whether or not you knew it was coming. In cyphers, you get feedback immediately. But then there are other instances where I've had to have people review my work who I don't even know. That can be a challenge. But because of the culture, I have thick skin.

*What about attitudes?*
I'm a KRS-One fan. In one of his talks, I think it is titled, "What does it mean to be hip-hop?", he goes into this metaphor of Super Jane. That you can't say your name is Jane, you've got to say it like, "I'm Super Janeskie. I come from here. I go over there." So there's that attitude, and I really believe that's why people are so attracted to hip-hop. Hip-hop gives you space to find out the different dimensions of attitudes that you can have. You don't have to singularly be one personality type. You can play around with different attitudes. But it requires you to always believe first, last, and in the middle, that you're better than everybody else. And that's not really my natural stance. But listen, when I'm on the stage, you can't tell me nothing. You can't tell me nothing. I don't believe there are many facilitators on this planet who are better than me. I know how to multidirectionally listen. I know how to build a space where people feel seen. And so I tell people now, "This my price, because you're not going to find someone better than me, period." My receipts might not be as long as CVS yet, but I know you will be a satisfied customer. You can't be doubtful. That's important especially if there haven't been other spaces or opportunities for you to experiment for even two seconds at being bigger than you're typically allowed to be.

*What beliefs about yourself do you get from hip-hop?*
I was very, very, very bossy as a child. She has a whole name. My family has a whole name for the person that I was as a child. Along the way, after a lot of insightful education, taking really meaningful classes, and having my world opened in beautiful ways, I did subdue a bit of that. But because in hip-hop you must believe that you're better than everyone else, hip-hop actually reminds me that she's still here. That sassy little girl was not an accident, I need her. Because I can have respect for everyone else and see other folks' work as amazing, but when it's my time to go, I have to remember that little feisty, bossy, short, little Napoleon complex-having little girl, she's in me and I need her. To even believe that everything you want, you can actually have, you need that fearless spirit. My friend and I were watching

a clip of Diddy when he found out that he got the MTV show and he jumps up and is like, "I'm a savage! If I want it, I get it!" We were like, "Yes!"

Hip-hop also reminds me to believe in humanity—that humans want to gather together in love and in peace. I've been able to see people gathered. I've gathered with people where there's no shared spoken tongue. While we can't even talk to each other, we can still vibe and feel each other. It helps me believe that evil is taught. In our natural state, we all want to two-step at the same time. I've seen how hip-hop can bring us together. It reminds me to believe that humanity is not utterly unsalvageable.

*What is professional success to you?*
Living at your fullest capacity, the capacity at which you were designed to live. I think it's possible to fulfill on all levels: financially, emotionally, spiritually, and even vocationally. This question comes to me at such a beautiful and real time, because I've experienced a lot of successes. But I am thirsty and ravenous to be full-out 100% on everything. So that flag ain't planted yet.

*Take a moment to do some trash-talking. Tell me about your greatest accomplishments.*
I'm very proud of being a professor at the Harvard Graduate School of Education. I'm from the north side of St. Louis, a part of St. Louis that is financially, economically decimated. When I grew up on the block, everything that I know and love about being Black, I got from that community. Of all the schooling that I've received, what I got out of that neighborhood, that block, that community, is really what has fortified me. It is what drives my teaching and my practice before any of the scholarship. But my neighborhood is literally gone now. So sitting here as a professor at Harvard and I don't have a PhD, is a big deal. I'm only one of a handful of people who have gotten lecturer appointments because of my experience and my innovative work. If I see a gap, I start thinking about ways to fill it. That little feisty, don't take nothing from nobody, tell everybody their business; that little girl who confused teachers because I always got straight As and also had the smartest mouth; the girl who grew up in a working-class family, who came to know what gentrification and urban renewal was not through a textbook, but through living it—she is a professor.

I'm also proud to follow in the legacy of women like Toni Blackman. I saw her on a hip-hop panel in DC and fast forward a few years later, I get a call from the State Department saying, "Hey, we have your profile. We see that you're fluent in Spanish. We see that you have a degree in conflict resolution, we want to send you to Honduras. Do you want to go?" Serving as a cultural envoy because of my work in dance, hip-hop, conflict resolution, Spanish language, things that don't really make sense to a lot of people when they see it on my resume, it finally made sense. I'm proud that I didn't try to keep putting myself into established holes.

*What about challenges? Have there been any challenges in embracing a hip-hop mindset or just being authentic?*
As a [dance] teacher, I definitely experienced some doubt, questioning, what am I teaching? Are they trying to pimp us out? Why do they always use me and my other Brown friend on all of these studio announcement covers? But they actually have all of these White jazz ladies teaching hip-hop to kids. I've realized that my approach won't always jive with every environment in which I'm earning a check. So I may have to make a decision. If they aren't going to make space for me to create the impact that I want and compensate me, then I've got to step away. Or, when I have these questions around race and representation, I may need to give myself and others a break to not have it all together all of the time. That doesn't mean that I'm abandoning the commitment to the cause.

*What's one word that best describes hip-hop culture?*
Beautifully real.

*What's your stage song?*
"Everything is Everything" by Lauryn Hill.

*Last question. Well, you're a dancer so I already know the answer. Can you dance?*
No. I've been faking it all this time! I'm a real good actress. Yes, absolutely. I actually believe one of my talents is that I can get just about everybody to dance. Even people who are adamant, "I will never dance. I will not two-step"—I can get you to do it. Because our bodies are not meant to be still. It's one of the most natural things we do. We take babies and we bounce them, and we puppet them around. We find joy in watching them dance and move. And then suddenly, we silence their bodies and we silence their access to their body. So I'm like, get free, shake your ass. Shake it. Twerk yourself to liberation!

## BARON DAVIS

*Senior Advisor, Digital Promise*
*Administrator, Educator, Community*
*Leader*
*Columbia, SC*

*This book is about understanding the utility of hip-hop culture. So talk to me about how you use hip-hop in your life, not just teaching it or studying it as a subject. Do you embrace it in how you show up in the world?*

Yes. I definitely embody hip-hop culture. The way that I act, the way that I carry myself, the things that I believe, my attitude, even down to a certain swag that we all bring to the work that we do—that's all hip-hop culture. Hip-hop helps you to understand the importance of being authentic. Hip-hop introduced me to the term *foogazy*. Fake, not real. In hip-hop there's this focus not just on the quality of your work, but also the quality of your self—your person, your reputation. Nothing can be fake. You must be genuine. You might gain some things by having a fake brand, but it's never going to sustain if it's not genuinely you. Hip-hop has taught us not to let society change you into a fake version of yourself—you can change society. Hip-hop changed American culture. Here in Columbia, Dawn Staley talks about this idea a lot: *doing it for the culture*—whatever that culture is. [Because Coach Staley's profession is sports] for her "the culture" is the sport [of basketball]. That's what many of us do as African Americans, as Black folks who grew up in the culture of hip-hop. Our embrace of it is a way of honoring it and acknowledging what it did for us.

*As a professional who embraces hip-hop, what are the skills that you get from hip-hop?*

Being innovative. Hip-hop is an innovative culture. It basically started as a subculture that had to fight its way to become mainstream. I can personally connect to that. I grew up living in housing projects in our city. In essence, we were a subculture within the city. It's crazy. You live 5 to 10 blocks from downtown, but you're not really a part of what's going on in downtown. You are physically close but socially and politically isolated to a point where it feels like you're living on an island. So you learn how to be innovative and creative. You make up your mind and determine the type of person you want to be and you just start moving that way in the community. I get being creative, being innovative, from hip-hop culture. The first thing that I created or innovated was my own future.

Now as a professional, I'm always looking for the next iteration of something. I never settle for achieving the bare minimum. While it's nice that something we are doing in the district is working well, I'm always looking at how we can push that further. There's a hustle mentality that comes from hip-hop. You learn to take what you've got and flip it, reinvent it, and then present it in a better way. And when that is successful, you are always looking for the next opportunity. That initial success becomes the launch pad, not the final destination.

*What about attitudes?*
Boldness. Fearlessness. Through the years, there was a real attempt to suppress hip-hop culture. So hip-hop's history teaches you that in order to be heard, you've got to be loud. I'm a superintendent, so of course I know there are a lot of spaces where young people are told not to be loud. But hip-hop gives me a different, philosophical understanding of loudness. When you play your hip-hop music, it doesn't sound the same when it's low. It doesn't have the same energy when it's played low. It has to have a certain decibel level in order for it to even sound right. So that's how I feel professionally. Sometimes you've got to have a boldness about your work. It also requires precision. I remember when the prep [dance] was out, we were so serious about it. You had to get your prep routine down for the dance battle at the hop [school dance]. You and your homeboy or homegirl would practice for hours and develop a little prep routine. You would perfect that routine so that you could stand out. It had to be tight. We got those ethics of hard work, attention to detail, perfection from hip-hop. Hip-hop built up so much excellence in us. But it also just brought us together in good times. Our friendships were made stronger and our community had a shared cultural experience.

One of my fondest values or attitudes from hip-hop is also the whole notion of being fresh. Fresh in the sense of always popping. I try to be fresh in all ways. With fashion, I started wearing bow ties a long, long time ago before it was trendy. When I'm wearing business attire or a suit, I'm putting colored laces in my dress shoes. So again, hip-hop is seeing every part of yourself as the brand—how you package yourself *and* how you package your work production. You want all of it stand out. That fearlessness that I express from the way I work to the way I dress communicates something: I'm here and I'm bringing you something different.

*What beliefs about yourself do you get from hip-hop?*
If you know hip-hop culture, you know that there are various forms of hip-hop, not just music. There's music, art, fashion. I adopt that belief—that I'm also an artist in the field of education. Educational leadership is about

creation. I am always asking myself, What am I creating that's going to leave some sort of lasting impression on the people that I serve? Typically, when you see a piece of art, you are inspired by it. When you hear certain songs, they resonate with you. The art can motivate you, encourage you. When you put on new clothes or fresh clothes, you feel good about yourself. Fashion can do that—make you feel good, not just cover your body. Artists are creating those types of lived experiences through their art. And that's what I want to create. I believe that we can create that same type of transformative beauty in the educational experience.

*What is professional success to you?*
Professional success to me is both achieving my goals and having the people view your work positively. When I say the people, I mean your contemporaries, your peers, the community. It's not about awards. There are a lot of artists that have won Grammys but they aren't on anyone's Top Five emcee list. And that community-based top five list matters. You don't necessarily spend all of your time just trying to be in the top five, but you spend your time trying to be the best at your craft. When you're recognized by your peers as being one of the best, there's not another level of professional success greater than that. There is a certain sense of pride that comes with having your name on that list because the list is created by the people who truly love the culture. So when I became superintendent, the first thing I said to our educators is that our goal is to strive to be premiere. When people are talking about who's doing it the best in education, our names should always be mentioned. I want us on that philosophical Top Five list. And that accolade comes with the requirement to perform. There's a lot of bragging in hip-hop, but there's also serious work required to back it up. You can't brag about being the best lyricist if you've got elementary rhymes. You can't brag about being the best producer if your beats are tired and lazy. To have a certain level of professional success you've got to put in the work. I'm on top of my goals virtually 24/7.

*Take a moment to do some trash-talking. Tell me about your greatest accomplishments.*
At my first graduation as superintendent, as part of my commencement speech, I shared what Tupac said about a rose that grew from concrete and I also shared Nikki Giovanni's poem about Tupac. The kids loved it. I received so much positive feedback from students. But I also received several emails from older White adults who thought that referencing Tupac was inappropriate. They also took issue with a portion of a J. Cole song that I shared in the speech. In their opinion, using rap in a graduation speech was inappropriate. So the next year, I upped the ante, and I quoted some Post Malone. The year after that, I focused on Nipsey Hussle. There were no complaints about the Post Malone, but with Nipsey the reaction was

once again negative. According to them, I was celebrating a gangster. Of course, they probably had to do research. Someone probably had to tell them who Nipsey was for them to even write these emails. There was no real understanding of who Nipsey was as a person, his evolution as a man and what he did for his community. At some level, he held some of the same values that many of the adults in that community had about entrepreneurship and business development. He embodied figuring out a way to reimagine who he was and having the hustle to get things done for his community. But because he was in a gang at one time in his life, that's all he could ever be. So I got into this little discussion with a group of people and I mentioned that I can walk into the Strom Thurmond federal building in South Carolina and no one has a problem with that. I can teach about one of the founding fathers who owned slaves. No one has a problem with that. You can forgive them for their atrocities. But you can't seem to forgive this person whose atrocity doesn't even remotely come close to the impact of White supremacy. Remaining authentic, bold, fearless, and standing my ground in that moment is my success. Those types of moments define your leadership and they decide who will really be leading on your watch.

*What about challenges? Have there been any challenges in embracing a hip-hop mindset or just being authentic?*
I guess you always have those thoughts in the back of your mind, how much of this should I reveal about myself? That's when the issue of being authentic comes in to play. When I start feeling like I'm not being authentic, I really start to struggle. If I feel like I acquiesced to make someone else feel satisfied, I have serious problems with that. If I must feel bad or less of myself in order to make you feel good, that's you making me go against the core of who I am. That's me shrinking so that you can stand tall. That's a problem. No one should be made to do that. But the desire to honor and preserve the culture also makes you careful about it. Because it can still be seen as unacceptable that your superintendent, who's 48 years old, listens to trap music. Is it appropriate for him to listen to Biggie Smalls? But I think back to when I was a principal, my kids were always playing hip-hop at the pep rallies and I was out there dancing to it. Kids watch you like hawks. They pay such close attention. They can see me mouthing the words. And then they talk amongst themselves, "Man, Dr. Davis knows all the words to every song." They're intrigued but they are also proud of that. It affirms that I truly value what they value. And they are right; I do know all of the words. I know every song, every word of the *Ready to Die* album. I can go word for word on *Reasonable Doubt*. It is good for kids to observe that, as a leader, I have cultural connections with them. We share some things. I'm trying to express that.

*What's one word that best describes hip-hop culture?*
Innovative.

*What's your stage song?*
"I Ain't No Joke" by Eric B. and Rakim. I just always loved this whole notion of—I'm on stage, I've got the microphone, and when I'm done there's nothing left. There's no coming behind me. So you better bring your A game if you're up next.

*Last question. Can you dance?*
Oh, yeah.

## MICHAEL BENITEZ

*Vice President, Office of Diversity and
    Inclusion, Metropolitan State
    University of Denver*
*Education leader, renowned speaker,
    community organizer, poet*
*Denver, CO*

*This book is about understanding the
utility of hip-hop culture. So talk to
me about how you use hip-hop in your
life, not just teaching it or studying it
as a subject. Do you embrace it in how you show up in the world?*
The first way it shows up for me is through creativity. I think outside the
box. I don't confine myself to what's in front of me or to whatever has been
presented to me. I break those boundaries and try to be innovative in my approach to programs and policy. It's no different than how a DJ approaches
music at a turntable—you see how these different musical productions can
work together to create something else. You take that same approach of
mixing and reinvention in education.

Another way I embrace hip-hop as a professional practice is my un-
apologetic way of owning who I am and my authenticity. I know what
I bring to the table, and I don't question it. There's an attitude of confi-
dence that hip-hop adds to the way I show up professionally. Especially
coming from humble beginnings and having navigated dominant culture.
When I think about where I've come from and where I am—making it from
Washington Heights, New York, through homelessness and section 8 in the
Lehigh Valley of Pennsylvania, to now being a vice president at a university,
I'm not going to denounce who I am. It got me here. When I see people
lean on assimilation, lean on losing oneself to get opportunity, that often
signifies a willingness to throw others under the bus. There is a lack of understanding the importance of solidarity and looking out for one another.
Assimilation isn't an individual act. You have to throw shade on your whole
community to assimilate. That means your colleagues, staff members, students who identify with your culture or race, when you deny yourself, you
are also denouncing all of them. They get sacrificed and the whole culture
gets thrown under the bus in the process. I can never get down with doing
that to other people.

*As a professional who embraces hip-hop, what are the skills that you get
from hip-hop?*
Entrepreneurship is a major one. We often talk about hip-hop as a culture that made something out of nothing. But really, for me, hip-hop is a

culture that never really looked at what others see as "nothing" as value-less. We took what we had around us and we learned how you leverage what we had or didn't have. Whether that was making the connections with somebody else's cable if you didn't have cable. Or whether that is saying, "Yo, if you're not going to let us in to traditional dance studios, we're just going to create our own joint outside. We will put down some cardboards and just start throwing down." There is no such thing as nothing—there's always something to work from. Entrepreneurship teaches you to be mind-ful of your own skills and how you leverage that skillset. There is also an independence associated with being entrepreneurial. You own your own stuff. Even if you are working for a company or organization, you under-stand that you have a particular brand; what you bring to the table is your personal genius. When you leave, that style goes with you.

I'd say the last skill I learned from hip-hop is stage presence or show-manship. You've got to see me in leadership team meetings. My colleagues are learning new ideas about what professionalism could look like. They are learning new language and expressions. They are learning to relax and be free. Working through a hip-hop lens, you show up with an energy that draws participants in similar to a concert crowd—active engagement as part of the community. The emcee needs the audience as much as the audience needs the emcee. I want them to get loud, not quiet, in their response and feedback.

*What beliefs about yourself do you get from hip-hop?*
Again, I will return to authenticity. It is important for me to show up as my unique self. My goal is to contribute to still hit the intellectual and engage the data without losing myself. I'm trying to disrupt norms about what is acceptable or not acceptable in spaces not used to realness. It's a form of resistance. I've also learned resiliency through hip-hop. There is this belief that nothing can stop you, nothing's going to get in the way. Hip-hop culture has such a go-getter, ambitious attitude. But it's not just about carv-ing your own path. Ambition in hip-hop is also about carving a path for your community. When you think about it from a literal standpoint, you can't be the only one in the space. Hip-hop requires a community—there has to be another ear listening or set of eyes watching. And the connected-ness that happens when that community gathers—there's nothing like it. The energy. Hip-hop culture can always find the smallest points of pride and blow them up to make them meaningful and important. For example, when DJs or emcees start calling out neighborhoods or street names, the crowd reacts to that because it's like their experience is in the spotlight. But honestly, I mean, it's a street sign. It's not even my name on the street sign. But because I walk that street daily, that street sign is a part of my history, my culture, and life experience. So if I hear it shouted out on stage, I'm like, "WOOORDDDD!" Someone is mentioning my neighborhood and letting everyone know it matters. New Yorkers do it a lot. And if I know

that corner, if I know that street, and you are an artist or famous person claiming that street, then the other thing I know about you is that you are resilient because we have that common struggle. I know exactly where you came from, and I can respect that you've persevered. You are showing me that nothing can stop greatness. That's hope right there.

*What about attitudes?*
I get an unbreakable attitude from hip-hop. It doesn't matter how great the effort to marginalize you or push you out, there is an attitude that nothing can hold you back. Hip-hop is about reclaiming, taking our stuff back. That might be reclaiming our voice, taking our power back, taking our emotions and spirits back, but it's recognizing that we have a right to those things. There's also a humility that is offered when you grow up hip-hop. There's a gratitude there for the opportunity to be put on. I say growing up hip-hop, because I do think there's something to having grown up living, practicing, and watching how hip-hop heads move humbly through spaces, at least in my younger years. You learn from it. When I close out educational sessions, one of the first things I extend is gratitude to the audience for trusting me with their time. That matters. There is a grace that comes with hip-hop mindfulness that I think is essential to who we are.

*What is professional success to you?*
Professional success is being at the top of my game. When I'm able to help shape an institutional direction or inform how the institution should be structured, leaving that legacy is a part of how I define success. I don't want to just inspire others. I'm here to be a partner in collective liberation. It's dope that when people hear me speak, they find my keynotes inspiring. Success is about honoring your gifts, honoring your passions, your brilliance. If you show up with your full brilliance, if you are engaging your passion, and if you really own who you are (meaning that some people are going to be down with you, but some people are going to be like, I want nothing to do with him), you can turn things out. But you have to show up like the mic is yours. I'm a good lyricist, or perhaps more of a poet, if I put it on paper. But I'm only okay at freestyling; I'm far from the best. But I am not going to show up to a freestyle session, get on the mic and start off by saying, "Just so y'all know, I'm kinda mediocre with freestyling." No. Even if I mess up, I'm going to be like, "Fuck it. I'm still throwing down and I'm nice." Showing up like you're the best is essential. It's a big part of what contributes to people's success. Now, there is also a prevalent confidence in highly White-supremacist spaces. But it is a different type of confidence—an arrogant type that you run up against quite a bit. Because the confidence you learn in hip-hop is about risk, learning, growth, and evolution. Any time you get in front of a crowd there is a public vulnerability that accompanies the confidence I own, but with a touch of humility. Hip-hop permits you the

audacity of a self-importance that demonstrates the balance between confidence, humility, intelligence, and introspection—I call it brilliance.

*Take a moment to do some trash-talking. Tell me about your greatest accomplishments.*
One of the most meaningful successes was probably the founding of the Diversity Monologues that my fraternity brothers (I was among the group) started at Penn State while I was still an undergrad. Once I became a director in student affairs, I was able to turn it into an institutional program, grow it, and create a Diversity Monologues Pedagogy, that has been adopted at different institutions across the country. With the Diversity Monologues we carved out a space for students to tell their stories and experiences, share their subjective narratives and present it in an aesthetic platform, like spoken word. People are now looking at the life struggles that these students are sharing as critical forms of scholarship, art, and knowledge production.

On a more grandiose scale, the cofounding of the Hip-Hop Pedagogy Institute at NCORE (National Conference on Race and Ethnicity) that's been running now for like 10 years is also a big success. It was an opportunity to bring hip-hop heads from the ground doing the work in their communities into this national conference. NCORE was a space that didn't think about the value hip-hop could offer within higher education at the time. With the Hip-Hop Pedagogy Institute it really opened the space to include hip-hop culture in a meaningful way.

*What's one word that best describes hip-hop culture?*
Transformative.

*What's your stage song?*
"I Got It Made" by Special Ed.

*Last question. Can you dance?*
Oh, yeah. I can't pull off the B-boy moves like I used to when I was 10 and 11, I can't spin anymore, but I can still get my dance on.

## WILLIAM BOYLES

*High School Science Teacher in South
    Carolina Public Schools*
*Educator, musician*
*Columbia, SC*

*This book is about understanding the utility of hip-hop culture. So talk to me about how you use hip-hop in your life, not just teaching it or studying it as a subject. Do you embrace it in how you show up in the world?*

I have seen how some of my Black peers sometimes feel inferior because of how society has social-ized everyone, including them, to believe that they are inferior. That's where hip-hop thinking comes in, it's all about knowing you're bad. It's about being free to be your bad self. My students do well because I let them. I let them do well. I let them be their bad selves. If you need to stand up and express yourself, then do it. If you need to make jokes about the type of socks I'm wearing that day to break the ice and make you feel comfortable, then you know what, I put them on just for you to pick at me today. Be a comedian. And if you can dish it, you better be able to take it. We will just go rounds cracking on each other. In general, it's really about relaxing and letting everybody, including yourself, have a good time.

*As a professional who embraces hip-hop, what are the skills that you get from hip-hop?*

Hip-hop culture is now the primary pop culture. If you look at the fashion, the language, the swag or the posture throughout the world, its overwhelm-ingly hip-hop. But social norms still teach folks to vilify Blackness. Folks can perform all this Blackness in pop culture but then can't say "Black Lives Matter." Truly embracing hip-hop is a form of freedom. It's not just listen-ing to the music or trying to copy the swag; I'm talking truly embracing your individuality and creativity, being free to be you. When you do that, you aren't shackled by society telling you who to value, how to talk, how to move. We are trained to look at certain types of students or certain cultural behaviors and see negativity. I had to break myself from that too. Expecting students to act one way in school and then *everything* else about them can be acted on at home or in their neighborhood—anywhere but school. We have to really ask ourselves, Why are we trying to conform? Who are we trying to please? Freedom is real.

*What about attitudes?*

I think an attitude that I get from hip-hop is that everybody can get down. Everybody can bring something to the table. If you want to draw it, you can draw it, if that's how you want to express yourself. If you want to dance, you can dance it. If you want to give attitude, you can give attitude. If you want to speak it, you can rap it. Actually, you can create your own language. I love the individuality that is at its core. I always try to make sure that I don't try to blend in. I'm trying to stand out. Hip-hop allows you to do that. Individuality in hip-hop isn't the same as European or White cultural norms where individualism is self-centered or about personal success, focusing on the "I" instead of the "we." That's not what I mean. Hip-hop individuality is about being unique or special. Your own flavor. We can be part of a community all day long and still each person is trying to contribute something unique and special to that community.

*What beliefs about yourself do you get from hip-hop?*

I think I get just believing in myself from hip-hop. I am at a school where I'm one of three African American men. I am not apologetic for who I am because they accept everybody else's normal. I be who I am and I dare anyone to say anything about it. I let my students know that I speak African American language and by doing that I am saying to them, "I want you to be who you are." I'm always trying to be culturally responsive, meaning that I can assess the culture, I can learn from the culture, and I can immerse in the culture. I need students to feel comfortable with me and I need them to feel comfortable with themselves. The only way that we can feel comfortable with each other is if we can communicate effectively—not in a foreign language that makes us feel even more less than. For example, I constantly use the phrase "ain't it." I didn't know that this was a South Carolina thing, but I constantly say "ain't it" about everything. When I'm asking a question or seeking affirmation, I always end my sentence with "ain't it?" When I taught in North Carolina, my students started doing it. They would be engrossed in a debate or raise their hands to ask a question and they would say, "Ain't it, Mr. Boyles? Ain't it?" Even when I went to Texas, my Mexican American babies started saying, "Ain't it, Mr. Boyles? Ain't it?" And I love that. It's all about engaging each other. They were showing me love. And with that love, I can teach them anything. Now me saying "Ain't it" isn't a hip-hop thing. It's more of a South Carolina thing. But hip-hop is about embracing your expressions regardless of what other people think. It's very accepting.

*What is professional success to you?*

Finding a way to use your gifts and talents to touch the world. That's success because my money ain't necessarily always successful. I've spent through some money. When I started creating a hip-hop science curriculum, I had a huge community of educators who wanted to learn more and paid me good money to train them. But there were other teachers looking at me like I wasn't professional. You can have all this money and still feel the need to be respected and valued. That will have a rich person feeling broke—or broken. When you stop worrying about what people think and how people perceive you, that's when you're mentally free. It's not that you don't see others or that you are blind. Hip-hop is good about people-watching, being observant and picking up on body language and cues. But there's a point where you just have to perform and not get caught up in looking at the one or two people in the audience not dancing. I got a room full of teachers dancing and I'm worried about the two teachers who don't like what I'm doing? No.

*What about challenges? Have there been any challenges in embracing a hip-hop mindset or just being authentic?*
There are a lot of challenges from the education system. They look at the image, but they don't look at the individual whether it's a teacher or a student. I do get disheartened because I can see the systematic racism in the education. If you go to the root of it, it starts in school. We teach these kids their lives don't matter starting in school. That's why I had to get out of administration because I'm not going to police my students and you're not going to police me. I'm not suspending a bunch of kids. If you send them out of your classroom, they're going to come in my office and we will talk it out and eventually have a good time. But they aren't going home. Be mad. I'm going to learn about the school from everyone's perspective including the kids getting sent to the principal's office. They will sit and tell me all that's going on in the whole school. I'm not kicking them out, I'm pulling them in. You have to engage culture. I'm trying to know everything about every student—illness, financial insecurity, family life, personality quirks, issues with teachers—I build relationships with students so that I don't just see the image of a disruptive student. I'm seeing who they are as a person. As a kid, I was bullied. My teacher called me a faggot when I was in high school. That thing hurt my feelings because he was actually my favorite teacher. I enjoyed his class. I remember how that made me feel and it has stuck with me. So I want to make sure that my struggling students know it's okay to be you.

*Take a moment to do some trash-talking. Tell me about your greatest accomplishments.*
When I first started teaching, I taught at West Charlotte High School. It's a historically Black high school that has a lot of rich tradition in Charlotte. My success story was that when I first came there, we ranked number 17 [out of 17 schools] in academic scores and performance. I immediately connected with the students. I was a music producer and moved to Charlotte after working professionally in New York with a record company. A lot of

us were laid off and I had a biology degree, so that's how I got into education. But I was still fresh. I was a radical teacher and my students learned. Before I left, we were number one in the science scores. Our school was considered the science school. I wrote this curriculum called Hip-hop Science in 2007. I basically started letting science teachers know that they have to translate science culturally.

*What's one word that best describes hip-hop culture?*
Individuality.

*What's your stage song?*
I Ain't Mad at Cha by Tupac

*Last question. Can you dance?*
In my head.

## CRYSTAL LEIGH ENDSLEY

*Associate Professor, Africana Studies,*
*    John Jay College of Criminal*
*    Justice*
*Director, International Day of the*
*    Girl Speak Out at the United*
*    Nations*
*Poet, performer, professor*
*New York, NY*

*This book is about understanding the utility of hip-hop culture. So talk to me about how you use hip-hop in your life, not just teaching it or studying it as a subject. Do you embrace it in how you show up in the world?*

Hip-hop has taught me how to show up with integrity. It's about becoming who we are at our core and living true to those values. It's also taught me multiplicity—how to be in relation with very different kinds of people. As an artist, my audience holds me accountable. As a teacher, my students hold me accountable. As a person, my friends and my family hold me accountable. Integrity matters to me. If I were to get up on stage and preach all these messages, write some good, inspiring poems, but then I'm a different person offstage, that's not right. And we all know artists that are like this; they are on their game when they are on the mic, and then in real life, they're nasty people. There has to be some alignment between your words and who you are as a person.

*As a professional who embraces hip-hop, what are the skills that you get from hip-hop?*

Hip-hop is not a solo project. It's about relationship. I am always aware of my relationships. When you look at Southern hip-hop artists as one example, Outkast, CeeLo, Mystikal—you could go down the list and they're all in relationship. Even if they come at their craft from different ways, the link is the relationship. They are building off of each other's sound to produce something that's distinct but still in conversation. Hip-hop culture also gives you a sort of social literacy, an ability to read the situation. Whether it's a workplace relationship and I'm dealing with my department chair or my coworkers, or if it's my students or the youth that I work with in the community, my ability to decipher how to move within each relationship is critical. It's also important to stress that it's not just about how I see others. It's also about recognizing how they see me. I do care if the community sees me as excellent, as outstanding. Because we reflect each other. If we are artists in a cypher doing what we love and I build off what you just spit and then you grow and get better from what you saw me do, then we are serving a purpose in each other's lives. And again, it's not just how I see my purpose, but also how the other person sees my purpose in their life. It's almost like in a romantic relationship. If I think we're dating, but you think we're just talking, there's a little misunderstanding there, or miscommunication, you know? But that misunderstanding can cause confusion about the whole nature of the relationship and that can cause real problems. What some students need a "professor" to be might be really different from how we have been taught that faculty should show up on campus. So that social literacy is really important if you are trying to truly serve a community.

*What about attitudes?*
Hip-hop taught me that it's okay to be a lot. I get called "intense" sometimes. Hip-hop taught me it's okay to perform in an extreme way, in a creative way or in a way that no one has seen before. I think of Missy [Elliott] and how she's fearless. She is fearless with it. She's so secure in who she is or at least she presents that way. Growing up watching her, I was like—oh, okay, this is a way to move in the world. Just extra bold. And then, Jay-Z is my number one emcee until the day I die. His calmness also taught me a lot—that you can be really serious and you can also have fun. It's okay to do both. I used to think I had to decide one way to be. But I've come to understand that you can be intense, but you can also still have fun. You also don't have to be perfect. You have to be excellent, but you don't have to be perfect. Hip-hop really reminds me of that lesson and taught me confidence.

Hip-hop–rich spaces also taught me when someone else is on stage and they do something really well, to applaud them. To have a generous attitude. In hip-hop "behaving properly" when I'm not the one on stage means giving the other performer the claps and response they need to feel good. Because as a performer, you feed off of that. When you're on stage, the audience reaction gives you life. So when you sit in the audience, you try to give that energy to other performers. Don't hold it back, don't save it for later. And that applies to regular life. If anyone in your life does something well or someone's having a really hard time, you show them real, vocal support. In an open mic, if a poet stumbles on their words, it's the audience that claps back up their confidence and gets them to start again. We've got to be that for our friends—being able to really embody support for people.

*What beliefs about yourself do you get from hip-hop?*
That all you've got to do is be really dope at whatever you do. Ain't no half-stepping. I'm not from New York City. I'm from a tiny rural town in Louisiana and then Virginia Beach. I don't have all of the typical experiences

you think of when you think of hip-hop. But when people talk about hip-hop authenticity or keeping it real, there is this expectation to always tell the truth. As long as you are telling the truth, with honor and with excellence, then that is hip-hop. I don't have to have *their* experience, I have to tell the truth about mine. It's all right to have some contradictions in your life. Hip-hop shows us that too. Hip-hop changes all the time—life changes all the time. I've learned from hip-hop to be okay when things in your life change. Believing and knowing that there is possibility is something I got from hip-hop.

*What is professional success to you?*
As a spoken word artist, professional success has been getting invited and paid to do what I love to do. I'm not constantly hustling for gigs or to make a name for myself anymore. And I think that's a very real form of validation. In spaces where I used to have to prove myself to be given a chance, I don't have to do that anymore. Being invited to go overseas to perform is a big deal. Being invited to come work with people's students or to keynote at conferences, that's a compliment to me and it's a manifestation of success. I'm successful because intermediary people trust me with their students. They vouch for me and that's a big deal for somebody to say, my students need this type of growth so let's bring in Crystal. I don't take it lightly. Another form of success has been more traditional—getting tenured and promoted doing exactly this type of work is a big deal. I don't feel as if I've compromised myself. I did what I loved and the academy came along. And I hope that my example just widens it for other scholars. I've added value to every space and every role I have been asked to fill and that is success to me.

*Take a moment to do some trash-talking. Tell me about your greatest accomplishments.*
Bringing spoken word poetry and girls from so many different communities to the United Nations. For years, I was a little nomad going to all these global communities working with girls through spoken word poetry. And now I'm the bridge. I'm bringing these girls' voices into this space because they matter and they're important and because I'm in a position to do so. The local New York City girls are literally memorizing the words of girls from across the globe and performing their stories in spoken word form. We've got hip-hop and spoken word poetry in the headquarters of the UN for two hours being performed by girls. And we have this spaced filled up unapologetically with girls—with all their little hormones and energy. Middle school, high school, college young women, they're all brought together to listen to each other's experiences and connect to their political power. To build these relationships with different communities of girls and to make

real impressions in their lives, to create one more opportunity for them to know and feel love, that's what it's all about.

*What about challenges? Have there been any challenges in embracing a hip-hop mindset or just being authentic?*
When I first proposed a spoken word class at my college, they were like, "Oh, is hip-hop still like a thing?" I get that a lot. I also get the questions about how I fit into any part of hip-hop culture because of the way that I look. I have to remember that it's natural for people who don't understand how culture works to be confused and project their discomfort onto me. And anything dealing with youth, girls of color, or the disenfranchised is automatically suspect in academia. And honestly, they should be suspicious. Authentic hip-hop culture is here to change the institution, not to remain static. So I better be my absolute best. I would never try to be slack or offer up something corny because I already have to deal with so much doubt about hip-hop in general. I can't prove them right. On a job I interviewed for before my current position, they looked at my scholarship and someone actually called it "flirty." I'm like, are we still talking about scholarship? I'm confused. These are publications—this is academic. What are you talking about, "flirty"? So the sometimes blatant lack of respect—that's definitely a challenge.

*What's one word that best describes hip-hop culture?*
Innovative.

*What's your stage song?*
Missy Elliott, "Lose Control," because of the energy that it has. It's a hype song. It's energetic. Missy is courageous to me. To her it's probably nothing, a regular day, but to me, I love it. It's something different. She pushes boundaries. It's creative, but it's also fun.

*Last question. Can you dance?*
I mean, not like a break dancer, but yeah, I can dance. We're taught to value and make a hierarchy—mind, body, spirit. But the more comfortable, alive, and in touch you are with your body, the happier you are. I was recently looking at a picture of me and Tony [Keith] from when we were in South Africa. It was the first night of our trip and we all went out to some club, a little hole in the wall. We danced so hard, in the picture we were dripping sweat, still dressed in our clothes from the plane. The lights were on full blast. It's not dark. They weren't trying to set a mood. My hair was so frizzy. And there we were—sweaty from dancing hard and just grinning at each other. Happy. And I'm like, that's free. That's the kind of liberation you're talking about in this project. Right? It's a form of healing.

## CHAPTER 7

# Air-Walking
## Concluding Thoughts

*Air-walking* relates to the magical way that hip-hop dancers seem to glide in the air—how they push the boundaries of what seems possible for the body to do.

Several years ago, Strife.TV filmed a segment on hip-hop and higher education at the College of William & Mary.[1] The focus was on the culture of break dancing and the values that it embodies. The students that were interviewed were B-boys and B-girls of all races and represented various academic disciplines. They were not art students. But these students perfectly articulated how the culture and community of hip-hop cultivated life and professional skills that they felt would propel them beyond the dance floor.

> Breaking gives you that extra free style creativity. You can think freely and come up with your own method of doing things. (Tigist, Biology and mathematics major).
> B-boying embodied three main traits that I'd really, really like to live my life by: hard work, determination, and just plain having guts. When you're out in the cypher you express all of these things in one dance. (Matthew, Physics major).
> Back in high school, you know, it was kind of just, you know, do my homework, get things done, but coming into college it's very different. Like believing in myself—definitely a different mindset, I guess. I can't go into a cypher just being like, I guess I can do this; I have to really believe in myself or it won't show through my dance. (Alice, Accounting major)[2]

There are so many gems in these interviews. What we should be wrestling with in the field of education is how we can create these types of environments in classrooms within schools and on college campuses where all students work hard, are determined, and have the guts to at least try their hand at being a scholar. Tigist was a math major and Matthew was a physics major—most folx wouldn't expect students who deeply love hard science to kill it on a dance floor. These students illustrate to us that hip-hop has something to give everyone. They also personify the idea of not limiting yourself. Yes, even a chemist has something to contribute to a hip-hop community. There is an incredible culture of belonging despite individual differences. While I understand the belief that rules, regulations, and standards might help to ensure that all students learn, in the professional development sessions that I have facilitated for P–12 teachers, it seems that no one hates and feels jailed by standards more than teachers themselves. Even teachers don't like what and how they are being made to teach. So why shouldn't students mentally check out?

We need schools to be safe and free of chaos, so there will always be a need for institutional rules and regulations. But perhaps there needs to be some relaxing of the ropes the closer that you get to the classroom. A horse can't trot if you are choking him with the reins. More than rules, there is a culture that guides and regulates a hip-hop cypher. If you are bringing something different, something no one has ever seen, you must have the confidence to jump in and show them something new. Youth who are involved in hip-hop show us what it means to not be intimidated, to put yourself out there. I have so much excitement about the type of scientists those students at William & Mary will become as a result of half of their heart belonging to hip-hop. How will they creatively change the spirit of their professional production? How might it give them the guts to resist conforming and to instead innovate and blaze trails—to not just be successful in their careers, but to "kill it." As educators, we should ask ourselves this question: Are you willing to get on the dance floor and show them what you've got?

Professor Ruth Nicole Brown sponsors a national tour through her organization, SOLHOT (Saving Our Lives, Hearing Our Truths) called Black Girl Genius Week, which is a programmatic outcome of her research and scholarship on Black girls (https://www.solhot.com/). In each city, Brown always includes a dancehall, a space for the girls and educators participating in the conference to just let loose and dance. Why? Because dancing is a function of joy and all people need joy in their lives. Often, teachers, administrators, counselors, and parents have become far removed from the young person that they used to be, the young boy practicing dance moves for the next party or the young girl trying to learn the latest line dance with her friends. Many of us used to love dancing, but have gone so far into adulthood, responsibility, titles, and professional respectability that we have forgotten how to dance. This is why I ended each interview in this book with the question, "Can you dance?" Remembering how to dance is a metaphor for remembering the core of who you are, remembering to have fun, remembering the importance of joy, and remembering to let go and take risks. There is nothing more intimidating than facing your turn in a soul train line. Remembering how to dance is synonymous with remembering to just jump in and try. It is also a form of freedom.

Tanisha "Wakumi" Douglas, a community-based leader of the S.O.U.L Sisters Leadership Collective in Florida, shared her personal story in Monique Morris's book *Sing a Rhythm, Dance a Blues*. She reflected on the role of dance in her own life to underscore how and why she uses it in her educational work with youth:

Freedom. That's the word that comes up for me when I think about dance—a space to just let go. This English isn't even our people's soul spirit language. It's language that was imposed on us, and there are so many ways in which it's so rigid. . . . We create spaces where people can just be free. One example with the Black Girls Matter work that's happening in Miami—the young people were really clear that yes, they want to organize, and yes, they want political wins, yes they want to change things that are going on with the schools, but they also just want to have fun and be free—and that's also radical and revolutionary for them.[3]

I bring dance into the conversation both physically and philosophically. One of my earliest memories of hip-hop was when my P.E. teacher in elementary school turned on "Planet Rock" by Afrika Bambaataa & The Soulsonic Force and instructed us to just dance. That is probably the only class session that I remember from elementary school some 40 years later. So yes, undoubtedly, making educational spaces more movement-friendly can do a lot to establish cultures of welcome, community, release, expression, and participation. If we can physically let loose, we might intellectually show out.

I also approach dance philosophically as an ethic or approach to life. My life's theme song (not to be confused with my hype-me-up stage song) is Michael Jackson's "Off the Wall." I love this song because it carries so much wisdom and inspiration regarding how to approach life. I am an introvert and very shy person, who for many years was intimidated by dance cyphers and soul train lines. Folx who know me now would never guess that I didn't dance at parties. My cornball claim to fame is that I have literally won "Thriller" dance contests at nightclubs across the country. But back in the day, I hated for all eyes to be on me on the dance floor; yet I loved to dance. At home, I was that child who watched all of the music videos and knew all of the dance routines. I perfected every dance—the wop, the prep, the running man, the Alf, the Steve Martin; I had them all down. But at parties, my shyness kept me on the wall watching. I watched others sweat, watched others laugh, and watched others let loose. I don't remember what exactly made me just get off the wall and start dancing. But at some point, I did. The intense pull of the dance floor won out over my personal insecurities and I made up my mind that I would always just get out there and dance. To this day, if I enter a party I will walk straight to the dance floor as a way to beat those personal insecurities before they start to creep up.

Because I know the experience of standing on the wall, I have a much more critical read of the whole party experience. Everyone at the party has a good time—enjoying the music, being in the scene. But there is a difference in the experiences of those who stand on the wall watching and those who jump on the floor and dance. When I finally got on the floor to dance, I wasn't just watching the party—I *was* the party. I felt connected and alive. I was experiencing it, not just observing or hearing about it. Even if I'm out dancing all by myself, I am fully experiencing that moment with my jam. And I realized that you leave the party with a completely different attitude. Those on the wall are still composed, still put together, smiling, and happy (the wall isn't a bad experience). But those who get out on the floor and dance—they leave the party exhilarated, talking loud, wet with sweat, and filled with memories. They created their good time and they are pumped by the work that they put in. Having clearly experienced the two different approaches, I vowed to live my life "off the wall." I don't want to sit on a couch watching other people's lives on TV. I don't want to watch other people be bold and daring and shine at work, while I sit waiting for someone to give me permission. I don't want to stand in place, leaning on the walls of my limited immediate surroundings. I want to travel and see the world. I don't want to observe life, I want to participate in it. I want to live it off the wall. And this is what I am suggesting about our approach to our professional life. Dance. Get off the wall and let loose, be free, and move in new, life-giving ways.

It also needs to be said: Give yourself permission to just relax. Life is serious. Our society is no joke. Our world is in severe need. But I have had no problems having fun while helping the world. Why do "service" and "social justice" have to feel so incredibly heavy? Oppression is heavy. Liberation should feel like love. Light. I'll put it this way, even Tupac made party songs. Tupac Shakur's lyrics will do everything from making you think deeply, opening your eyes politically, and hyping you up socially. Some of his lyrics might even incite a riot (if you blast "Hit'em Up" to just the right volume and you're in just the right mood, it might actually make you want to hit somebody up); but nothing is more memorable than Tupac's smile. He was a great talent, but he was also a full, flawed human being. He showed us all sides of himself—anger, lust, love, and fun. He was thoughtful, critical, political, sexist, aggressive, ignorant, funny, silly, excited, ambitious, confident, the list could go on. He was someone who could party hard at a club on Friday and then speak at an activist rally on Saturday. And his fans wouldn't view those two engagements as hypocritical. Those two very different sides of himself weren't in conflict. They were allowed to coexist. We need to free ourselves professionally from showing up as titles and positions and allow ourselves to show up as whole humans. One of the most critical professional development challenges within the field of education is to effectively close the distance between who an educator thinks they are and who they actually are in order to make their practice more genuine and authentic.

While this discussion on the benefits of being free has primarily focused on body movement, it is important to acknowledge the role of mental freedom. The benefits of cultural freedom can be reaped in two directions. If you take that physical step to move differently, then that movement frees your mind and opens new possibilities. Conversely, if you first shift your mindset to embrace new ways of being and doing, then you will be more willing to get up and move differently. The group Funkadelic's title to their 1970 classic album says it all: *Free Your Mind . . . and Your Ass will Follow*. This makes the point plainly and clearly—change your mindset and you will change your movements, your actions. Every movement your body makes is directed by your mind. Your brain tells your hand to scratch, your legs to walk, and your eyes to open. Once we change the way that we think about ourselves, our students, our abilities, our purpose, and our expectations regarding how work should look and feel for all involved, only then can we take the action to actually transform things. Only then can we create spaces of true power within education. What do I mean by spaces of power? Research into the educational benefits of hip-hop–based cultural spaces have shown them to be (1) spaces of self-created belonging; (2) spaces that give students permission to use their voices as tools of advocacy, action, or as allies; (3) spaces for students to sit with words, experiences, or ideas that make them uncomfortable; (4) spaces for students to sit with words, experiences, or ideas that they absolutely understand; (5) spaces for students to be experts of their own experience; and (6) spaces for educators to be human and to commune with students.[4] The idea of creating "something out of nothing" is a powerful mindset to adopt, and necessary in the realm of educational transformation. In the same way that Black folx turned leftover mess and scraps of food into soul food, we need to transform the mess and scraps within education into spaces of love, life, and power. There is a sort of magical mindset that you need to do this. I think people are being real when they use phrases like "Black girl magic." When you look across all historically oppressed people—African, Indigenous, Latinx, Asian, Jewish, impoverished people, women, etc.—and you truly grasp what they have endured, how they have prevailed, and where they are now, it does look like magic. Hip-hop is proof that the culture and the people that created it are indeed talented, exceptional, and brilliant—we simply need a healthy space to shine.

As educators, we often teach students that, to be great, they need school. It is actually the other way around. For educators to be great, we need to better understand students and their cultures. We have much to gain from sitting at the feet of our students' cultures. Black culture has been providing space for Black boys and girls to shine for decades. Traditionally minoritized communities already clearly understand how to survive in a racist world. They understand how to tap their brains to create, innovate, and develop things that the world will devour. In my personal life, I often share that although I was exceptional at math in school, no math teacher can touch my father who taught me the ability to make ragged ends meet. When you can make a $40,000 total household income fill every need of a family of four, and come out of that experience with a home that you own, perfect credit, a savings account, and two highly educated children, you have skills.

Folx just need a healthy platform to demonstrate those skills and someone willing to hand them the mic.

The academic field is indeed a performance. I have a 9-year old son who is incredibly shy and often chooses not to speak, which means teachers aren't able to accurately evaluate him. So my focus has not only been on teaching him academic content, but also massaging his confidence to perform—to, as I tell him, "Show them what you've got." That is at the core of every standardized test, every class assignment, every school competition. Show them what you've got, or they will think you don't have anything to offer. Because of those power differentials mentioned earlier where academic standards are set by those in power (which often lean toward White, wealthy norms), minoritized students (or professionals) who don't speak, write, test, and think the way the power structure expects are seen as having nothing to offer. We could have a genius sitting in our class and never know it because we don't give them a culturally respectful and meaningful platform to display their genius.

I often wonder, what did DJ Kool Herc's teacher at the Alfred E. Smith Career and Technical Education High School in the Bronx think of him? This is a vocational school that offers automotive, home construction, plumbing, and heating/air conditioning programs. It was originally built as the Bronx Continuation School for students who left the school system and became a vocational school by the time that Herc attended. The focus of the school on trade skills affirms that many of the students enrolled there weren't "performing" in traditional schools, so they were tracked into vocational programs. I'm just assuming here, but I'm probably right. So here we have a kid being prepared to become an HVAC or plumbing professional, to whom we can now trace responsibility for creating a global culture. Starting in 1971, Herc and his sister began hosting annual back-to-school parties in the rec room of their apartment building to make money to buy school clothes. He was a 16-year-old high school student. It was at one of these back-to-school parties that Herc developed the DJing style of extending "the break" or instrumental beat so that people could dance longer and he could freestyle rap over the beat while they were dancing. This became the blueprint for hip-hop music. In the introduction to Jeff Chang's book on the history of hip-hop, *Can't Stop Won't Stop: A History of the Hip-Hop Generation*, DJ Kool Herc wrote this about hip-hop:

> When I started DJing back in the early 70s, it was just something that we were doing for fun. I came from "the people's choice," from the street. If the people like you, they will support you and your work will speak for itself. . . . To me, hip-hop says, "Come as you are". . . . People talk about the four hip hop elements: DJing, B-boying, MCing, and graffiti. I think that there are far more than those: the way you walk, the way you talk, the way you look, the way you communicate.[5]

When he talks about "the people's choice," this reiterates the point that I am making about performance. Who "the people" are will determine how your performance is evaluated. To his community in the Bronx this kid was outstanding, something special. To his school system, probably not so much. And he wasn't the only one. Jay-Z, Biggie, Busta Rhymes, and DMX all attended the George Westinghouse Career and Technical School in Brooklyn. Like Herc's Bronx school, George Westinghouse (https://westinghousehs .org/) started as a continuation school for students who were no longer enrolled to come back to school and complete their education. The school now explicitly has in its mission a "focus on students' academic, social and emotional health and growth." It continues to serve as a career-prep school offering industry-based training and certifications. Four of the biggest names in hip-hop attended this school. I'm not sure what happened in their classes, but I can imagine the lunchroom rap battles were something crazy.

Students can indeed perform well. They are simply struggling to perform in your theatre (school or classroom). They aren't catching your beat (instructional strategy). They are standing on the wall ready to leave your dance. But in their neighborhood, that same kid might be seen as the modern-day hip-hop king. We can learn a lot from the communities that we teach if we would allow them to speak freely and to fully be themselves. We have so much to absorb if we, as educators, allow ourselves to listen, watch, and learn. If a classroom could be filled with the magic and energy of those parks in New York where cyphers were born in the 1980s, imagine what might be the next great thing young people develop. What's more, imagine how professionals might perform if we wore more comfortable clothes (in other words, used more flexible practices and created more open environments).

Ian's and Timothy's stories about their greatest professional successes resonated with me because the moments that they shared were also meaningful to them—not just their students. They participated and had fun, developed, and gained confidence as artists. Often, in education, there is pressure to act as if the students are the only ones who matter. "Oh, I'm just working for the kids." But I think educators need to understand that they need to be fed too. Otherwise, we are walking models of why not to further your education. If the educators in a students' school went to college, worked hard, and earned degrees in careers they chose, and then got jobs in which they now seem miserable or uninspired, how is that inspirational? Why would a young person be motivated to do that? I truly believe that my educational initiatives are successful because they also give me life. I have fun. I enjoy them. I want to be there too. I find points of connectivity between my cultural experience and my students' cultural experiences, and I create community within that overlap. The result is transformational for all of us. The reality is when you serve people food that you don't eat, you really aren't as invested in how good it tastes. But when everyone's favorite dish is the macaroni and cheese, including the chef, you better believe it will be delicious. You must also be personally invested.

DJ Kool Herc's point about there being many more elements of hip-hop beyond the standard five is critical to the foundation of this book. This book is centered on those who aren't artists—those who do not DJ, emcee, dance, tag, or write lyrics, but who are still quintessentially hip-hop in how they show up in the world. This includes both students and the educators who teach them. It is also about helping others outside of the culture to more deeply understand it and potentially find a point of connection. Some professionals who read this book might wrestle with what to do with it, particularly if they aren't into hip-hop. During our interview, Edmund Adjapong and I had a meaningful side conversation about this very issue. He commented, "I think my biggest trouble as a teacher educator is trying to figure out, how do we get more teachers to use hip-hop? But then I struggle with authenticity. I don't want you doing hip-hop if you're not authentic—if you're not willing to try to really understand the culture. I struggle with people using it as a tool. I think there needs to be a lot of deep self-awareness, self-reflection, identity work before you can engage in this culture. I know some scholars who are dope, but then we have a conversation and they can't even say the word Black. So even if you have your own personal connection to hip-hop culture, there's also connection that's required with these communities." Edmund's statement is poignant because it is not cool to love hip-hop and hate the communities of people that created it. My attempt in this text was to contribute to the body of scholarship that pushes professionals to wrestle with these issues—better understanding and appreciating the culture, connecting more deeply, valuing the youth communities that created it, and determining points of congruence and connection. This pulls me back to the story about Tony Keith's visit to Tanzania. Many of the readers of this book may not identify with hip-hop culture. Many of the practices shared might not feel comfortable for everyone to adopt. But are there a few elements of the mindset that inspire you? Can you re-examine your levels of creativity in your work? Can you reflect on your approach as a professional—how you command attention or claim space in your professional environments? We began the discussion by asking, how hungry are you? If the hip-hop mindset pushes you to elevate your goals and your confidence in your ability to achieve them, that is an authentic benefit that you derived from hip-hop culture. All of hip-hop isn't for everyone, but I do believe that we can all learn important insights from the culture. If you are an ambitious person, there is no way that you can come away from this book not bobbing your head just a little bit to the hip-hop mindset.

We need to put the stakes explicitly out there. Our world needs professionals willing to turn the tables, challenge the needles, and extend the break. When you extend the break, you are essentially taking the best part of the song and giving the audience more of it. We need professionals who can take the best of themselves and give the world more of that. When we look at many of the hip-hop icons discussed in this book, they *believed* they had something to give—even if their schools or society were telling them differently. As Timothy David Jones so brilliantly put it, "Hip-hop taught me that I could believe my own words." Hip-hop youth have taught us that if we dare to try, if we dare to attempt the outlandish or impossible, we can indeed change the world. A professional approach rooted in a hip-hop mindset provides professionals a freedom of sorts: the permission to be imaginative and creative, the agency to not ask for permission at every turn, a strong sense of cultural self-value, and a competitive spirit that makes even the teacher want to shine.

I depart this project full of joy. You know that a phenomenon is powerful when even researching it is fun, inspiring, and joyful. These conversations have helped to paint a full portrait of hip-hop that is vibrant and insightful. We can now see and understand that there are concrete skills that are developed through the hip-hop mindset, like being creative, clear, and accurate in the work we produce. Hip-hop also enhances one's presentation and performativity in really important ways. Posture matters. All educators from administrators to teachers perform and present (when we instruct, when we lead meetings, when we speak publicly). Hip-hop teaches us to command attention and claim our space. It molds how we move, speak, and captivate through our words and actions. Hip-hop drives the commitment to search and discover (what we call research). It underscores the value of putting in time to dig through crates for that undiscovered gem (read, learn, knowing the archives) and engage with peer communities of practice (cyphers and squads) who push us to be better. Approach is about remixing, innovating, or reimagining our practice. Originality. Authenticity. It is about mining our students' culture for the gold that you know is present there. Finally, hip-hop teaches us to have drive—to seek to not only show up at work, but to show out. It was this fundamental ethic of excellence, hunger, and ambition to be the best that made me first fall in love with hip-hop. But one of the absolute nuggets of wisdom that came out of this project was clearly seeing how hip-hop minds see, speak, and live their goals as if they are happening now. Whatever you wish for your school, your classroom, your department, your institution, you must live your experience there "as if" it is already the school of your dreams. As the group Outkast reminds us, opportunity is rarely handed to the marginalized. We must bake and make our own piece of the pie. I don't personally care for apple pie, but I will put my foot in some lemon meringue. That is most definitely a hip-hop mindset: remixing the American dream. Do you, and stop waiting for your plate to be served.

Ultimately, what we learn from this deep exploration of hip-hop culture (the music, documentaries, scholarship, student and educator voices) is that our students don't need to be saved. The marginalized are actually magical and have much to contribute. Embracing *their* powerful mindsets by becoming more free, flexible, dynamic, and authentic just might elevate our own expectations. It might propel us to reach beyond simply meeting standards set by the unimaginative, and instead dream, believe, grind, and create careers that allow us to walk on air.

# Glossary

**Cypher:** A group of artists or performers (rappers, beatboxers, break dancers, poets) typically gathered in a circle and engaged in an extemporaneous performance. Artists in the circle often take turns performing in the middle. Spectators are also a critical part of the circle as their attention, reaction, and support helps to maintain the energy and sense of community.

**Dope:** Very good

**Down:** Included or a part of; knowledgeable; in agreement

**Fly:** Stylish

**Folx:** Respelling of the word folks; the "x" is used to signal the inclusion of groups that are often marginalized.

**Fresh:** Fashionable, cool, interesting, different

**GOAT:** Abbreviation for "Greatest of All Time"

**Kill it:** To do something extremely well; amazing or perfect performance

**Mic:** Abbreviated term for microphone

**Ratchet:** Unrestricted, free, uninhibited

**Show out:** Do your best; be seen and make a lasting impression

**Slay:** Impress, succeed, or do something amazing

# Notes

## Chapter 1

1. Isabel Wilkerson, *Caste: The Origins of Our Discontents* (New York, NY: Random House, 2020); Ibram X. Kendi, *Stamped from the Beginning* (New York, NY: Avalon Publishing Group, 2016).

2. Toby S. Jenkins, "What Would Brother Malcolm do? Police & Race in America," Huffington Post, 2016, http://www.huffingtonpost.com/entry/what-would -brother-malcolm-do_us_57803625e4b0f06648f4d1ff; M. E. Johnson, "The paradox of black patriotism: double consciousness," *Ethnic and Racial Studies* 41, no. 11 (2018): 1971–1989, doi: 10.1080/01419870.2017.1332378; A. Alleyne, "Book Banning, Curriculum Restrictions, and the Politicization of U.S. Schools," Center for American Progress, report published Sept 19, 2022, https://www.americanprogress .org/article/book-banning-curriculum-restrictions-and-the-politicization-of-u-s -schools/; Toby Jenkins, "Patriotism: A Love Story," *Journal of Black Masculinities* 1, no. 1, 12–21.

3. Adrian Leftwich, *What is Politics? The Activity and Its Study* (United Kingdom: Polity Press, 2004); Toby Jenkins, "De (Re) Constructing Ideas of Genius: Hip Hop, Knowledge, and Intelligence," *The International Journal of Critical Pedagogy* 4, no. 3 (2013a): 11–23.

4. Tara Yosso, "Whose Culture Has Capital? A Critical Race Theory Discussion of Community Cultural Wealth," *Race Ethnicity and Education* 8, no. 1 (2005): 69–91, https://doi.org/10.1080/1361332052000341006; Toby S. Jenkins, *"Imagination, Power and Brilliance: Hip-hop as a Politic of Educational Survival,"* E. Adjapong & I. Levy (Eds.); *HipHopEd: The Compilation on Hip-Hop Education* (Vol. 2, *Hip-Hop as Praxis & Social Justice*, pp. 87–102) (Peter Lang, 2020); Toby S. Jenkins, *My Culture, My Color, My Self: Heritage, Resilience, and Community In the Lives of Young Adults,* (Philadelphia, PA: Temple University Press, 2013b).

5. Paulo Freire, *Pedagogy of the Oppressed* (New York, NY: The Continuum International Publishing Group, Inc., 2008).

6. Patricia Thandi Hicks Harper, "Understanding Youth Popular Culture and the Hip-Hop Influence," *SIECUS Report* 28, no. 5 (2000): 21.

7. TEDx Talks. (2013, May 14). The cipher, the circle, and its wisdom: Toni Blackman at TedXUMassAmherst. [Video]. YouTube. https://www.youtube.com/watch ?v=WYdb5snA1Jc

8. Sam Seidel, *Hip Hop Genius: Remixing High School Education* (New York: R&L Education, 2011).

9. Christopher Emdin, "Pursuing the Pedagogical Potential of the Pillars of Hip-hop through Sciencemindedness," *International Journal of Critical Pedagogy* 4, no. 3 (2013): 85.

10. Emery Petchauer, "Framing and Reviewing Hip-Hop Educational Research," *Review of Educational Research* 79 (2009): 946, https://doi.org/10.3102 /0034654308330967

11. Tricia Rose, *Black Noise: Rap Music and Black Culture in Contemporary America* (Hanover, NH: University Press of New England, 1994).

12. Sean McCollom, Hip-Hop: A Culture of Vision and Voice, Kennedy Center Website, 2019. https://www.kennedy-center.org/education/resources-for-educators /classroom-resources/media-and-interactives/media/hip-hop/hip-hop-a-culture-of -vision-and-voice/

13. Gloria Boutte and Nathaniel Bryan, "When Will Black Children Be Well: Interrupting Anti-Black Violence in Early Childhood Classrooms and Schools," *Contemporary Issues in Early Childhood Education* 22, no. 3 (2019): 232–243.

14. Jazelle Hunt, "Symbols Are Important to Black America," NNPA: Washington, DC, 2015.

15. Toby Jenkins, "A Beautiful Mind: Black Male Intellectual Identity in Hip-Hop Culture," *Journal of Black Studies* 42, no. 8 (2011): 1231–1251, https://doi.org /10.1177/0021934711405050; Crystal Glover, Toby Jenkins, Stephanie Troutman, *The Invisible Backpack: Narratives of Family, Cultural Gifts and Community Assets on the Academic Journey* (MD: Lexington Books/Rowman & Littlefield, 2018).

16. Yosso, "Whose Culture"; Norma González, Luis Moll, and Cathy Amanti, *Funds of Knowledge: Theorizing Practices in Households, Communities, and Classrooms* (New Jersey: Lawrence Erlbaum Associates Publishers, 2005).

17. Joshua J. Mark, The Great Pyramid of Giza, *World History Encyclopedia*, December 19, 2016, https://www.worldhistory.org/Great_Pyramid_of_Giza

**Chapter 2**

1. Mathers, M., Bass, J., & Resto, L. (2002). *Lose yourself in 8 Mile: Music from and inspired by the motion picture*. Shady/Aftermath/Interscope.

2. Jay-Z, *Decoded* (New York, NY: Random House, 2010).

3. Jay-Z, *Decoded*, 75.

4. Miriam Pawel, *The Crusades of Cesar Chavez: A Biography* (London, UK: Bloomsbury Press, 2015).

5. Victoria Moorwood, "Kanye West breaks record as producer with most hip hop No.1 hits," Revolt TV, https://www.billboard.com/artist/kanye-west/chart -history/hsi/, October 20, 2021; J. Valdez, "'Not for sale': Kanye West claims his music catalog was put up without his knowledge," *Los Angeles Times*, 2022, https:// www.latimes.com/entertainment-arts/story/2022-09-20/not-for-sale-kanye-west -claims-his-music-catalog-was-put-up-without-his-knowledge

6. Jay-Z, *Decoded*, 9.

7. Michael Warren, Erin Gamble, Eli Holzman, Jay-Z, and Meek Mill, *Free Meek* (New York, NY: Roc Nation & The Intellectual Property Corporation, 2019).

8. Warren, Gamble, Holzman, Jay-Z, and Meek Mill, *Free Meek*.

9. Norbert Juma, "85 Biggie Smalls Quotes and Lyrics about Life and Death," accessed December 11, 2020, https://everydaypower.com/biggie-smalls-quotes-and -lyrics/

10. Alexa Epitropoulos and ASCD, "10 Signs of a Toxic School Culture," *ACSD Education Update* 6, no. 9 (2019); *Education World*, "Is Your School's Culture Toxic or Positive?," n.d., https://www.educationworld.com/a_admin/admin/admin275.shtml

11. Grace Chen, "10 Major Challenges Facing Public Schools," *Public School Review*, November 5, 2020 (updated 5/18/22), https://www.publicschoolreview.com/blog/10-major-challenges-facing-public-schools

12. Jay-Z, *Decoded*, p. 86

13. Andre M. Perry, *Know Your Price: Valuing Black Lives and Property in America's Black Cities* (Washington, D.C.: Brookings Institution Press, 2020).

14. Perry, *Know Your Price*, 38.

15. Perry, *Know Your Price*, 39.

16. Quoted in Sam Dunn, Scot McFadyn, and Darby Wheeler, *Hip-Hop Evolution* S3, E3, 12:41, 2019 (Toronto, Canada: Banger Films).

17. Lauren Lazin, Paramount Pictures Corporation, and Amaru Entertainment, *Tupac: Resurrection* (Hollywood, CA: Paramount, 2003).

18. Nancy Yuen, *Reel Inequality: Hollywood Actors and Racism* (New Brunswick, New Jersey, London: Rutgers University Press, 2017).

19. Karen Attiah, "America Hates to Let Black Women Speak," *Washington Post Online*, October 8, 2020, https://www.washingtonpost.com/opinions/2020/10/08/america-hates-let-black-women-speak/; Jacqueline Koonce, "Oh, Those Loud Black Girls!: A Phenomenological Study of Black Girls Talking with an Attitude," *Journal of Language and Literacy Education* 8, no. 2 (2012): 26–46; Venus Evans-Winters, Billye M. Waters, and Bettina Love (eds.), *Twenty Years of "Miseducation" and Black Girlhood: The Lauryn Hill Reader* (New York, NY: Peter Lang, 2018); Venus Evans-Winters and Bettina Love (Eds.), *Black Feminism in Education: Black Women Speak Back, Up, and Out.* (New York, NY: Peter Lang, 2015); Morris, Monique, *Pushout: The Criminalization of Black Girls in Schools* (New York, NY: The New Press, 2016); Monique Morris, *Race, Gender and the School to Prison Pipeline: Expanding our Discussion to Include Black Girls* (Quincy, MA: Schott Foundation for Public Education, 2012); Monique Morris, *Sing a Rhythm, Dance a Blues: Education for the Liberation of Black and Brown Girls* (New York, NY: The New Press, 2019).

20. Henry Giroux, "Racial Justice and Disposable Youth in the Age of Zero Tolerance," *International Journal of Qualitative Studies in Education* 16, no. 4 (2003): xvii.

21. Monique Morris, *Pushout: The Criminalization of Black Girls in Schools* (New York, NY: The New Press, 2016); https://pushoutfilm.com/

22. Patricia Williams, "Spirit-Murdering the Messenger: The Discourse of Fingerpointing as the Law's Response to Racism," *University of Miami Law Review* 42 (1987): 127.

23. Shaun Harper and Walter Kimbrough, "Staffing Practices, Professional Preparation Trends, and Demographics among Student Affairs Administrators at HBCUs: Implications from a National Study," *NASPA Journal* 8, no. 1 (2005): 8–25.

24. Erin Blakemore, "The Woman Who Schooled the Civil Rights Movement," *Time Magazine Online*, February 16, 2016, https://time.com/4213751/septima-clark-civil-rights-movement/

25. Blakemore, "The Woman."

26. Mia Reddy, "Can I get a Window Seat? Erykah Badu as a Site of Expression, Resistance, and Erotic Power," *Words, Beats & Life: The Global Journal of Hip-Hop Culture 5*, no. 1, 14–23.

27. Reddy, *Can I*, 17.

28. Reddy, *Can I*, 17.

29. Nick Levine, "Why Lizzo Was the Star Who Defined 2019," *BBC Culture*, December 27, 2019, accessed December 1, 2020, https://www.bbc.com/culture/article/20191218-why-lizzo-was-the-star-who-defined 2019

30. Levine, "Why Lizzo."

31. T. A. Hoppe, A. Litovitz, K. A. Willis, R. A. Meseroll, M. J. Perkins, Hutchins, B. I., . . . & Santangelo, G. M. (2019), "Topic choice contributes to the lower rate of NIH awards to African-American/black scientists," *Science Advances 5*, no. 10.

32. Love, Bettina L. *Hip Hop's Li'l Sistas Speak: Negotiating Hip Hop Identities and Politics in the New South* (New York, NY: Peter Lang, 2012), 30.

33. Love, Bettina L., "Complex Personhood of Hip Hop & the Sensibilities of the Culture that Fosters Knowledge of Self & Self-Determination," *Equity & Excellence in Education* 49, no. 4 (2016a): 414–427; Love, Bettina L., "Good Kids, Mad Cities: Kendrick Lamar and Finding Inner Resistance in Response to Ferguson USA," *Cultural Studies—Critical Methodologies* 16, no. 3 (2016b): 320–323. https://doi.org/10.1177/1532708616634837

34. Love, Bettina L. *Hip Hop's Li'l Sistas*.

35. WE 102.9, "Nicki Minaj is One of the Highest Selling Artists Ever," https://www.wehiphop.com/nicki-minaj-is-one-of-the-highest-selling-artists-ever/?doing_wp_cron=1608521932.8611040115356445312500

36. Elaine Richardson, "Developing Critical Hip Hop Feminist Literacies: Centrality and Subversion of Sexuality in the Lives of Black Girls," *Equity & Excellence in Education* 46, no. 3 (2013): 327–341; Tamura Lomax, "In Search of Our Daughters' Gardens: Hip Hop as Womanist Prose," *Bulletin for the Study of Religion* 40, no. 3 (2011): 15–20, https://doi.org/10.1558/bsor.v40i3.004; Patricia Hill-Collins, *Black Sexual Politics: African Americans, Gender, and the New Racism* (New York, NY: Routledge, 2004); Aisha Durham, "Check on it:" Beyoncé, Southern Booty, and Black Femininities in Music Video," *Feminist Media Studies* 12, no. 1 (2012): 35–49, https://doi.org/10.1080/14680777.2011.558346; Gwendolyn Pough, "What it do, Shorty?: Women, Hip-Hop, and a Feminist Agenda," *Black Women, Gender, and Families* vol 1, issue 2, pp. 78–99; Tracey Sharpley-Whiting, *Pimps Up, Ho's Down: Hip Hop's Hold on Young Black Women* (New York, NY: New York University Press, 2007); Adilia James, "The Black Girl Body as Site of Sexual Terrorism" in *Wish to Live: The Hip-Hop Feminism Pedagogy Reader,* edited by Ruth Nicole Brown and Chamara Jewel Kwakye, 55–69 (New York, NY: Peter Lang, 2012).

37. Nick Soulsby, "Nicki Minaj is the Greatest Rapper of the Decade Bar None," *Pop Matters Magazine Online* (May 11, 2020), https://www.popmatters.com/nicki-minaj-greatest-rapper-decade-2645966150.html

38. Soulsby, "Nicki Minaj."

## Chapter 3

1. Chang, *Can't Stop*.

2. Chang, *Can't Stop*, 106.

3. Merriam-Webster, "Revolution" in Merriam-Webster.com Dictionary, accessed October 12, 2020, https://www.merriam-webster.com/dictionary/revolution

4. Boyd Rossing, *Identifying, Mapping and Mobilizing Our Assets* (Madison, WI: University of Wisconsin-Madison, 2000).

5. Marc Lamont Hill, *Nobody: Casualties of America's War on the Vulnerable, from Ferguson to Flint and Beyond* (New York, NY: Atria Books, 2016).

6. Kathy Iandoli, "The Lost Art of Cratedigging," *Cuepoint/Medium*, September 24, 2014 accessed November 12, 2020, https://medium.com/cuepoint/the-lost-art-of-cratedigging-4ed652643618

7. Sean Combs, *We Invented the Remix* (New York, NY: Badboy/Arista Records, 2002).

8. Lauryn Hill, "Doo Wop," on *The Miseducation of Lauryn Hill* (1998).

9. Carter G. Woodson, *The Mis-Education of the Negro* (Trenton, NJ: Africa World Press, 1933/1990); Molefi Asante, *The Afrocentric Idea* (Philadelphia: Temple University Press, 1998); Love, *Hip Hop's Li'l Sistas*; Gloria Boutte, *Educating African American Students: And How are the Children?* (New York, NY: Routledge, 2016).

10. Woodson, *Mis-Education of the Negro*, xiii.

11. Jay-Z, *Decoded*, 9.

12. Yosso, "Whose Culture."

13. Sam Dunn, Scot McFadyn, and Darby Wheeler, *Hip-Hop Evolution* (Toronto, Canada: Banger Films, 2016–2020).

14. Jay-Z, *Decoded*, 77.

15. Toby Jenkins, "Mr. Nigger: The Challenges of Educating African American Males in American Society." *Journal of Black Studies* 37, no. 1 (2006): 127–155. https://doi.org/10.1177/0021934704273931

16. Dante Smith, "Mr. Nigga." On *Black on Both Sides* [CD], (United States: Rawkus, 2002).

17. Robert Spuhler, "The 1977 NYC Blackout and the Hip-Hop Spark that Ignited Soon After." *AMNY*, July 12, 2017. https://www.amny.com/entertainment/the-1977-nyc-blackout-and-the-hip-hop-spark-that-ignited-soon-after-1-13796834/

18. bell hooks, *Teaching to Transgress: Education as the Practice of Freedom* (New York, NY: Routledge, 1994), and *Teaching Community: A Pedagogy of Hope* (New York, NY: Routledge, 2003).

19. William Griffin, Christopher Martin, and Louis Barrier, *Waiting for the World to End*. On *The Master* (New York, NY: Universal Music Group, 1999).

## Chapter 4

1. Nikki Giovanni, *Racism 101* (New York, NY: William Morrow, 1994).

2. Merriam-Webster, *Swag*, Merriam-Webster dictionary, https://www.merriam-webster.com/dictionary/swag

3. Merriam-Webster, *Swag*.

4. Ben Younger, *Boiler Room* (Los Angeles, CA: New Line Cinema, 2000).

5. Younger, *Boiler Room*.

6. Merriam-Webster, *Posture*, Merriam-Webster dictionary.com, https://www.merriam-webster.com/dictionary/posture

7. Urban Dictionary, *Bling*, Urbandictionary.com, https://www.urbandictionary.com/define.php?term=bling

8. Joshua Mark, "Color in Ancient Egypt," *Ancient.eu.com*, January 8, 2017, https://www.ancient.eu/article/999/color-in-ancient-egypt/

9. Mark, "Color in Ancient Egypt."

10. Ainé Cain, "Here's What It Was Like to Be Mansa Musa, Thought to Be the Richest Person in History," *Business Insider*, February 14, 2016, http://www.businessinsider.com /mansa-musa-the-richest-person-in-history-2016-2

11. KRT, "The Evolution of 'Bling'," *Chicago Tribune*, August 9, 2005, http://articles.chicagotribune.com/2005-08-09/news/0508090309_1_hip-hop-artists-bling-bling-cred.

12. RZA, *The Tao of Wu* (New York, NY: Riverhead Books, 2010), 145.

13. Open Bible, "Power of the Tongue," https://www.openbible.info/topics/power_of_the_tongue; Sohaib Sultan, "Ramadan, Day 25: Restraining the Tongue," *Time Magazine Online*, July 22, 2014, https://time.com/3014362/ramadan-day-25-restraining-the-tongue/

14. KRS-One, *The Gospel of Hip Hop*, 34.

15. Shawn Carter and Kanye West, *"Ni**as in Paris"* on *Watch the Throne* (New York, NY: Roc-a-Fella Records/Def Jam, 2011).

16. Jenkins, "A Beautiful Mind," 17.

17. George R. R. Martin, *A Song of Ice and Fire* (New York, NY: Bantam Books, 1996); David Benioff and D. B. Weiss, *Game of Thrones* (Los Angeles, CA: HBO Studios, 2011).

18. Erika Ramirez, "Jay-Z Talks 'Watch the Throne' & Calls Beyoncé 'The Second Coming,'" *Billboard Online*, August 15, 2011, https://www.billboard.com/music/music-news/jay-z-talks-watch-the-throne-calls-beyonce-the-second-coming-467908/

19. Toby Jenkins, *Enlivening Learning in Graduate School.* In T. Jenkins (Ed.), *Reshaping Graduate Education through Experiential Learning & Innovation* (Hershey, PA: IGI Global Publishing, 2020), p. xxii.

### Chapter 5

1. Jeff Chang, *Can't Stop Won't Stop: A History of the Hip-Hop Generation* (New York: St. Martin's Press, 2005).

2. Gloria Boutte, George Johnson, Nathaniel Bryan, Kamania Winter-Hoyte, and U. E. Uyoata, "Using African Diaspora Literacy to Heal and Restore the Souls of Young Black Children," *International Critical Childhood Policy Studies Journal* 6, no. 1 (2017), pp 66–79.

3. Bouette et al., "Using African Diaspora Literacy"; A.W. Boykin, "Afrocultural Expression and its Implications for Schooling," in E.R. Hollins, J.E. King, & W.C. Hayman (Eds.), *Teaching Diverse Populations: Formulating a Knowledge Base* (Albany, NY: State University of New York Press), pp 243–273; J. Hale, *Learning While Black: Creating Educational Excellence for African American Children* (Baltimore, MD: Johns Hopkins University Press, 2001); J. King, "A reparatory justice curriculum for human freedom: Rewriting the story of African American dispossession and the debt owed," *African American History*, 102 (2017), 213–231.

4. Etienne Wenger-Trayner and Beverly Wenger-Trayner, "Introduction to Communities of Practice," June 2015, http://wenger-trayner.com/introduction-to-communities-of-practice

5. Wenger-Trayner and Wenger-Trayner, "Communities of Practice," 2.

6. Halifu Osumare, "Global Breakdancing and the Intercultural Body," *Dance Research Journal* 34, no. 2 (2002): 30, https://doi.org/10.2307/1478458.

7. Osumare, "Global Breakdancing," 31.

8. Monique Morris, *Sing a Rhythm, Dance a Blues: Education for the Liberation of Black and Brown Girls* (New York, NY: The New Press, 2019).

**Chapter 7**

1. "Academia and Hip-Hop Dance," Strife TV, 2012, https://www.youtube.com/watch?v=TC-D8b2cbSo.

2. "Academia & Hip-hop Dance," 2012.

3. Morris, *Sing a Rhythm*, 141.

4. Toby Jenkins, Crystal Endsley, Marla Jaksch, and Tony Keith, *The Open Mic Night: Campus Programs that Champion Student Voice and Engagement* (Sterling, VA: Stylus Publishing, 2017); Morris, *Sing a Rhythm*; Christopher Emdin, "Pursuing the Pedagogical Potential of the Pillars of Hip-hop through Sciencemindedness," *International Journal of Critical Pedagogy* 4, no. 3 (2013), pp. 83–99.

5. Chang, *Can't Stop*, xi.

# References

Alleyne, A. (2022). *Book banning, curriculum restrictions, and the politicization of U.S. schools*. Center for American Progress. https://www.americanprogress.org/article/book-banning-curriculum-restrictions-and-the-politicization-of-u-s-schools/

Asante, M. (1998). *The Afrocentric idea*. Temple University Press.

Attiah, K. (2020, October 8). America hates to let Black women speak. *The Washington Post*. https://www.washingtonpost.com/opinions/2020/10/08/america-hates-let-black-women-speak/

Benioff, D., & Weiss, D. B. (2011). *Game of Thrones*. HBO Studios, 2011.

Blakemore, E. (2016, February 16). The woman who schooled the Civil Rights Movement. *Time Magazine*. https://time.com/4213751/septima-clark-civil-rights-movement/

Boutte, G. (2016). *Educating African American students: And how are the children?* Routledge.

Boutte, G., & Bryan, N. (2013). When will Black children be well? Interrupting anti-Black violence in early childhood classrooms and schools. *Contemporary Issues in Early Childhood Education, 22*(3), 232–243.

Boutte, G., Johnson, G., Bryan, N., Winter-Hoyte, K., & Uyoata, U. E. (2017). Using African Diaspora literacy to heal and restore the souls of young Black children. *International Critical Childhood Policy Studies Journal, 6*(1), 66–79.

Boykin, A. W. (1994). Afrocultural expression and its implications for schooling. In E.R. Hollins, J.E. King, & W.C. Hayman (Eds.), *Teaching diverse populations: Formulating a knowledge base* (pp. 243–273). State University of New York Press.

Cain, A. (2016, February 14). Here's what it was like to be Mansa Musa, thought to be the richest person in history. *Business Insider*. http://www.businessinsider.com /mansa-musa-the-richest-person-in-history-2016-2

Carter, S., & West, K. (2011). Ni**as in Paris [Song]. On *Watch the throne*. Roc-a-Fella Records/Def Jam.

Chang, J. (2005) *Can't stop won't stop: A history of the hip-hop generation*. St. Martin's Press.

Chen, G. (2020, November 5; updated May 18, 2022). 10 major challenges facing public schools. *Public School Review*. https://www.publicschoolreview.com/blog/10-major-challenges-facing-public-schools

Combs, S. (2002). *We invented the remix* [Album]. Badboy/Arista Records.

Dunn, S., McFadyn, S., & Wheeler, D. (2016–2020). *Hip-hop evolution* [Television series]. Banger Films.

Durham, A. (2012). "Check on it": Beyoncé, Southern booty, and Black femininities in music video. *Feminist Media Studies, 12*(1), 35–49. https://doi.org/10.1080/14680777.2011.558346

*Education World.* (n.d.). Is your school's culture toxic or positive? https://www.educationworld.com/a_admin/admin/admin275.shtml

Emdin, C. (2013). Pursuing the pedagogical potential of the pillars of hip-hop through sciencemindedness. *International Journal of Critical Pedagogy, 4*(3), 83–99.

Epitropoulos, A., & ASCD. (2019). 10 signs of a toxic school culture. *ACSD Education Update, 61*(9). https://www.ascd.org/el/articles/10-signs-of-a-toxic-school-culture

Evans-Winters, V., & Love, B. L. (Eds.). (2015). *Black feminism in education: Black women speak back, up, and out.* Peter Lang.

Freire, P. (2008). *Pedagogy of the oppressed.* Continuum International Publishing Group.

Giovanni, N. (1994). *Racism 101.* William Morrow.

Giroux, H. (2003). Racial justice and disposable youth in the age of zero tolerance. *International Journal of Qualitative Studies in Education, 16*(4), 553–565.

Glover, C., Jenkins, T., & Troutman, S. (2018). *The invisible backpack: Narratives of family, cultural gifts and community assets on the academic journey.* Lexington Books/Rowman & Littlefield.

González, N., Moll, L., & Amanti, C. (2005). *Funds of knowledge: Theorizing practices in households, communities, and classrooms.* Lawrence Erlbaum.

Griffin, W. (Rakim), Martin, C., & Barrier, L. (1999). Waiting for the world to end [Song]. On *The Master.* Universal Music Group.

Hale, J. (2001). *Learning while Black: Creating educational excellence for African American children.* Johns Hopkins University Press.

Harper, P. T. H. (2000). Understanding youth popular culture and the hip-hop influence. *SIECUS Report, 28*(5), 19–23.

Harper, S., & Kimbrough, W. (2005). Staffing practices, professional preparation trends, and demographics among student affairs administrators at HBCUs: Implications from a national study. *NASPA Journal, 8*(1), 8–25.

Hill, L. (1998). The miseducation of Lauryn Hill [CD]. Ruffhouse/Columbia, Doo-Wop.

Hill, M. L. (2016). *Nobody: Casualties of America's war on the vulnerable, from Ferguson to Flint and beyond.* Atria Books.

Hill-Collins, P. (1986). Learning from the outsider within: The sociological significance of Black Feminist Thought. *Social Problems 33*(6), S14–S32. https://doi.org/10.2307/800672

Hill-Collins, P. (2004). *Black sexual politics: African Americans, gender, and the new racism.* Routledge.

hooks, b. (1994). *Teaching to transgress: Education as the practice of freedom.* Routledge.

hooks, b. (2003). *Teaching community: A pedagogy of hope.* Routledge.

Hoppe, T. A., Litovitz, A., Willis, K. A., Meseroll, R. A., Perkins, M. J., Hutchins, B. I., . . . Davis, A. F., Lauer, M. S., Valentine, H. A., Anderson, J. M., & Santangelo, G. M. (2019). Topic choice contributes to the lower rate of NIH awards to African-American/black scientists. *Science Advances, 5*(10).

Hunt, J. (2015). Symbols are important to Black America. *The Madison Times.* https://themadisontimes.themadent.com/article/symbols-are-important-black-america/

Iandoli, K. (2014, September 24). The lost art of cratedigging. *Cuepoint/Medium*. https://medium.com/cuepoint/the-lost-art-of-cratedigging-4ed652643618

Jackson, O. Sr. (1988). Fuck tha Police [Song]. On *Straight Outta Compton*. Priority/Ruthless Records.

James, A. (2012). The Black girl body as site of sexual terrorism. In R. N. Brown & C. J. Kwakye (Eds.), *Wish to live: The hip-hop feminism pedagogy reader* (pp. 55–69). Peter Lang.

Jay-Z. (2010). *Decoded*. Random House.

Jenkins, T. S. (2006). Mr. Nigger: The challenges of educating African American males in American society. *Journal of Black Studies, 37*(1), 127–155. https://doi.org/10.1177/0021934704273931

Jenkins, T. S. (2010). Patriotism: A love story. *Journal of Black Masculinity, 1*(1), 12–21.

Jenkins, T. S. (2011). A beautiful mind: Black male intellectual identity in hip-hop culture. *Journal of Black Studies, 42*(8), 1231–1251. https://doi.org/10.1177/0021934711405050

Jenkins, T. S. (2013a). De (re) constructing ideas of genius: Hip-hop, knowledge, and intelligence. *The International Journal of Critical Pedagogy, 4*(3), 11–23. https://libjournal.uncg.edu/ijcp/article/view/529

Jenkins, T. S. (2013b). *My culture, my color, my self: Heritage, resilience, and community in the lives of young adults*. Temple University Press.

Jenkins, T. S. (2020). Enlivening learning in graduate school. In T. S. Jenkins (Ed.), *Reshaping Graduate Education through Experiential Learning & Innovation* (p. xxii). IGI Global Publishing.

Jenkins, T. S. (2020). Imagination, power & brilliance: Hip-hop as a politic of educational survival. In E. Adjapong & I. Levy (Eds.), *HipHopEd: The Compilation on Hip-Hop Education* (Vol. 2, *Hip-Hop as Praxis & Social Justice*, pp. 87–102). Peter Lang.

Jenkins, T. S. (2016, July 9). What would brother Malcolm do? Police & race in America. *Huffington Post*. http://www.huffingtonpost.com/entry/what-would-brother-malcolm do_us_57803625e4b0f06648f4d1ff

Jenkins, T. S., Endsley, C., Jaksch, M., & Keith, T. (2017). *The open mic night: Campus programs that champion student voice and engagement*. Stylus Publishing.

Johnson, M. E. (2018). The paradox of black patriotism: double consciousness. *Ethnic and Racial Studies, 41*(11), 1971–1989. doi: 10.1080/01419870.2017.1332378

Juma, N. (Ed.) (2022). *Biggie Smalls quotes and lyrics about life and death*. Everyday Power. https://everydaypower.com/biggie-smalls-quotes-and-lyrics/

Kendi, I. X. (2016). *Stamped from the beginning*. Avalon Publishing Group.

King, J. (2017). A reparatory justice curriculum for human freedom: Rewriting the story of African American dispossession and the debt owed. *African American History, 102*, 213–231.

Knopper, S. Afrika Bambaataa: Crate-digger, collector, creator. *Chicago Tribune*, May 5, 2011. Tribune Publishing.

Koonce, J. (2012). Oh, those loud Black girls!: A phenomenological study of Black girls talking with an attitude. *Journal of Language and Literacy Education, 8*(2) (2012), 26–46.

KRS-One. (2008). *The gospel of hip hop: The first instrument*. PowerHouse Books.

KRT. (2005, August 9). The evolution of 'Bling.' *Chicago Tribune*. http://articles
.chicagotribune.com/2005-08-09/news/0508090309_1_hip-hop-artists-bling
-bling-cred

Lazin, L. (Director). (2003). *Tupac: Resurrection* [Film]. Paramount Pictures
Corporation.

Leftwich, A. (2004). *What is politics? The activity and its study*. Polity Press.

Levine, N. (2019, December 27). Why Lizzo was the star who defined 2019. *BBC
Culture*. https://www.bbc.com/culture/article/20191218-why-lizzo-was-the-star
-who-defined 2019

Lomax, T. (2011). In search of our daughters' gardens: Hip Hop as womanist prose.
*Bulletin for the Study of Religion, 40*(3), 15–20. https://doi.org/10.1558/bsor
.v40i3.004

Love, B. L. (2012). *Hip hop's li'l sistas speak: Negotiating hip hop identities and
politics in the New South*. Peter Lang.

Love, B. L. (2016a). Complex personhood of hip hop & the sensibilities of the culture that fosters knowledge of self & self-determination. *Equity & Excellence
in Education, 49*(4), 414–427.

Love, B. L. (2016b). Good kids, mad cities: Kendrick Lamar and finding inner
resistance in response to FergusonUSA. *Cultural Studies—Critical Methodologies, 16*(3), 320–323. https://doi.org/10.1177/1532708616634837

Mark, J. J. (2016). The Great Pyramid of Giza. *World History Encyclopedia*. https://
www.worldhistory.org/Great_Pyramid_of_Giza

Mark, J. J. (2017). Color in ancient Egypt. *World History Encyclopedia*. https://
www.worldhistory.org/article/999/color-in-ancient-egypt/

Martin, G. R. R. (1996). *A song of ice and fire*. Bantam Books.

Matthers, M., Bass, J., & Resto, L. (2002). *Lose yourself in 8 Mile: Music from and
inspired by the motion picture*. Shady/Aftermath/Interscope.

McCollom, S. (2019). *Hip-Hop: A culture of vision and voice*. The Kennedy Center.
https://www.kennedy-center.org/education/resources-for-educators/classroom
-resources/media-and-interactives/media/hip-hop/hip-hop-a-culture-of-vision
-and-voice/

Merriam-Webster. (n.d.) Revolution. In *Merriam-Webster.com dictionary*. https://
www.merriam-webster.com/dictionary/revolution

Merriam-Webster. (n.d.) Posture. In *Merriam-Webster.com dictionary*. https://www
.merriam-webster.com/dictionary/posture

Merriam-Webster. (n.d.). Swag. In *Merriam-Webster.com dictionary*. https://www
.merriam-webster.com/dictionary/swag

Moorwood, V. (2021, October 20). Kanye West breaks record as producer with most
hip hop No.1 hits. Revolt TV. https://www.billboard.com/artist/kanye-west
/chart-history/hsi/

Morris, M. (2012). *Race, gender and the school to prison pipeline: Expanding our
discussion to include Black girls*. Schott Foundation for Public Education.

Morris, M. (2016). *Pushout: The criminalization of Black girls in schools*. The New
Press.

Morris, M. (2019) *Sing a rhythm, dance a blues: Education for the liberation of
Black and Brown girls*. The New Press.

Open Bible. (n.d.). *Power of the Tongue*. https://www.openbible.info/topics/power
_of_the_tongue

Osumare, H. (2002). Global breakdancing and the intercultural body. *Dance Research Journal, 34*(2), 30–45. https://doi.org/10.2307/1478458

Pawel, M. (2015). *The crusades of Cesar Chavez: A biography.* Bloomsbury Press.

Perry, A. (2020). *Know your price: Valuing Black lives and property in America's Black cities.* Brookings Institution.

Petchauer, E. (2009). Framing and reviewing hip-hop educational research. *Review of Educational Research, 79*, 946. https://doi.org/10.3102/0034654308330967

Pough, G. D. (2007). What it do, Shorty?: Women, hip-hop, and a feminist agenda. *Black Women, Gender, and Families, 1*(2), 78–99. https://www.jstor.org/stable/10.5406/blacwomegendfami.1.2.0078

Ramirez, E. (2011, August 15). Jay-Z talks 'Watch the Throne' & Calls Beyoncé 'The Second Coming.' *Billboard Online.* https://www.billboard.com/articles/columns/the-juice/467908/jay-z-talks-watch-the-throne-calls-Beyoncé-the-second-coming

Reddy, M. (2013). Can I get a window seat? Erykah Badu as a site of expression, resistance, and erotic power. *Words, Beats & Life: The Global Journal of Hip-Hop Culture, 5*(1), 14–23.

Richardson, E. (2013). Developing critical hip hop feminist literacies: Centrality and subversion of sexuality in the lives of Black girls. *Equity & Excellence in Education, 46*(3), 327–341.

Rose, T. (1994). *Black noise: Rap music and Black culture in contemporary America.* University Press of New England.

Rossing, B. (2000). *Identifying, mapping and mobilizing our assets.* University of Wisconsin–Madison.

RZA. (2010). *The tao of Wu.* Riverhead Books.

Seidel, S. (2011). *Hip hop genius: Remixing high school education.* R&L Education.

Sharpley-Whiting, T. D. (2007). *Pimps up, ho's down: Hip hop's hold on young Black women.* New York University Press.

Smith, D. (2002). Mr. Nigga. On *Black on Both Sides* [CD]. Rawkus.

Soulsby, N. (2020, May 11). Nicki Minaj is the greatest rapper of the decade bar none. *Pop Matters Magazine Online.* https://www.popmatters.com/nicki-minaj-greatest-rapper-decade-2645966150.html

Spuhler, R. (2017, July 12). The 1977 NYC blackout and the hip-hop spark that ignited soon after. *AMNY.* https://www.amny.com/entertainment/the-1977-nyc-blackout-and-the-hip-hop-spark-that-ignited-soon-after-1-13796834/

Strife.TV. (2012, August 19). *Academia & hip-hop dance* [Video]. YouTube. https://www.youtube.com/watch?v=TC-D8b2cbSo

Sultan, S. (2014, July 22). Ramadan, day 25: Restraining the tongue. *Time Magazine Online.* https://time.com/3014362/ramadan-day-25-restraining-the-tongue/

TEDx Talks. (2013, May 14). *The cipher, the circle, and its wisdom: Toni Blackman at TEDxUMassAmherst.* [Video]. YouTube. https://www.youtube.com/watch?v=WYdb5snA1Jc

Urban Dictionary. *Bling.* Urbandictionary.com.

Valdez, J. (2022). 'Not for sale': Kanye West claims his music catalog was put up without his knowledge, *Los Angeles Times.* https://wwwlatimes.com/entertainment-arts/story/2022-09-20/not-for-sale-kanye-west-claims-his-music-catalog-was-put-up-without-his-knowledge

Warren, M., Gamble, E., Holzman, E., Jay-Z, & Meek Mill. (2019). *Free Meek* [Television series]. Roc Nation & The Intellectual Property Corporation.

Waters, M. B., Evans-Winters, V. E., & Love, B. L. (Eds.). (2018). *Celebrating twenty years of Black girlhood: The Lauryn Hill reader*. Peter Lang.

WE 102.9. Nicki Minaj is one of the highest selling artists ever. https://www .wehiphop.com/nicki-minaj-is-one-of-the-highest-selling-artists-ever/?doing _wp_cron=1608521932.8611040115356445312500

Wenger-Trayner, E., & Wenger-Trayner, B. (2015, June). *Communities of practice: A brief introduction*. http://wenger-trayner.com/introduction-to-communities-of -practice

Wilkerson, I. (2020). *Caste: The origins of our discontents*. Random House.

Williams, P. (1987). Spirit-murdering the messenger: The discourse of fingerpointing as the law's response to racism. *University of Miami Law Review, 42*, 127.

Woodson, C. G. (1933/1990). *The mis-education of the Negro*. Africa World Press.

Yosso, T. (2005). Whose culture has capital? A Critical Race Theory discussion of community cultural wealth. *Race Ethnicity and Education, 8*(1), 69–91. https:// doi.org/10.1080/1361332052000341006

Younger, B. [Director]. (2000). *Boiler Room* [Film]. New Line Cinema.

Yuen, N. (2017). *Reel inequality: Hollywood actors and racism*. Rutgers University Press.

# Index

# About the Author

*Toby S. Jenkins* is a professor of Higher Education Administration and Interim Associate Dean of Diversity, Equity & Inclusion in the Graduate School at the University of South Carolina. Jenkins has published five books focused on culture, diversity, and inclusion in education. Prior to becoming a professor, Dr. Jenkins worked for 10 years as a student affairs administrator in the areas of diversity and inclusion, student leadership, student activities, fraternity and sorority life, and education abroad. Her research, teaching, and professional studies have taken her to over 35 countries. She is a mom of a super-active 8-year-old son, a wife, daughter, sister, and friend. She is a breast cancer survivor who is also living with lupus. Culture, in the form of art, poetry, music, storytelling, elder wisdom, historical resilience, and street knowledge, feeds her soul.